N. Blattner · H. Genberg
A. Swoboda (Eds.)

Competitiveness in Banking

With 28 Figures

Physica-Verlag Heidelberg
A Springer-Verlag Company

Prof. Dr. Niklaus Blattner
Forschungsstelle für Arbeitsmarkt-
und Industrieökonomik (FAI)
Leonhardsgraben 3
CH-4051 Basel

Prof. Dr. Hans Genberg
International Centre for Monetary and Banking Studies (ICMB)
Avenue de la Paix 11A
CH-1211 Geneva

Prof. Dr. Alexander Swoboda
Institut Universitaire de Hautes Etudes Internationales (IUHEI)
Rue de Lausanne 132
CH-1211 Geneva

ISBN-13: 978-3-7908-0607-6 e-ISBN-13: 978-3-642-48846-7
DOI: 10.1007/978-3-642-48846-7

CIP-Titelaufnahme der Deutschen Bibliothek

Competitiveness in banking / N. Blattner ... (ed.) - Heidelberg
: Physica-Verl., 1992
(Studies in contemporary economics)

NE: Blattner, Niklaus [Hrsg.]

Studies in Contemporary Economics

Preface

Oliver Landmann

> "Once upon a longish time ago, Swiss bankers were solemn men to whom you took the money stashed under your mattress so they could stash it under theirs. Not now".
>
> (The Economist, February 2nd, 1991)

As The Economist has recognized, the banking business is subject to thorough change. Traditional competitive advantages are lost, new ones must be sought. And above all, the rapid globalization of financial markets in the recent past has greatly intensified international competition in banking. In view of these developments, the issue of competitiveness in banking has become an urgent research priority.

The contributions collected in this conference volume present the first results of a joint research project of the Labour and Industrial Economics Research Unit at the University of Basel, the International Centre for Monetary and Banking Studies, and the Graduate Institute for International Studies in Geneva on the Swiss Financial Sector. The Conference was held in Basel on May 16 - 17, 1991. The research project, directed by Professors Alexander Swoboda, Niklaus Blattner and Hans Genberg, is part of the National Research Programme Nr. 28, commissioned by the Swiss Government and administered by the Swiss National Science Foundation. The programme is devoted to the external economic challenges faced by Switzerland.

The notion of competitiveness is at the very core of this research programme. Therefore, the conceptual issues that are raised by several contributors to this volume with regard to the definition and measurement of competitiveness are of importance far beyond the specific applications to the banking sector. Too often, competitiveness is simply identified with easily observable indicators of performance such as growth rates, productivity or market shares. The empirical studies in this volume teach us to look behind such indicators for the complex conditions that generate the often contradictory developments in different measures of performance. By taking the perspective and using the tools of industrial economics rather than financial and monetary economics, this volume is opening an interesting and potentially rewarding avenue of research on Switzerland's banking industry. Considering this industry's substantial role as a contributor to Swiss employment and value added (well documented in this volume), the foundations of its present strength and the preconditions of its future viability in international competition are certainly worth investigating.

Although the empirical research reported in this volume centres on the case of the Swiss banking sector, the general results and the research methodology are of interest for much more than what they teach us about Switzerland. This research is part of a mostly young, but promising literature on the nature of the international competitive advantages of financial firms and the attractiveness of financial centres. With the ongoing global integration of the markets and an evolving regulatory environment, these advantages are bound to shift and established structures are being transformed. It is to an understanding of these processes that the strand of research advanced in the present volume can make a contribution.

Table of Contents

Introduction

Niklaus Blattner, Hans Genberg, Alexander Swoboda

These are not the times for complacency in the world of finance. In many ways and everywhere the party is over now. After many years of exceptional growth and success, private investors are cruelly reminded of the sometimes forgotten positive relationship between profits and risk. At the same time the professionalism and the performance demands of the increasingly weighty institutional investors keep growing. In addition, events of singular importance like the crisis of the Banque de Crédit Commercial International increase the likelihood of re-regulation with uncertain effects for an industry that was just about to accomplish the adaptations required by the international move towards deregulation that started in the Eighties. And also, the macroeconomic outlook is rather tarnished, with inflation still not mastered and interest rates persistently high. The growth effects of the restructuring of the former communist economies in Eastern Europe also might take longer to materialise than initially hoped for.

Furthermore and significantly, the potential of telecommunication and other innovations as a source of increased efficiency in finance is by no means exhausted. As a consequence, the providers of financial services have increasingly been struggling with overcapacity in the recent past, and one might safely foresee more structural change and an ever increasing drive for cost-effectiveness in financial markets and banking everywhere.

Not surprisingly therefore, the notion, the definition, the measurement, and the explanation of competitiveness in banking have increasingly caught the attention of researchers as well as of policy makers, particularly in countries where financial intermediation and securities trading contribute importantly to value added, exports and employment. Switzerland is, without any doubt, among those countries. Viewed from the beginning of the Nineties the banking industry in Switzerland is a leading contributor to economic prosperity and has been for many years and in many ways.

The research project, of which this volume is the outcome, carries the title "The Swiss Financial Sector at the Turn of the Century". It is financed by the Swiss

National Science Foundation. The background is described by Oliver Landmann in the Preface. Our research seeks to contribute to an increased understanding of the performance of the banking firm in general, of the competitive processes at work in banking markets, of the effects of the regulatory activities and international trade policies of governments on banking and, in particular, of the links between the characteristics of competition in the financial markets and the monetary and exchange rate policies of the central bank.

This is clearly a vast programme. Our research teams at the University of Basel, at the International Centre for Monetary and Banking Studies, and at the Graduate Institute for International Studies in Geneva, were given two years to master several tasks. The output of the first year of work was presented to a distinguished group of economists at a conference in May 1991. The papers and the comments are contained in this volume. While in this first conference the main interest was the definition, the measurement, and the explanation of competitiveness in banking, a second conference, that will take place in the spring of 1992, will be devoted to banking performance at the firm level and to a number of specific trade, monetary, and exchange rate policy issues.

The present volume falls into six parts. Part I contains a survey of selected recent contributions to defining, measuring, and explaining competitiveness by Niklaus Blattner. He also discusses research priorities and thereby provides an introduction to a number of other papers on competitiveness, many of them contributed by his colleagues at the University of Basel. The term of competitiveness is clearly loose. It requires clarification. The position taken can be summarised as follows: First, the definition of competitiveness should be clearly linked to those attributes of a firm, an industry, or a country which stand for its economic viability. Second, the definition ought to be precise enough to become an endogenous variable in an analytical model. Third, the definition should be easily translatable into empirically measurable indicators. Precisely defined, competitiveness can be analysed. Short of definitional efforts any discussion is vain. The survey shows that a number of interesting attempts were made to empirically measure and explain competitiveness in the past. These are he starting point for the investigations contained in this volume, especially when they address the issue of a financial centre's attractiveness either to banks headquartered elsewhere or to depositors from other countries.

Part II provides the local background. It is devoted to the description of the Swiss banking sector as it has developed over the past ten years. Andreas Bossard, Matthias Wirth, and Niklaus Blattner try to explain what happened and add some thoughts on the sector's outlook for the Nineties. In particular, the discussion draws the attention to the importance of what was called "relative attractiveness" by Jones (1980). Today, when most of the economically important factors of production are internationally highly mobile, it is very important to understand what determines the attractiveness of a country to these highly mobile factors of production. The competitiveness of an individual firm depends not least on its ability to select the most attractive location or mix of locations from which to offer its services. Not only individual firms but also whole industries are internationally mobile. This is particularly true for banking services, the production of which depends less on real than on human capital. This implies that business operations tend to be run from a particular country only if it offers special advantages. Put differently, bankers must face challenges everywhere. Whether they continue to do so from Switzerland depends on how far that country meets its own challenges as an industrial location in the coming years.

Directly linked to these considerations is the theoretical discussion contained in Part III. Thomas Helbling contributes to the modelling of the determinants of international trade in banking services and especially stresses the importance of the regulatory framework. He analyses the effects of alternative regulatory regimes as well as that of liberalising market entry by banks on trade flows in banking services. According to his model, a country's specialisation in banking depends on three main factors: the degree of tradability of banking services, the international mobility of the production factors specific to banking, and the proportion of risk in total service cost. The model thus helps to clarify the implications of the perspective of "relative attractiveness" underlined before.

In Part IV the focus shifts back to the empirical considerations. Ulrich Camen analyses the Swiss share in the market for international non-bank deposits since 1970. He finds that foreign depositors who select Switzerland nevertheless stick to US-dollar denomination for their accounts. Other factors than just the stability of the Swiss franc must additionally explain the attractiveness of Swiss banks to foreigners. The empirical results point to the importance of the institutional framework, i.e. tax advantages on fiduciary accounts, bank secrecy, and the safety of Swiss banks. These factors appear to outweigh the macroeconomic stability of Switzerland. From this the author concludes that it is important to distinguish between the competiveness of Swiss banks and the attractiveness of Switzerland as a financial centre when discussing the future of banking in this country.

George Sheldon contributes to the same issue in a cross-country perspective. A general conclusion of the study is that some determinants of the shares in the market for international bank deposits differ from country to country and depend on the currency denomination and on the particular nature of the deposit instrument chosen. Explanations for changes in market shares common to all countries are the importance of trade flows and the control of the free flow of capital. Other explanatory factors show less homogeneous effects. Results are documented for each country separately.

What decides on the cross-country distribution of bank offices? This issue, closely linked to the question of the attractiveness of international financial centres, is addressed in Part V by Matthias Jeger, Urs Haegler, and Roland Theiss. The attractiveness of international financial centres to banks is investigated empirically. The results suggest some interdependence in locational decision making. Centres are also more attractive when their general economic potential is large. Hence, large centres like London, New York, and Tokyo appear to be in a privileged position. But the authors point to a number of other factors which suggest that lesser centres might well continue to prosper.

In Part VI a model of monopolistic competition is chosen by Hans Genberg, Thomas Helbling, and Salih Neftci in order to better understand what determined interest rate movements in Switzerland over the past years. It is shown that the domestic rates increasingly followed the Euro Swiss franc rates. This and other evidence points to a decreasing degree of monopoly power over local deposit rates. As a result, the influence of monetary policy over the differential between international and domestic interest rates is eroding. This in term implies a change in the impact of monetary policy which needs to be taken into account in its formulation.

The authors revised their papers after the conference and in the light of the discussants' and the other participants' comments. Thanks are due to all for their suggestions.

The editors also wish to extend particular thanks to the Swiss National Science Foundation, especially to the National Research Programme Nr. 28 and its executive director Professor Oliver Landmann whose support continues to be vital to our research. Warm thanks are also due to Professor Gottfried Bombach from the University of Basel who encouraged us to submit the conference papers to the publisher. Finally, we gratefully note that Mrs. Silvia Antognini, Basel, was helpful not only in preparing the conference but also in picking up the bits and pieces that remained of the papers and comments after the conference and helped us make a book out of them.

Literature

Jones, R.W. (1980), "Comparative and Absolute Advantage", in: Schweiz. Zeitschrift für Volkswirtschaft und Statistik, 116, 3.

Part I: Competitiveness in Banking

Competitiveness in Banking: Selected Recent Contributions and Research Priorities

Niklaus Blattner

1. Introduction

There has hardly been a topic in recent years that has attracted more public attention in economics than that of competitiveness. Competitiveness is taken as the essence of what market processes are about. Whether one discusses the economics of a single firm, an industry, a country or even of a continent, sooner or later the question of its competitiveness is raised.

The ubiquity of the term does not match the clarity of the concept, however. Does competitiveness mean efficiency or simply ability to sell? Or should one rather look at the attractiveness of a firm, an industry or of a country to highly mobile factors of production such as human or financial capital? Connected with these questions are those on how to explain competitiveness theoretically and on how to measure and explain it empirically.

All these questions have been addressed by many authors before. For a recent discussion based on experience won while researching the case of Switzerland in general, see Blattner (1990). In this paper, the focus is more restricted, since all of the studies subsequently discussed are linked to competitiveness in banking only.

As a result of a brief survey of a number of recent studies it should be possible to clarify the notion of competitiveness in banking and to identify more precisely the research priorities described in the first part of the project "The Swiss Financial Sector at the Turn of the Century", financed by the Swiss National Science Foundation (No. 4028-28127). This project is pursued in a common effort by two teams of researchers from the University of Basel (Labour and Industrial Economics Research Unit, FAI) and the University of Geneva (International Centre for Monetary and Banking Studies, ICMB, at the Graduate Institute for International Studies).

2. Prerequisites for International Financial Centres

Reed (1981, p.1) gives the following definition of a financial centre and its economic advantages: "A financial center is generally defined as a central location where the financial transactions of an area are coordinated and cleared. By centralizing its financial transactions, the financial community benefits from the efficiencies inherent in various functional economies of scale. The benefits of centralization include (1) quick and easy access to the knowledge and services of complementing and competing institutions; (2) rapid clearing and exchange processes for checks, drafts, and stock certificates; and (3) highly developed financial markets capable of providing large amounts of capital and relatively cheap rates for borrowers and great liquidity for lenders."

While Kindleberger (1974) endeavours to identify the prerequisites for the formation of financial centres by assembling and interpreting verbally a large amount of economic, political and institutional evidence, more recent studies utilise quantitative methods.

Reed (1981) uses cluster analysis and stepwise multiple discriminant analysis in his effort to reveal what he calls the hierarchical structure of international financial centres and its development over time, to rank the centres and to determine the responsible factors. The study covers the period from 1900 to 1980. Every interval of five years is analysed separately. The basic units of observation are 76-80 cities ranging from Alexandria to Zurich. These cities are chosen on the basis of their historical and/or current reputation for financial importance.

In the cluster analysis the financial centres are grouped according to their homogeneity with respect to several variables for which the following can serve as examples: number of large and internationally active banks headquartered in the centre, number of all private banks, number of internationally active foreign banks with an office in the centre, and total amounts of foreign financial assets and liabilities held in the centre. The first set of variables indicates the banking infrastructure of a centre, while the second measures its portfolio management activities. The cluster analysis yields, e.g. in the last subperiod ending in 1980, a first group made up by London alone, a second by New York and Tokyo and a third by Paris, Frankfurt, Zurich, Amsterdam, San Francisco, Chicago, Hamburg and Hong Kong. Group four contains 30 centres and group five incorporates the remaining 39 centres.

Table 1 gives additional information on the relative position of selected financial centres as they evolved over time. From period to period the relative importance of the variables for the clustering changes. In 1980 the structure was mainly determined by two variables: the number of large and internationally active banks headquartered in the centre and the amount of foreign financial liabilities held in the centre.

The cluster analysis is carried out on the basis of variables characterising individual financial centres, i.e. cities. In a further step, utilising discriminant analysis, the author attempts to find out whether other variables describing the macroeconomic, industrial, political etc. qualities of the centres' home countries also contribute to the classification. 41 variables are considered, ranging from gross fixed capital formation, money supply, interest rates, to the number of industrial corporations among the world's 200 largest that are headquartered in the centres' home nations, their total amount of direct investment and the number of international telegrams sent and received. Home nations are assigned to clusters according to the location of the highest ranking financial centre in the clusters. It is then checked whether the home country variables discriminate among the home countries in the same way as the financial centre variables among the international financial centres. This test is carried out for the periods 1955, 1965, 1975 and 1980. Only in 1955 and 1965 are the two sets of organisational ordering identical.

From the observation "that London emerged in 1975 as the world's only preeminent international financial centre without the United Kingdom also becoming preeminent", Reed (1981, p. 48) infers that "other (less quantitative) variables are important to organizational structure and rank." Other remarkable conclusions are: "... once a center's international banking machinery is in place, it is extremely difficult - short of mounting a direct military invasion - to impair that center's international banking eminence drastically. Financial eminence, on the other hand, is obviously more mobile and thus more volatile than banking eminence. Because financial eminence is granted in large part on the basis of relatively subjective factors such as trust, many influences beyond the financial system as such affect an international financial center's status. This study also makes it quite clear that political and economic hegemony does not necessarily lead to financial hegemony ..." (p. 54). And, finally, Reed concludes: "A center's banking infrastructure is obviously important. However, power and influence (preeminence) is derived primarily from

Table 1: Classification of International Financial Centres According to their Inclusion in Hierarchical Clusters

Centre	1955	1960	1965	1970	1975	1980
London	2	1	1	1	1	1
New York	1	1	1	1	2	2
Tokyo	3	2	2	2	2	2
Paris	2	2	2	2	2	3
Frankfurt	3	2	2	2	2	3
Zurich	4	2	3	2	3	3
Basel	4	2	2	2	2	4
Geneva	4	3	3	3	5	5
Total number of clusters	**4**	**3**	**3**	**3**	**5**	**5**

Source: Reed (1981), Table A.7 **FAI**

the center's global portfolio management activities, which usually requires that the center be successful in attracting relatively large amounts of foreign financial liabilities. Because of the potential volatility associated with international finance (foreign financial liabilities and assets), I believe it is reasonable to conclude that the behavior and activities of international financial centers cannot be adequately explained or predicted by analysing international banking centers. Therefore, analyses of international financial centers that focus only on 'banking' dimensions are just as inadequate as analyses that exclude banking and focus mainly on 'finance' (capital flows and foreign lending)." (p. 56)

While the Reed (1981) study is noteworthy because of its quantitative nature it suffers from the thoroughly descriptive quality of the methods employed. The explanatory power of the results is extremely limited. There is a practically total absence of theoretical analysis. Consequently, any testing of hypotheses in the traditional sense of empirical research is lacking.

More in line with traditional economic research is the work by Goldberg, Helsley, Levi (1989). Their work initially aimed at identifying the determining factors giving rise to international financial centres in order to reply to the practical question whether "the city of Vancouver has the 'right stuff' to grow as an international financial center." (Goldberg et al., 1989, p. 49.) The published report on their research is not comprehensive. But what there is can be described as follows.

Goldberg et al. (1989) attempted to explain the variations in the size of international financial activity on the basis of cross-sectional, time-series and pooled data. Cross-sectional analysis is carried out at the level of 42 countries for the year 1984, at the level of 50 US states and of 31 international cities (year not given). Time-series analysis is applied to the US (1900-84), the UK (1960-84) and Canada (1975-84). Estimates with pooled data cover 16 OECD countries over the period 1975-84. From the Swiss point of view it is important to note that Switzerland as well as Zurich are included in the respective samples.

No explicit theoretical modelling can be detected in the study. The selection of righthand variables in the equations appears to be justified by its plausibility alone. Data were taken from published sources. Selected results are summarised in **Tables 2-3**.

Table 2: Financial Activity Explained - Results of Cross-sectional Data and Pooled Data Estimations

Explanatory variables	Cross-sectional data Foreign assets, 42 countries, 1984	Pooled Data Foreign assets, 16 countries, 1975-84
GDP per capita	(+)	(-)
Imports	++	++
Exports	-	-
Saving rate	(-)	(+)
Total debt	(-)	(+)
Foreign debt	(+)	...
Investment		
abroad	(+)	++
foreign	(-)	(-)
Reserve ratio	(+)	++
Offshore dummy	++	...
Constant	(-)	...
Years 1975-84 (dummies)	...	(-)

two signs = significant at the 1% level
one sign = significant at the 5% level
sign in brackets = not significant
... = not included

Source: Goldberg et al. (1989), pp. 52 and 56 **FAI**

Table 3: Financial Activity Explained - Results of Time-series Estimation

Explanatory variables	United States, 1900-84 Labour force (%)	United Kingdom, 1960-84 Labour force (%)	Canada, 1946-84 Labour Force (%)
GDP per capita	++	++	++
Lagged dependent variable	++	...	...
Imports	(+)	(+)	++
Exports	-	(-)	--
Saving rate	(-)	++	(+)
Total debt	(-)	(-)	--
Foreign debt	(+)	...	...
Investment			
abroad	(-)	(-)	(-)
foreign	(-)	(-)	+
portfolio	(-)	++	+
Reserve ratio	-	(+)	-
Unemployment rate	++	...	++
Number of banks	++	...	...
Constant	(-)	--	++

two signs = significant at 1% level
one sign = significant at 5% lvel
sign in brackets = not significant
... = not included

Source: Goldberg et al. (1989), pp. 55-6 **FAI**

The list of the explanatory variables in the tables is indeed quite plausible. GDP per capita is taken to measure economic development. One naturally expects a positive sign. Only in the case of the pooled regression is this not confirmed. Imports require a lot of financial paperwork. So the positive sign is in line with expectations. By the same token one would expect a positive sign in the case of exports. But here, the empirical results are opposite. The authors give ad hoc explanations: a zero-sum game situation with respect to resources might prevail, or exporters might cover their demand for financial services abroad rather than at home. Nevertheless, the negative result for exports remains puzzling. A number of variables that ought to catch intermediation, i.e. the saving rate, total debt, foreign debt and several forms of investment, also deliver disappointing results. In general one would have liked to see positive signs, since with an increase in these variables the demand for financial services should rise. Only in rare cases can this be found, while the empirical relationships remain insignificant in general. As a proxy for the severeness of the regulatory regime the average bank reserve ratio is included in the study. Here, the pooled data reveal a positive relationship, but the time-series analysis for the US and for Canada strongly support a negative sign. This again raises interesting questions, e.g. on whether in some countries (like e.g. Switzerland) that are included in the pooled data, banking security is a stronger marketing argument than in the US and Canada. The offshore dummy, a proxy for the existence of "tax havens" produces less controversial results, however. Financial activity is indeed positively linked to tax advantages for foreigners.

Whenever possible, the authors regress the explanatory variables on two types of dependent variables. **Table 2** contains the results with respect to one type only, namely the volume of foreign assets taken from the balance sheets of the banks. Results with respect to the percentage of the labour force in the financial sector (banking, insurance, real estate) are not included. The explained variance of those estimates is generally lower. This is not surprising, since employment is an even weaker proxy for the size of international financial activity than foreign assets. Time-series estimates were limited to the employment proxy, however. As can be seen from **Table 3** this required the inclusion of additional variables like the unemployment rate and the number of banks to control for the effects of the weaker activity proxy taken.

In their article the authors also report on the findings of their cross-sectional analysis of the data of 31 international cities. The results are similar to those at the national level, although the equations clearly show the considerable difficulties the authors had in finding adequate proxies for the explanatory variables. One might therefore doubt very much whether the authors' application of their findings to the question whether the Alaskan city of Anchorage had good prospects as an international financial centre is warranted.

The third study dealt with in this section of this paper addresses still another question. How can the location pattern of offices of the world's largest banks be explained? Choi, Tschoegl, Yu (1987) first draw on Reed (1980) to identify 14 international financial centres: London (LO), New York (NY), Paris (PA), Frankfurt/Hamburg (FH), Tokyo (TO), Singapore (SI), Hong Kong (HK), Los Angeles/San Francisco (LS), Zurich/Geneva (ZG), Amsterdam (AM), Brussels (BR), Panama (PN), Milan/Rome (MR) and Toronto/Montreal (TM). For these centres, To/From matrices are constructed for 1970 and 1980. The diagonal elements contain the number of the world's Top 300 commercial banks headquartered in the centres. The off-diagonal elements show the number of those banks having an office, branch or subsidiary in the respective other centre. Centres are ranked according to the column totals, i.e. the total number of offices including headquarters of the world's biggest banks located in a given centre. **Table 4** contains these data and rankings from which the authors pursue their analysis further.

First, they calculate four measures of interconnectedness, all of which point in the same direction: the interconnectedness increased between 1970 and 1980. "Not only are there more connections between centers so that the number of pairs with no direct connection has fallen, but also the links are more intensive. From table 1 (here **Table 4**) we can calculate that while the number of banks represented has increased by only 3 percent, the number of foreign offices has increased by 90 percent." (Choi et al., 1987, p. 51)

Choi et al. (1987) then go on to explain the attractiveness of a centre to offices from other centres. The dependent variable in their empirical models is some form of the number of offices from banks headquartered in centre i with offices in centre j (Y_{ij}). Apart from the better known ordinary-least-squares method (OLS) they also

Table 4: Head Offices of Major Banks and Their Representation in Other Centers, 1970 and 1980*

FROM \ TO	LO	NY	PA	FH	TO	SI	HK	LS	ZG	AM	BR	PN	MR	TM	Σ
LO	14 *8*	9 *8*	8 *6*	4 *5*	4 *8*	1 *4*	1 *7*	2 *4*	1 *3*	7 *3*	2 *4*	0 *1*	2 *2*	0 *4*	55 *67*
NY	10 *9*	13 *10*	8 *8*	7 *8*	8 *8*	3 *9*	6 *8*	0 *7*	3 *5*	5 *3*	4 *4*	2 *4*	5 *7*	1 *4*	75 *94*
PA	5 *11*	3 *13*	7 *14*	3 *8*	3 *9*	1 *6*	1 *9*	1 *4*	1 *2*	4 *5*	3 *3*	1 *3*	4 *8*	0 *2*	37 *97*
FH	3 *4*	2 *6*	1 *2*	12 *12*	1 *4*	1 *3*	0 *5*	0 *1*	0 *0*	0 *0*	0 *1*	0 *1*	0 *1*	0 *2*	20 *42*
TO	8 *14*	8 *15*	2 *7*	2 *10*	17 *23*	2 *11*	2 *8*	6 *11*	1 *4*	1 *2*	1 *3*	0 *2*	1 *1*	1 *6*	52 *117*
SI	0 *1*	0 *1*	0 *0*	0 *0*	0 *1*	1 *1*	1 *1*	0 *0*	0 *0*	0 *0*	0 *0*	0 *0*	0 *0*	0 *0*	2 *5*
HK	1 *1*	1 *1*	1 *1*	1 *1*	1 *1*	1 *1*	1 *1*	1 *1*	0 *1*	0 *1*	0 *0*	0 *0*	0 *0*	0 *1*	8 *11*
LS	5 *4*	4 *4*	1 *3*	2 *4*	5 *4*	1 *4*	5 *4*	8 *4*	1 *1*	1 *1*	2 *1*	1 *1*	1 *2*	0 *2*	37 *39*
ZG	1 *3*	1 *3*	1 *2*	0 *0*	1 *3*	1 *2*	1 *3*	1 *3*	3 *5*	1 *1*	0 *0*	0 *0*	0 *0*	1 *2*	12 *27*
AM	2 *2*	2 *3*	0 *0*	0 *0*	1 *2*	0 *2*	2 *2*	1 *2*	0 *0*	3 *4*	0 *1*	0 *1*	0 *1*	0 *0*	11 *20*
BR	0 *3*	1 *3*	0 *1*	1 *1*	0 *3*	0 *3*	0 *2*	0 *0*	0 *2*	0 *0*	3 *7*	0 *0*	0 *2*	0 *0*	5 *27*
PN	0 *0*	0 *1*	0 *0*	0 *0*	0 *0*	0 *0*	0 *0*	0 *0*	0 *0*	0 *0*	0 *0*	1 *1*	0 *0*	0 *0*	1 *2*
MR	4 *7*	5 *7*	4 *4*	5 *6*	0 *5*	1 *4*	0 *3*	1 *4*	2 *0*	0 *0*	3 *4*	0 *0*	12 *10*	1 *3*	38 *57*
TM	5 *5*	5 *5*	2 *4*	2 *4*	4 *5*	0 *4*	4 *5*	4 *5*	1 *1*	1 *1*	2 *1*	0 *2*	1 *2*	7 *5*	38 *49*
Σ	58 *72*	54 *80*	35 *52*	39 *59*	45 *76*	13 *54*	24 *58*	25 *46*	13 *24*	23 *21*	20 *29*	5 *16*	26 *36*	11 *31*	391 *654*
Rank	1 *3*	2 *1*	5 *7*	4 *4*	3 *2*	11 *6*	8 *5*	7 *8*	11 *12*	9 *13*	10 *11*	14 *14*	6 *9*	13 *10*	

[a] The figures for 1980 are shown in italics below the figures for 1970. - Sum of main diagonal: 102 in 1970 and 105 in 1980.

Source: The Banker [1971; 1981]; The Bankers' Almanac and Yearbook [1970-1971; 1980-1981].

Choi et al. (1987), p. 50. **FAI**

applied the non-linear-weighted-least-squares method (NLWLS) which to them is better suited when the dependent variable consists of count data.

The theoretical position of Choi et al. (1987) is quite traditional. They assume profit seeking behaviour on the part of banks. Whether or not a bank would like to have an office in another centre depends positively on the revenues and negatively on the costs of such offices. The revenues stem from two conceptually different sources: "First, there are those activities for which the center provides a convenient location, but which are independent of the presence or absence of other banks. Second, there are the activities which are a consequence of the agglomeration of institutions." (Choi et al. 1987, p. 52). With respect to the second source of returns the authors mention the emergence of interbank markets, e.g. foreign exchange or money markets, and the possibility that "the presence of several sellers of similar but not identical services in one location can reduce search costs for buyers." (Choi et al. 1987, p. 53). Costs are connected with the distance between home and host centres, regulatory obstacles and competitive response by incumbant banks.

Table 5 gives a summary of the Choi et al. (1987) results for the year 1980, again abstracting from the statistical details. In general models performed better in 1980 than in 1970.

Irrespective of the statistical technique used the results are quite similar and the number of significant and "correctly" signed coefficients is impressive. - TO is a proxy for the attractiveness of a centre j in terms of the agglomeration effects mentioned above. It stands for the number of banks in j from centres other than i. Alternatively, CGNP is a measure of a centre's share in national GNP and also a proxy for the attractiveness of the centre. The empirical results clearly confirm the existence of positive agglomeration effects. FROM controls for the number of banks headquartered in centre i as a potential source for offices elsewhere. Centre i cannot send out more offices than it harbours headquarters. The expected positive sign of the coefficient is confirmed, too. DIST stands for the airline distance between two centres. Since the theoretical expectation is ambiguous, the insignificant results do not disturb. Greater distance might reduce the likeliness of service exchange, but at the same time a local office might help to reduce costs. Y_{ji} stands for the reverse "flow" of the dependent variable Y_{ij}, i.e. for the number of offices from the destination centre j in the source centre i. This is taken as a proxy for an "exchange of threat"-behaviour: "If you enter my backyard I enter yours!" The expected sign is

Table 5: Explaining the Attractiveness of an International Financial Centre to Offices of Banks Headquartered Elsewhere in 1980

	OLS-models		NLWLS-models	
	II	III	II	III
ln $\hat{TO}$	...	+	...	+
ln CGNP	+	...	+	...
ln FROM	+	+	+	+
ln DIST	(+)	(+)	(-)	(+)
ln $\hat{Y}_{ji}$	+	+	+	+
JPN	-	(-)	-	(-)
EURO	-	-	-	(-)
SWISS	-	-	-	-
FHZH	-	-	...	...
Constant	-	-	-	-

^ = estimated numbers (two-stage least squares procedure)
one sign = significant at 5% level
sign in brackets = not significant
... = not included

Source: Choi et al. (1987), pp. 59-60. **FAI**

positive. The empirical results are again in line with what was expected. JPN is a dummy variable which is equal to one if the sending centre is Tokyo. Despite some relaxation in past years, Japanese banks are still not completely free to open offices abroad. The estimated negative coefficients are in line with expectations. Competition between centres might also be reduced through other channels. Cooperation between European banks might slow down the interpenetration of banking. EURO, again a dummy variable, is one if both relevant centres are located within the EC. The empirical results confirm this pessimistic view on anticompetitive tendencies in Europe. Furthermore, the authors suspect Swiss banks systematically to shy away from going abroad ("... the banks have been content to let their customers come to them. Customers seeking Swiss banking secrecy may not have found Swiss bank branches in their own countries of any great value to them." - Choi et al. 1987, p. 53). Empirical results do not contradict this hypothesis. The dummy variable SWISS is one whenever the link goes from Zurich/Geneva to one of the EC destinations, i.e. Paris, Brussels, Amsterdam, Frankfurt/Hamburg and Milan/Rome. Finally, the authors believe there exists a "mutual nonaggression pact" between Zurich/Geneva and Frankfurt/Hamburg. Here, the dummy is FHZG. It is one in all cases in which both centres are linked together. Again, the results are as expected. But the authors think that this "Swiss-German entente" is about to break down: "A replication of this study with 1990 data then may well show no such effect." (Choi et al. 1987, p. 61).

Comparing the description of the economic advantages that characterise international financial centres given by Reed (1981) and quoted at the beginning of this section with the empirical studies presented, one cannot help noting quite considerable discrepancies. Reed (1981) himself does not even try to explain the performance of the centres. Rather, he concentrates on the description of their characteristics in terms of fairly general factors. His deeper conclusions follow much more from what his analyses were not able to explain than from what they in fact revealed. More pertinent to the explanation of the competitiveness of financial centres are the studies by Goldberg et al. (1989) and Choi et al. (1987). But there again limitations are obvious. In the case of Goldberg et al. (1989) both the dependent and the independent variables are too general to be considered good proxies of either the performance in financial services or its determinants. The strongest of all is the Choi et al. (1987) study. As mentioned in the Introduction competitiveness can be equated with attractiveness. Insofar, the Choi et al. (1987) study points to promising areas for further research. The explanatory variables are also quite suggestive.

Important first steps are undertaken to quantify the impact of competition and regulation. But many questions still remain open, of course. Some answers are provided by Jeger, Haegler, Theiss (1991).

Essayyad (1989, p. 14) quotes Conninx from a letter written in 1987 in which he points out "that bankers as well as corporate and private investors are usually drawn to places which are politically stable, have excellent communications, have a supply of qualified human resources (unless it is a postbox), fall within a time zone permitting at least minimal daytime contact, and have something special to offer, like low or no taxes (e.g., the Bahamas, Channel Island), a banking secrecy law (e.g., Switzerland and Panama), or an activity in which they have a very strong, almost monopolistic position (e.g., financial futures in Chicago, currency options in Philadelphia, etc.)".

In further studies on the prerequisites for international financial centres one should certainly try to incorporate still further the institutional and structural factors mentioned by Conninx. At the same time one should increasingly take into account the special characteristics of universal banking. The studies discussed in this section more or less concentrated on commercial banking. Universal banking has been a distinguishing feature of important international financial centres in Europe (e.g. in Germany and in Switzerland) for many decades already, and it is of growing importance worldwide, today. Off-balance sheet activities increasingly determine bank profitability. Regulators have long become aware of this and are currently adapting and extending their rules for prudential supervision as a consequence. With respect to the research on the prerequisites for international financial centres this means that their performance and/or attractiveness cannot be convincingly explained without taking into account the conditions affecting not only commercial but also investment and trust banking as well as the availability and the access to efficient and liquid stock and bond markets.

3. The Market for International Bank Deposits

In the studies on international financial centres the perspective is global. Other studies are of a more restricted scope, but they contribute to the same discussion. What explains the strength of a given country in attracting bank deposits from abroad? The special treatment of the market for international bank deposits is easily justified. Deposits are not only the most important source of funds for commercial banks, but they also show a wide variation with respect to their origins. The proportion of liabilities owned by non-residents varies between over 80 % to below 12 % of the total of deposits in European banks in 1985. There is also considerable variation in the percentage of the country share in the world total of bank deposits over time. (Grilli, 1989, pp. 397- 400).

Grilli (1989) attempts to explain these developments empirically. His results are summarised in **Table 6**. The countries of which data are included are Belgium/Luxemburg, Canada, France, Germany, Italy, Japan, The Netherlands, Switzerland, the UK and the US. The time period runs from 1972-1987. The data are pooled.

The dependent variable is the stock of deposits in the banks of a given country owned by non-resident banks and non-banks, respectively. The specification of two separate models is justified on the grounds of assumed differences in the fund-placing motives of bank and non-bank agents. The selection of explanatory variables is the same in both models, though. The variables follow from ad hoc reasoning. The empirical proxies sometimes demand considerable trust in the author's ability to transform qualitative into quantitative information.

TaxI and TaxD stand for the rates of withholding tax on interest and dividend income of non-residents. A negative sign is expected in both cases, but it is not always significant. Regulatory restrictions on capital inflows are condensed into the dummy CapitalIn. The expected negative sign is confirmed. CapitalOut measures restrictions on capital outflows. This dummy ought to have a negative coefficient since such restrictions reduce the freedom of exit once a depositor has placed his funds. The estimated signs are not significant, however. On the other hand the coefficient of the Secrecy dummy is clearly positive and highly significant, especially in the non-bank model. This is no surprise. But the quantitative proxy for

Table 6: Factors Explaining International Bank Deposits

	Non-bank deposits	Inter-bank deposits
TaxI	- -	(-)
TaxD	(-)	- -
CapitalIn	- -	-
CapitalOut	(-)	(+)
Secrecy	+ +	+
GNP	-	+ +
Time	+ +	+ +
Constant	+ +	+ +

two signs = significant at 1% level
one sign = significant at 5% level
in brackets = not significant

Source: Grilli (1989), p. 405 **FAI**

banking secrecy begs a number of questions. GNP is a catch-all variable. It not only measures the size and development of the economic activity in a country but it is also supposed to act as a proxy for what the author calls "thick market externalities", i.e. the agglomeration effects already treated by Choi et al. (1987). GNP is a very crude approximation of externalities in financial "hot spots". Finally, the variable Time controls for the time trend in the data.

It is evident that the Grilli (1989) study cannot provide more than a first clue when explaining the market for international bank deposits. It is certainly welcome that he considers intensively the influence of regulatory differences on the distribution of international bank deposits. But the specification of the models is extremely simplified and data problems abound. It is quite certain that not only empirically but also theoretically more refined concepts will have to be applied if progress were to be hoped for. Sheldon (1991) and Camen (1991) report on work in this direction.

4. Investment Banking and Securities Trading

Clearly, investment banking and securities trading are important dimensions of the financial services in general and for universal banks in particular. Investment banking and securities trading are connected but each is important in its own right and displays many particularities. Here, they are treated in the same section because the studies subsequently discussed are of a rather descriptive nature. A more detailed presentation is not required.

Walter, Smith (1989, 1990) distinguish three activities specific to investment banking: Underwriting new issues of securities, i.e. equities and bonds, fee-based advisory services associated with corporate finance transactions, i.e. mergers and acquisitions, take-over defense, leveraged buy-outs and other financial restructurings, and, finally, secondary market brokerage and trading. Walter, Smith (1989) even include portfolio management for institutional and private investors as a fourth type of activity.

Especially with respect to the first two activities and with regard to the effects of European integration and of European securities industry regulation the authors provide valuable insights. But since the authors refrain from systematic empirical analysis, their work is more useful as a source of background information than as a collection of theoretical and empirical results.

Commenting on Walter, Smith (1990), Carter (1990, p. 150) specifically mentions placing power as "a key success factor in the issue and underwriting of securities", and he goes on: "In general the US and Japanese investment banks and security houses have a clear competitive edge in placing securities, including those issued by European corporations, in their home markets." But not only US and Japanese institutions benefit from their placing power. Swiss banks are also known to manage sizeable portfolios for their domestic as well as international clients. Indicators of placing power are very likely to contribute considerably to the explanation of the success in investment banking.

Furthermore, the existence of well developed stock markets presumably has a great impact on the attractiveness of international financial centres. This is part of the widely received wisdom in the field. But, as was noted before, the studies discussed in the second section of this paper do not account for the existence and quality of stock markets and of markets for derivative financial instruments like options and futures in their empirical analysis of the prerequisites for international financial centres. In this respect, Pagano, Roell (1990) and Hawawini, Jacquillat (1990) provide particularly useful information.

Hawawini, Jacquillat (1990) restrict themselves to the economic, structural and regulatory aspects of equity and derivative markets within the EC. Apart from the obvious information on the size and activity of the markets, on commissions and taxation as well as on regulation they also include clearing and settlement systems in the list of explanatory variables. The latter are deemed of considerable importance for the efficiency and safety of secondary securities trading.

In their discussion of the relative competitiveness of European financial markets Pagano, Roell (1990) especially deal with the efficiency of equity trading in Europe. First, they rank stock markets in terms of market capitalisation and turnover. Market shares are measured by local turnover as a percentage of European equity turnover.

The number of foreign companies listed is also used as an indicator of the attractiveness of a market for foreign participants. In their attempt to explain the pattern revealed by these indicators they concentrate on transaction costs and on liquidity. They develop a "synthetic measure of explicit round trip transaction cost", i.e. "the sum of commissions and taxes that one has to pay on the purchase and sale of the same amount of stock, as a percentage of the value of trade." (Pagano, Roell, 1990, p. 77) More difficulties are encountered in finding a proxy for liquidity. The authors refer to bid-ask spreads, which is easy enough in dealer markets but necessitates estimation in the case of auction markets where there are no posted buying and selling prices from specialists or market makers. Pagano, Roell (1990) do not formally estimate equations to explain stock market shares or rank. The scarcity of the data only allows for a descriptive analysis.

In his comment Danthine (1990, p. 106-7) takes the cases of Zurich and Frankfurt as a starting point for his criticism of the reliance of Pagano, Roell (1990) on the explanatory power of transaction costs and liquidity. Zurich is said to have been "largely bypassed by the winds of reform" so far but still displays a high turnover ratio. Frankfurt is shown to be more resistant to competition from London than other European centres despite rather high transaction costs. Germany and Switzerland are both noted for their rapid and safe settlement systems, however. "One may hypothesize that as is the case in many other industries, the Germans (and probably the Swiss as well) are concentrating on selling a higher quality, higher price service. But then the notion of 'competing on transaction costs' becomes quite misleading." Danthine (1990, p. 107) invokes still another notion. The German (and Swiss) product could also include a larger dose of intermediation; "for example, it could very well be sold as a package with other services, as one would plausibly expect from an exchange managed by banks." Apart from economies of scale, economies of scope also enter the picture.

Finally, as an example of a study of a particular market, Davis (1988) deserves to be mentioned especially. He discusses the primary Eurobond market in terms of industrial economics, i.e. he tries to apply not only the traditional paradigm "structure-conduct-performance" but also the more recent ones of contestability and strategic competition. But Davis (1988) utilises these concepts more as a tool to organise his still descriptive analysis and not as a source of theoretical modelling preceding econometric analysis.

5. Regulation

Financial services are one of the most heavily regulated industries. Regulation affects the competitiveness of the industry. Levich (1990, p. 374) makes this quite clear when he defines Net Regulatory Burden (NRB) as the difference between costs and benefits of regulation placed upon private firms: "As regulations act to promote public confidence in financial institutions, restrict entry into the industry or supply ancillary services (e.g. deposit insurance, wire transfer) below their costs, private firms benefit. On the other side of the equation are the costs that hit private firms, such as foregone interest in required reserves, foregone earnings from excessive capital requirements, and foregone revenues from limits (e.g. geographic and product line) in their activities."

Private firms aim to reduce NRB. They can innovate, adapt and relocate as a result of regulatory changes. Levich (1990, p. 374) considers the Eurocurrency market as an example, i.e. as "a natural outgrowth of differential natural regulation set in a world with declining barriers to capital movements and increasing capabilities in telecommunication and data processing."

Levich (1990, p. 387) also states: "Private firms monitor their NRB and transfer activities into another regulatory regime when, ceteris paribus, their NRB can be reduced. In a perfect capital market with no entry or exit costs, no transaction costs, no barriers between countries and no sovereign risk, we predict that all banking activities would migrate to the country with the lowest NRB inclusive of taxes." This implies not only competition among regulators but also international coordination, e.g. in the framework of the BIS, the EC, IOSCO etc.

Despite the obvious relevance of regulation for the explanation of the attractiveness of international financial centres, econometric research has only rarely and then only in a rudimentary way accounted for it. This follows from the first two sections of this paper. Verbal treatments dominate.

In the area of policy evaluation things are slightly different. Short of econometric tests, Tonks, Webb (1989) analyse the effect of the Big Bang on the London stock market in 1986. Their theoretical background is the "structure-conduct-performance" paradigm of industrial economics. By comparing pre and post Big Bang indicators they address questions like: Has the number of transactions altered? What has been the effect on the number of market makers relative to the number of jobbers? Have costs of transactions, bidask spreads and liquidity been affected? Has price volatility increased? Typical indicators of market structure are the number of participants on both sides of the market, the types of transactions and the settlement systems. Conduct variables are spreads and commissions. Performance is measured by indicators like turnover, liquidity, volatility and profitability.

Econometric studies are available for the US. Bendeck (1988) analyses the effect of regulation on commercial bank valuation in the case of reserve requirements. The regulation analysed concerns the imposition of changes in the discount rate surcharge and in capital requirements as well as bank deregulation of 1980 (Depository Institutions and Monetary Control Act) and 1982 (Germain Act). Policy effects were measured either as announcement effects on the shareholders wealth (share prices) or as alterations in the systematic risks, i.e. the betas of the banking firms. Harris (1987) attempted to find out whether the profitability profiles in terms of selected financial ratios of commercial banks reacted to the deregulation of 1980. Several fairly sophisticated statistical techniques were successfully applied on pre and post 1980 firm level data.

6. Other Firm Level Studies

Both the Bendeck (1988) and Harris (1987) studies make clear that in the US, econometric work with firm level data continues to be of interest to researchers in banking. Rhoades (1982) is able to report on 26 studies within the "structure-conduct-performance" framework which were published between 1977 and 1982. Most of these studies focused on banks as the units of observation. Most of them estimated a structure-performance relationship. Structure was mostly measured by some index of concentration. Performance indicators were either prices or profits. Clearly, such exercises presuppose the availablity of ample firm level data.

In Europe, firm level data are not so readily available. San Paolo (1989, 1990) are to be welcomed greatly, therefore. The data base of these studies cover growth, profitability and capitalisation and other quantitative information of Europe's 100 biggest banks in terms of assets from 1984-89. By applying comparatively simple statistical methods the authors arrive at many interesting findings. Examples from the 1989 study are: Smaller banks achieved the best average performance. Only few banks managed to combine high asset growth with good profits and improved equity positions. Performance is more similar within countries than across countries. There is no simple link between the degree of internationalisation and profitability, etc. In the most recent 1990 report the authors especially address two major questions: What are the characteristics of cross-border operations, which they define as the opening of new branches and subsidiaries, the acquisition of a controlling or minority interest, cross holding agreements, joint ventures, cooperative agreements etc., and which strategies do Western banks pursue with respect to the new Eastern European banking markets? The perspective particularly of the 1990 study is complementary to the one of Choi et al. (1987) treated in section 2. The Italian study focuses on reactions of individual banks to the opportunities offered by alternative financial centres while Choi et al. (1987) concentrate on explaining the attractiveness of given centres to banks from other centres. Interesting findings for the 1988-1989 period are: "An 'autonomous' expansion strategy seems to prevail. The establishment of new branches or the acquisition of holdings in other financial companies outnumbers the cooperative agreements ... The crossborder expansion follows well-defined patterns. The opening of a representative office is usually the first step for dealing in foreign markets. Acquisition of local dealers may just follow later on ... Agreements, and particularly joint-ventures, are mainly used for expansion in new market sectors." (San Paolo, 1990, p. i). - The potential of the data used in the San Paolo (1989, 1990) studies, which will be updated annually, is clearly great and invites further research.

7. Research Priorities

As a starting point for a brief discussion of research priorities in the competitiveness chapter of the common FAI/ICMB-project, **Tables 7-8** provide an overview of the main indicators of competitiveness and explanatory variables in the literature surveyed in this paper. Additional sources are mentioned in **Table** 7 because of the potential usefulness in future investigations.

Table 7 illustrates that there are many different indicators of competitiveness in banking and securities markets available. Readily useable data are the exception,

Table 7: Indicators of Competitiveness in Banking

Attractiveness:	Location pattern of offices (Choi et al., 1987; San Paolo, 1990)	M
	Bank deposits (Grilli, 1989; Sheldon, 1991)	G
	Fiduciary accounts (Bridel, 1984)*	G
	Custodian accounts**	-
Performance:	Efficiency and technical change (Elyasiani, Mehdian, 1990)*	M
	Market value, assets, profitability (Bendeck, 1988; San Paolo, 1989, 1990)*	M
	Profitability profiles (Harris, 1987)	M
	Profitability, interest margins (OECD)*	G
	Profitability (Davis, Kay, 1990)*	M
	Ratings (Moody's, etc.)*	M
	Foreign assets, % of total employment (Goldberg et al., 1989)	G
	Foreign assets (Bridel, 1984)*	G
	Bond issuing and underwriting (Walter, Smith, 1990; Davis, 1988)	G
	Securities markets capitalisation, turnover, liquidity, spreads, volatility, costs, (Pagano, Roell, 1990; Hawawini, Jacquillat, 1990; Tonks, Webb, 1989)	G

M= micro data *** = not included in the survey**
G = grouped data **** = pro memoria** **FAI**

however. Very often the studies quoted use quite particular sets of data, restricted in time or otherwise, so that the data cannot fruitfully be exploited by other researchers. Remarkable exceptions are Choi et al. (1987) with regard to the location pattern of bank offices and San Paolo (1989, 1990), where for 30 of the largest European bank groups comprehensive information is given. Comparable international information on profitability, costs and margins in banking can be found in OECD publications (e.g. Revell, 1985). Bridel (1984) is an example of how one can measure market shares of international financial centres such as Switzerland in terms of foreign assets. His source are the BIS statistics. The same source also permits the quantitative description of the other side of the coin, i.e. market shares in foreign liabilities. The latter are used in Grilli (1989) and Sheldon (1991).

Ratings do not apppear to have been widely used as an indicator of competitiveness in banking yet. This is surprising, since the safety of a bank might clearly be taken as a sign of its strength and attractiveness. Information in individual banks ability to service and repay debt is contained e.g. in Moody's (1987) and should prove very useful in future research.

Data appear to be weakest with respect to indicators of a bank's attractiveness to clients seeking portfolio management services. For Switzerland information is available for fiduciary accounts, but the volume of funds placed in custodian accounts etc. is virtually unknown. Figures sometimes given for those funds which do not appear in the balance sheets of the banks vary between SFR 1,000- 2,000 billion. To compare, the balance sheet total of all banks in Switzerland amounted to SFR 1,000 billion in 1989. Placing power in primary securities markets is decisively affected by the size of the portfolios managed by the banks in Switzerland. These portfolios are also the source of most of the sizeable annual streams of commissions and fee income to the banks (SFR 10.2 billion of a gross income total of SFR 29.7 billion in 1989, see SNB, 1990). Given the lack of data on the volume of portfolios managed by banks, research will have to concentrate on data on income streams instead.

Grouped data are based on micro information, of course, but very often published sources do not give the micro details.

Table 8 shows that the paradigm of "structure-conduct-performance" has gained some prominence in the economics of banking in Europe recently. As Muldur (1991) shows, **Table 8** does not give a complete coverage. Alone for France there are a

Table 8: Explanatory Variables

Macroeconomics:	GDP, international trade, savings, investment, debt, unemployment (Goldberg et al., 1989)
Structure:	Number of banks (Choi et al., 1987), concentration ratios (Davis, 1988)
	Competitive interdependence, collusion (Choi et al., 1987)
	Distance between financial centres (Choi et al., 1987)
	Agglomeration effects, externalities (Choi et al., 1987, Grilli, 1989)
	Costs (Pagano, Roell, 1990; Davis, 1988)
	Regulation (Choi et al., 1987; Grilli, 1989; Levich, 1990; Bendeck, 1988; Harris, 1987)
	Taxation (Grilli, 1989; Levich, 1990)
	Secrecy (Grilli, 1989)
	Trading systems (Pagano, Roell, 1990)
Conduct:	Spreads, commissions (Tonks, Webb, 1989)

FAI

number of studies that use the concepts of industrial economics in the analysis of the banking sector. According to Rhoades (1982) this has been a distinguishing feature of research in the US for many years. There remains the issue of the quality of the proxies chosen as indicators of structure and conduct. Its solution very likely will decide on the success of further research along these lines of industrial economics.

Within the framework of the common FAI/ICMB-project, a number of pertinent research proposals can be made, two of which have already been effectuated during the past months. Others will be realised in the period ending in March 1992, after which the results will be presented at a second conference in May 1992. **Table 9** gives a summary.

A first group of projects deals with the explanation of the financial centres international attractiveness. Project 1 starts from the data on the location pattern of bank offices given by Choi et al. (1987). By updating the matrix, by developing an explicit theoretical model and by applying other empirical methods Jeger et al. (1991) have produced interesting comparisons and new results. Similarly, new results on the explanation of foreign bank deposits (project 2) can be presented today (Camen, 1991, and Sheldon, 1991).

A second group of projects (project 3) aims at the explanation of the performance of banks. Different dependent variables are proposed. The efficiency variable implies the application of a recently developed method to measure efficiency and technical change (Elyasiani, Mehdian, 1990). With respect to profitability it is also intended to apply new measurement concepts (Davis, Kay, 1990).

In a third group of projects (project 4) the performance of secondary securities markets, i.e. of secondary brokerage and trading stands in the centre. In principle, attempts should also be made to analyse primary securities markets, i.e. the issue and underwriting of bonds and the issue of equity. At present it is not possible to say whether this will be within the limits of the current research programme, however.

On the other hand it ought to be possible to evaluate regulatory change by comparing coefficients estimated first with data from the period before the change

Table 9: Competitiveness in Banking - Research Priorities

	Dependent variables	Main independent variables
Attractiveness of financial centres	(1) Location pattern of offices	Demand (customers), externalities, regulatory regimes, taxation, securities trading volumes
	(2) Bank deposits	like (1) plus ratings of main banks or capital ratios
Performance of banks	(3) Efficiency, profitability, market value	like (1) plus size of banks, concentration and factor costs
Performance of securities markets	(4) Market capitalisation, turnover liquidity	like (2) plus spread and commissions
Regulation evalued	(5) Like (1) - (4)	Time, before and after regulatory change

FAI

and second with data from after the change (project 5). This could be done in the case of all examples of regulation already treated in projects 1-4 provided the necessary information was available.

It has to be admitted that information contained in **Table 9** on the proposed explanatory variables is less than abundant. Clearly, the choice of variables will ultimately depend on theoretical arguments and, not least, on the availability of the relevant statistical information. In any case specific efforts are intended to include externalities and the existence and quality of securities markets in the explanation of the attractiveness of financial centres and of the performance of universal banks.

Apart from international data which can be of cross-sectional, time-series or pooled nature, it is intended to analyse firm, i.e. bank specific data. This particularly applies to project 3. It might be worthwhile to explain empirically the performance of different groups of Swiss banks, ranging from private banks to the large banks in the Top 4 group. It appears also to be of interest to analyse whether such groups are likely to be affected differently by imminent regulatory and economic change.

Literature

Bendeck, Y.M. (1988), The Effects of Regulation on Commercial Bank Valuation, Arizona State University.

Blattner, N., Genberg, H., and Swoboda, A. (eds.) (1992), Competitiveness in Banking, Heidelberg.

Blattner, N. (1990), "Defining and Explaining Competitiveness: Lessons from Research in Switzerland", OECD Conference on the Consequences of the Technology Economy Programme for the Development of Indicators, Paris, July 2-5, unpublished manuscript (available on request from FAI).

Bridel, P. (1984), "Essai d'estimation de la part suisse à l'activité financière internationale 1975-1983", in: Geld, Währung und Konjunktur, Vol. 2, 3.

Camen, U. (1991), "Measuring and Explaining the Swiss Position in Markets for International Bank Deposits", in: Blattner et al. (1992).

Carter, N. (1990), "Comment", in: Dermine (1990).

Choi, S.-R., Tschoegl, A.E., and Yu, Ch.-M. (1987), "Banks and the World's Major Financial Centers, 1970-1980", in: Weltwirtschaftliches Archiv, Bd. 122.

Danthine, J.-P. (1990), "Comment", in: Dermine (1990).

Davis, E.P. (1988), Industrial Structure and Dynamics of Financial Markets, the Primary Eurobond Market, Bank of England Discussion Papers, No. 35.

Davis, E., and Kay, J. (1990), "Assessing Corporate Performance", in: Business Strategy Review, Summer.

Dermine, J. (ed.) (1990), European Banking in the 1990s, Oxford.

Elyasiani, E., and Mehdian, S.M. (1990), "A Nonparametric Approach to Measurement of Efficiency and Technological Change: The Case of Large US Commercial Banks", in: Journal of Financial Services Research, 4.

Essayyad, M. (1989), "The Feasibility of Establishing an International Financial Center: the Case of Anchorage", in: Park, Essayyad (1989).

Goldberg, M.A., Helsley, R., and Levi, M.D. (1989), "The Prerequisites for an International Financial Center", in: Park, Essayyad (1989).

Grilli, V. (1989), "Financial Markets", in: Economic Policy, Vol. 4, No. 2.

Harris, J.D., Jr. (1987), Changes in the Financial Profile of Large Commercial Banks' Profitability to Compensate for Deregulation, Michigan State University.

Hawawini, G., and Jacquillat, B. (1990), "European Equity Markets: Towards 1992 and Beyond", in: Dermine (1990).

Jeger, M., Haegler, U., and Theiss, R. (1991), "The Attractiveness of International Financial Centres", in: Blattner et al. (1992).

Kindleberger, C.P. (1974), The Formation of Financial Centres: A Study of Comparative Economic History, Princetown.

Levich, R.M. (1990), "The Euromarkets After 1992", in: Dermine (1990).

Moody's (1987), Bank Credit Opinions, New York.

Muldur, U. (1991), Efficience et compétition dans les marchés bancaires, manuscript.

Pagano, M., and Roell, A. (1990), "Stock Markets", in: Economic Policy, Vol. 5, No. 1.

Park, Y.S., and Essayyad, M. (eds.) (1989), International Banking and Financial Centers, Dordrecht.

Reed, H.C. (1981), The Preeminence of International Financial Centres, New York.

Reed, H.C. (1980), " The Ascent of Tokyo as an International Financial Center", in: Journal of International Business Studies, Vol. 11, No. 3.

Revell, J.R.S. (1985), Cost Margins in Banking: Statistical Supplement 1978-1982, OECD, Paris.

Rhoades, St.A. (1982), "Structure-Performance Studies in Banking: An Update Summary and Evaluation", in: Federal Reserve Bulletin, Washington.

San Paolo Group (1989, 1990), Europe's Main Banking Groups: Growth and Strategies, Torino.

Sheldon, G. (1991), "Measuring and Explaining the Swiss Position in the Market for International Bank Deposits", in: Blattner et al. (1992).

SNB (1990), Das schweizerische Bankwesen im Jahre 1989, Nr. 74, Zürich.

Tonks, I., and Webb, D. (1989), "The Reorganisation of the London Stock Market: The Causes and Consequences of 'Big-Bang'", Special Paper No. 20, LSE Financial Market Group Special Paper Series.

Walter, I., and Smith, R.C. (1989), Investment Banking in Europe, Oxford.

Walter, I., and Smith, R.C. (1990), "European Investment Banking: Structures, Transactions Flow and Regulation", in: Dermine (1990).

Comment on
Niklaus Blattner: "Competitiveness in Banking: Selected Recent Contributions and Research Priorities"

Martin Hellwig

1. Introduction

In his survey of recent contributions to the analysis of competitiveness in banking, Niklaus Blattner observes that (i) 'hardly a topic in recent years has attracted more public attention in economics than that of competitiveness', and (ii) 'the ubiquity of the term does not match the clarity of the concept'. In the following comment, I will start from this observation and expand a bit on the semantics of the word 'competitiveness'.

The importance of semantics may be illustrated by an example. As a student, reading a book of logic, I was saddened to learn that 'about five percent of all prime numbers die within three years of their birth, some from a typhoid fever and some of the square root of a mock turtle'. This unhappy sentence reminds us that a word is typically defined in a certain context, and that a sentence which uses a word outside its definitional context tends to be meaningless even though it may be syntactically correct. To be sure, following Humpty-Dumpty in his conversation with Alice in "Through the Looking Glass", we may choose to give a word an additional meaning in another context - so that, e.g. 'glory' may also mean 'a nice knockdown argument' (Carroll, 1965, p. 269) -, but then we have to make it clear that this is a meaning with a new definitional context. If one fails to make the proper distinctions, one may end up with statements that are just as meaningful as the above statement about the sad prospects for newly-born prime numbers.

As a case in point, consider the following passage from one of the contributions to the early post-war debate on the Pigou effect: 'It is interesting to note that the Pigou effect ... implies a curious type of money illusion .... For an increase in the real value of cash-balances makes society no wealthier in 'real' terms, that is in goods ...' (Eisner, 1958, p. 718 n.). This passage overlooks the fact that the definitional context of the word 'wealth' depends on whether one is referring to 'individual wealth' or to 'societal wealth'. The notion of 'wealth' as a measure of the power to command goods and services belongs to the context of the individual who can buy these goods and services in the market. Indeed the notion involves an implicit presumption that the individual in question is a price-taker. For a non-price-taker, i.e., a monopolist or an oligopolist, a conventional measure of 'wealth' - at given prices - will not provide an unambiguous indication of the power to command goods and services in the market. For society as a whole, the notion of 'wealth' as a measure of the power to command goods and services makes even less sense: First it is not clear whose power to command goods and services is to be measured - although the word 'society' is a substantive, it hardly denotes a subject that is active in the market. Secondly, the concept of 'society' as a whole leaves no room for the trading partners that are required for market transactions; moreover 'society' as a whole can hardly take prices as given. These considerations do not imply that the concept of 'societal wealth' itself is meaningless.[1]

However, the definitional context of 'societal wealth' differs from the definitional context of 'individual wealth', and a sentence which disregards this difference is likely to be just as meaningful as a sentence about the square root of a mock turtle.[2]

Like the word 'wealth', the word 'competitiveness' has a certain rhetorical appeal. Therefore it is used quite often, sometimes in widely differing contexts. The transfer to new contexts tends to be motivated by a desire to profit from the rhetorical appeal of the word in this original context. For us it is all the more important to make the proper distinctions between the different uses of the word and to develop a certain awareness of differences in the underlying issues and phenomena. This is the object of the following notes.

---

1 One may define 'societal wealth' quite mechanically as the sum of all individual wealth levels in the economy. If all individuals take prices as given, and if there are no 'distribution-effects', this 'societal wealth' variable properly measures the wealth argument in the aggregate demand functions for goods and services. If individuals do not take prices as given, or if there are 'distribution effects', the 'societal wealth' variable probably is without analytic interest - in spite of the propagandistic appeal and time-honoured tradition of the word.

2 The reader who wonders about the inclusion of worthless paper in 'Society's real wealth' should try Eisner's argument for machines. After all, machines make society hardly wealthier in terms of current consumption goods, so presumably the inclusion of machines in society's 'real' wealth must reflect a curious type of machine illusion.

2. 'Competitiveness' of a Firm

The notion of 'competitiveness' originates in the area of sports. When we refer to Stefan Edberg as a 'competitive' tennis player, we think of him as a player who is willing and able to compete successfully at the game of tennis. He may not win every match or every tournament that he plays in. However, ex ante he is a good bet to win any tournament that he enters.

What about 'competitiveness' in economics? If we think of competition in terms of the Bertrand model of price competition in a single homogeneous market, we can transfer the concept of 'competitiveness' from sports to economics without change. Like a tennis tournament, price competition à la Bertrand in a single homogeneous market has a single winner, namely the firm with the lowest marginal cost of production.[3] A firm with low production costs is likely to win any Bertrand competition that it enters and may thus be called 'competitive'.

However, the Bertrand model covers only a very special case. The moment one looks at other models of competition, the meaning of the term 'competitiveness' is less clear. To see this, consider first the Cournot model of competition among quantity-setting firms in a single market. In this model, it doesn't make sense to say that any one firm 'wins' the competition. To be sure, in equilibrium the firm with the lowest production cost has the largest market share and the highest profit, but this does not preclude the higher-cost firms from also being active and earning positive profits. In contrast to a tennis tournament or to the Bertrand model of price competition, the Cournot model puts less of a premium on relative performance; in particular, winning is not 'the only thing'.[4]

---

3 Recall that the Bertrand model assumes constant marginal and average costs so that both are actually equal.

4 See McCloskey 1990, pp. 43-49, for a very perceptive account of how the sporting metaphor with its emphasis on winning distorts one's assessment of economic performance.

If we allow for product differentiation, the matter becomes still more difficult. Regardless of whether we think of competition in terms of price setting à la Bertrand or in terms of quantity setting à la Cournot, equilibrium market outcomes will depend on product characteristics as well as costs. Moreover the market outcomes themselves will be multidimensional in that equilibrium profits and equilibrium market shares will not always be perfectly correlated. If Volkswagen has the larger share of the automobile market and Daimler-Benz earns the larger profits, which one are we to consider the 'more competitive'?

At this point, it is tempting to assess market outcomes solely in terms of profits so that a firm is deemed to be 'competitive' if it can expect to earn high profits. However, in the absence of a complete system of contingent-securities markets, firms' objective must be taken to be multidimensional, involving considerations of risk avoidance as well as of profitability, considerations of profitability in the future as well as the present. How then are we to assess the 'competitiveness' of a firm that does very well in its markets at present, but has little ability to adapt to a substantial change in its environment? In assessing the 'competitiveness' of Stefan Edberg as a tennis player, should we take account of the fact that he is likely to win rather less if the rules of the game are changed so as to substitute ping pong bats for tennis rackets? To any tennis fan, this question is absurd. Its analogue though is of great concern to analysts looking at Volkswagen in the late Sixties or at continental stock markets today.

In summary, the sporting metaphor works well for the simplest model of Bertrand competition, but becomes strained as one departs from that model. The underlying issue is that firms do not compete in a sport with well-defined rules and a clear definition of what it means 'to win'. To some extent they choose their own objectives and make their own rules. The analyst tries to account for this by looking at competition among firms in terms of many different types of games. But then it seems as though the definition of 'competitiveness' has to be newly adapted each time one looks at a new model of competition among firms. This makes it doubtful that there should be any simple set of factors to explain 'competitiveness' in a wide variety of contexts.

3. 'Competitiveness' and the Role of Prices

Discussions of competitiveness frequently involve prices, in particular factor prices and exchange rates. High wages in Switzerland are said to reduce the competitiveness of Swiss firms. A high value of the German Mark is said to reduce the competitiveness of German firms.

Such statements raise the question to what extent the prices referred to can be regarded as exogenous. If they must be regarded as endogenous, then it makes no sense to have them 'explain' a firm's competitiveness or the lack thereof. Within a given product market, this point is well understood. Hardly anybody will claim that the high price of a Mercedes reduces the competitiveness of Daimler-Benz relative to Volkswagen. Indeed one is tempted to interpret their high prices as an indication of the attractiveness of their products and hence a signal of their 'competitiveness'. What would one say though if overnight their demand schedules became more elastic and they chose to lower their prices? In a situation in which actual prices are the results of conscious decisions in the process of competitition, an assessment of 'competitiveness' must rely on the underlying demand and cost schedules rather than the particular price-quantity combinations that are observed.

To some extent, these considerations apply to factor markets and factor prices as well. After all, firms must attract the suppliers of their inputs as well as the demanders of their outputs. Indeed if a scarce input is essential for production, competition on the input market can be more important and fiercer than competition on the output market. For instance, Stahl (1988) and Yanelle (1988) show that in a Bertrand model of price competition on input and output markets, a firm may want to bid inputs away from other firms - not because it needs them, but because it wants to obtain and exploit a monopoly position on the output market. In the absence of job differentiation, this competition for inputs is won by the firm with the lowest input-output coefficient, which can afford to pay the highest price for the input. High factor prices, in particular a high wage rate must thus be the result of high competitiveness in the input market rather than a source of low competitiveness in the output market.

To be sure there are cases when it is appropriate to focus solely on competition in output markets, taken input prices as given. This may be because input prices in fact are determined exogenously, without regard to market conditions, as in the case of

East German wages since fall 1990. Alternatively, the firms and the sector under study may be so small relative to the input markets that they have practically no effect on input prices.

In the latter case though, one must be aware of the partial-equilibrium nature of the analysis. From a partial-equilibrium perspective, it may make sense to say that high wages reduce the competitiveness of a single firm or even of all firms in a small sector. However, it doesn't make any sense to say that high wages in Switzerland reduce the competitiveness of Swiss firms as a whole. At this level of aggregation, the wage rate - and, similarly, the exchange rate - cannot be regarded as exogenous. Once one endogenizes it, one is likely to find that the high wage rate itself is caused by the high degree of efficiency of certain firms in the economy. Thus by the same logic as in the Stahl-Yanelle argument, a high equilibrium wage must be seen as the result of high competitiveness on the input market rather than a source of low competitiveness on the output market.

4. Competition among Financial Centers

I now turn to the notion of competition among financial centres. In what sense can we say that Zurich and London are 'competing financial centers'? How meaningful is a statement that doubts the 'competitiveness of Switzerland as a financial center' over the years to come?

The first question here is who competes. In sports, we think of competitors as individuals or teams playing against other individuals or teams. A team is ideally characterized by a high degree of internal coordination and a shared objective of the team members. In practice, the team may stop short of the ideal, i.e., coordination may not work, or a disgruntled team member may want to annoy the others rather than to win. Such instances however are seen as deviations from the ideal which do not lead us to question the ideal itself. Indeed coordination failures or member disaffection are seen as weaknesses which tend to reduce the 'competitiveness' of the team relative to other teams.

Competition among firms is thought of in much the same vein. The firm is seen as an individual or a team competing against other firms, and ideally all activities on behalf of the firm are well coordinated and are motivated by the same objectives. To the extent that incentive problems or communication failures lead to frictions, this is seen as a weakness which tends to reduce the 'competitiveness' of the firm.

In contrast, it is a priori not clear what one means when one refers to 'competition among financial centers'. A financial center involves many different firms which do not usually act as a team. In the absence of a local cartel agreement, there is little coordination between them. They compete among each other as much as they compete with firms in other financial centers. In contrast to the case of a football team, the lack of coordination and the lack of a common objective among the firms in a given center are considered to be the rule rather than the exception (except perhaps by an adherent of the medieval guild system). Hence it seems that the notion of 'competition among financial centers' is rather akin to the square root of a mock turtle - unless of course we provide a new definition with a well-specified definitional context.

I see three possible definitions:

a. Without thinking of financial centers as competitors, we can refer to 'competition among financial centers' in terms of aggregate indices of the noncoordinated activities of the different firms in the different centers.

b. We can think of 'competition among financial centers' in terms of explicit competition among certain institutions at different centers, e.g., competition between the London stock market and the Zurich stock market.

c. We can think of 'competition among financial centers' in terms of explicit competition between the regulatory and fiscal authorities of different countries as they try to attract certain activities - and to profit from them.

I will briefly discuss each of these possibilities in turn, hoping to show that they involve quite different notions of 'competition among financial centers'.

ad a. If we think of uncoordinated competition between financial firms anywhere in the world, there is a priori no reason why the fates of firms in a given center should be correlated and why any kind of aggregate index of the 'competitiveness' of firms in a given center should be meaningful. Such an index is meaningful only if there are common factors driving, e.g., the fates of Crédit Suisse and UBS in Zurich so that their market positions are more highly correlated that the market positions of Crédit Suisse and Crédit Lyonnais. As possible common factors, we have

- the common institutional, regulatory, and fiscal framework, within which the firms of a given center operate,

- the common factor prices which the firms of a given center face in their domestic factor markets,

- the possible thick-market externalities whereby the success of one firm enhances the chances of the second firm.

If we look at the recent literature, e.g., Grilli (1989), we find that - apart from the obvious tax factors, e.g. the stamp duty - much attention is paid to the factors that we don't understand so well, namely institutional and regulatory factors and thick-market externalities, whereas less weight is given to factor prices. In this era of the 'new international economics' are we so sure that Ricardin comparative advantage is altogether irrelevant?[5]

Among the factors listed, the thick-market externalities are perhaps the most interesting one - and the one that is least understood. Grilli (1989) stresses the role of skilled labour: With many firms in a financial center, I am more likely to find skilled labour when I need it. This argument presumes that the supply schedule for skilled labour is downward sloping so that the pecuniary externality from the other firms' labour demand goes in the direction of lowering the wage that I have to pay. Such a downward-sloping supply schedule for skilled labour is not impossible, but presumably it rests on the presence of economies of scale in the underlying education system. I am not sure that such economics of scale are sufficiently large to counteract the more direct effect whereby the other firms' labour demands make labour more scarce and force me to pay a higher wage.

---

5 As a further aside on the semantics of the word 'competitiveness', the reader may note that the Ricardian theory militates against the notion of 'competitiveness of an entire economy'. See McCloskey (1990), pp. 156ff., for a critical assessment of such rhetoric.

ad b. If we think of a stock exchange as a firm, then in principle we can analyse competition among the exchanges in different locations in terms of the framework discussed in Section 2. Presumably the 'competitiveness' of a given exchange will depend on the product it offers: its organization, the set of available contracts, the settlement procedure, etc. As in the general case of competition with product differentiation, an assessment of 'competitiveness' here requires detailed information about customers' tastes, i.e., about their tradeoffs between the different characteristics of 'the product'.

In this context, it is perhaps intersting to note that the competition between exchanges may give rise to some rather unexpected effects. Thus Pagano, Roell (1990) note that the recent reform of the Paris bourse may in part have benefitted the competitiveness of London market makers because the improved transparency of the bourse provided them with a better information basis for setting their bid and ask prices.

ad c. Competition among regulatory and fiscal authorities is akin to competition among exchanges; however, the authorities' objectives are less clear. On the one hand, they may be concerned about the customers of the financial firms. On the other hand, they may be concerned about their own tax revenues. From this perspective, taxes - such as the stamp duty or the withholding tax on interest income - appear as fiscal prices that have to be paid for the right to transact in a certain jurisdiction. Whereas a Swiss bank or the Zurich stock exchange interpret the stamp duty as an impediment to their 'competitiveness', the Swiss finance minister may regard the stamp duty as a proper reward for the high attractiveness of Switzerland as a financial center - just as Daimler-Benz charges a high price because its cars are so attractive.

Unfortunately, we have as yet little understanding of how competition among the regulatory authorities of different centers works. However, the preceding remarks should make it clear that our assessment of 'competition among financial centers' and of the factors explaining 'competitiveness' depends very much on which of the three interpretations of 'competition' we are using.

To conclude these notes, I recall Humpty-Dumpty's remark to Alice: "When I make a word do a lot of work like that, I always pay it extra." The preceding discussion suggests that the word "competitiveness" needs to be paid extra quite a lot.

References

Carroll, L. (1965), Through the Looking Glass, in: L. Carroll, The Annotated Alice, ed. by M. Gardner, Penguin, Harmondsworth.

Eisner, R. (1958), 'On Growth Models and the Neo-Classical Resurgence', Economic Journal, 68.

Grilli, V. (1989), Europe 1992: 'Issues and Prospects for the Fiancial Markets', Economic Policy, 9.

McCloskey, D. (1990), If You're So Smart: The Narrative of Economic Expertise, University of Chicago Press, Chicago.

Pagano, M., and Roell, A. (1990), 'Trading Systems in European Stock Exchanges: Current Performance and Policy Options', Economic Policy, 10.

Stahl, D. (1988), 'Bertrand Competition for Inputs and Walrasian Outcomes', American Economic Review, 78.

Yanelle, M.O. (1988), On the Theory of Intermediation, Diss., University of Bonn.

Comment on

Niklaus Blattner: "Competitiveness in Banking: Selected Recent Contributions and Research Priorities"

Thomas Gehrig

In his selective survey on competitiveness in banking Blattner concentrates on the interesting issue of the competitiveness of market places or financial centres rather than the competitiveness of individual firms. While the notion of competitiveness of an individual firm seems to be well understood by economists they generally feel quite embarrassed when it comes to define competitiveness of a market place, a financial centre or even the competitiveness of a nation. In each case competitiveness of the subject quite intuitively would seem to suggest some sort of economic viability of this subject. Obviously, the viability will depend very much on the conduct of this subject in a given environment as well as on the nature of the environment itself. Therefore, one feels tempted to define competitiveness of a market place basically as the ability of this market to attract positive market shares and hence the ability to survive in a given economic environment. In the sequel I would like to argue that it is the interplay of the market place with its economic environment, which makes the competitiveness issue a particular interesting and politically important one.

The empirical studies surveyed by Blattner are largely studies on the attractiveness of financial centres. By identifying factors of attractiveness also factors of viability of these market places are singled out. Not surprisingly in the empirical work surveyed, but also in the work to be presented during the course of this conference, variables related to regulatory intervention into the market mechanism are found to exert significant explanatory power in determining the attractiveness of market places. Actually, it seems to me that the notion of competitiveness is intimately related to the political discussions about government interventions into the internal functioning of markets. For example the discussion about the competitiveness of European financial centres has intensified after London's Big Bang has succeeded in diverting market volumes from continental European stock exchanges. Likewise the discussion about the competitiveness of the financial market place Switzerland can be largely seen as a response to the deregulation wave in

Europe and pending changes in the regulatory framework of the Common Market. The discussion typically is directed at influencing government regulators to react in a way as to secure domestic competitiveness. On the other hand governments may have an incentive to participate at the revenues generated in the market place. This interest typically poses a burden on the market place. The many facets of competitiveness thus result from different notions of the process of competition against which ultimately the competitiveness of a market place will have to be judged and from different notions about the division of revenues.

Blattner repeatedly complains about a lack of theoretical modelling. Therefore, in the present note I would like to fill in some gaps to show how the competitiveness of a market relates to government interests. While not offering a fully fledged model here I want to argue that theory can contribute to sharpening our understanding of the notion of competitiveness of markets. Although stylized the following ideas may help to focus the discussion on some elements which seem important in our understanding of competition between markets[1].

So consider two market places, each comprising a number of firms active solely on the respective market place. Each market is organized by some independent regulator. The first feature which seems crucial and which lays the basis for the political discussion is the existence of a conflict of interest between the regulator and the individual firms. Regulators may intervene for prudential reasons or for reasons of some market failure. Alternatively, regulators may simply be interested in collecting taxes, such as the stamp duty for example. It is not the purpose of this note to discuss respective merits of alternative regulatory rules. Therefore, assume that regulators only care for tax revenues derived from transactions taxes. By imposing taxes such as the stamp duty regulators increase the effective prices of financial services offered by firms in the market under consideration and accordingly they will affect consumer choice. (In this note we shall not consider lump sum taxation for the well known information problems in the imposition of this tax)

Consumers are located evenly on a line between the two market places. When travelling to a market place they incur costs proportional to their distance. Now assume at the moment consumers have to decide, which market to choose they still are not aware of the specific contract they need to buy (i.e. the maturity of a futures

1 For a full description of the theoretical argument, see Gehrig (1991).

contract say). At the moment of decision however the consumer do know exactly the type of contracts offered by each firm in each market place as well as the corresponding prices. If the consumer has chosen a market and finds that the maturity desired is not available he will have to move to the closest substitute, which again is costly. So his choice will be the market place which minimizes his expected total costs of travelling. His choice does not need to be the market place, which is geographically closer. Firms in the farther market may offer better prices and more variety in the sense of more maturities. In this example the market with more active firms will typically offer better insurance possibilities. Therefore, if prices and travelling distance are identical consumers will prefer the market with more active firms because of increased risk pooling. Hence in the words of Grilli we find a natural thick market externality. It is quite different to the type of externality he considers, but it will have the same effect.

Given consumers minimize expected travelling costs firms compete against each other for market shares. Let us assume that each firm will select a single commodity, i.e. one variety (contract) in one market. Now given firms locations price competition between firms has two components:

i) There is competition between firms in a market place. If the firm offering a 3 month contracts charges significantly lower prices than a firm offering 6 months contracts the low price firm may succeed to capture a client who ideally would like a 5 months contract, which is not on offer in the market considered.

ii) Furthermore there is competition against firms in the foreign market place. By lowering domestic prices domestic firms will steal market shares from domestic rivals but in addition they reduce the average prices on the domestic market thus attracting additional consumers to the market place. Domestic rivals may be partially compensated from this increase in the international market share of the whole market place.

The rivalry between firms for international business induces a rivalry between regulators. Naturally, regulators are interested in large market shares for the domestic market place, since they will gain handsomely on transaction taxes. On the other hand imposing such taxes will increase prices and therefore reduce the attractiveness of the market place to international investors. Thus by imposing taxes regulators implicitly subsidize foreign firms by allowing them to gain larger market shares. Accordingly, regulators in their attempt to maximize tax revenues are caught in a competitive game against the foreign regulator. The equilibrium level of transactions taxes will depend inter alia on the physical transportation costs between the market places.

In a free entry equilibrium the number of active firms in each market is determined by a zero profit condition. Entry will occur as long as it is profitable. Regulatory intervention in this model will affect both, the margins charged and the corresponding profits earned by firms and the number of active firms.

Now what can be said about equilibrium in such a model?

First, given the levels of transactions taxes in a symmetric equilibrium more firm will locate in the market with lower taxes. Interfirm rivalry will be stronger in the low intervention market but at the same time the corresponding low general level of prices will attract a large portion of international business. In this sense the low tax market does attract more business than the high tax market and hence seems to be more competitive.

In this case however the total market share of the low tax market exceeds the total market share of the high tax market. Nevertheless, each individual firm in the low tax market will enjoy a smaller market share than a firm in the high tax market. This directly stems from the zero profit condition, according to which high tax firms do need larger market shares in order to fund the tax requirements. Furthermore, provided the markets are small enough such that wage determination in each country remains unaffected, per capita income would typically be larger in the low tax market. While the above statement cautions to use market shares crudely as indicators for competitiveness, per capita income, an indicator proposed by Blattner et al. (1987) matches well with domestic market share as an indicator of competitiveness in this framework. On the other hand further indicators such as return on capital or profits trivially remain uninformative.

Second, we have already hinted to one type of thick market externality embodied in our framework. A direct consequence of this externality is that entry barriers for further market places are created. Entry at an intermediate position between the two established market places will be rather costly and may be possible only if sufficient varieties are offered.

Third, we should note that the model offers a natural rationale for the observed deregulation wave. A drastic reduction in transportation costs does reduce firms price cost margins drastically. In such a case also regulators have larger incentives to undercut each other. The original equilibrium therefore cannot be maintained and a new equilibrium at significantly lower transactions taxes should be reached. Since regulatory changes seem to move rather slowly relative to immediate behaviour of market participants (see Kane, 1991) this framework can easily explain the dramatic losses of market shares, when one of the regulators moves late.

This story may closely be reminiscent of the rivalry between the London and Paris stock markets. London moving first in reducing transactions taxes could increase market shares so dramatically that Paris was forced to react most urgently and reform the Paris stock exchange in just one year.

Finally, how does attractiveness relate to welfare?

Not surprisingly also here there does not seem to be any obvious link. Several components of welfare have to be considered. From a domestic point of view domestic consumer surplus, profits of domestic firms and domestic tax revenues are the variables of concern. Typically, there are tradeoffs in the relative importance of these components.

A small country generating a lot of foreign business for example might be tempted to weigh profits of domestic firms plus domestic tax revenues quite highly relative to domestic consumer surplus. These profits and revenues are being paid largely by foreigners and add to domestic income. In this case it seems quite plausible for the regulators of the small country to select a high tax policy, which among others serves as to impede entry and hence keeps the industrial structure quite profitable. An alternative policy with similar ends is a restriction to entry. As argued above, however, such a policy may be severely constrained by competition from low tax markets. In particular, such policies will reduce the impact of thick market externalities. The regulator will have to strike the balance between welfare losses in domestic consumer surplus against the gains from market power against foreign consumers.

Literature

Blattner, N., Maurer, M., Weber, M. (1987), Voraussetzungen der schweizerischen Wettbewerbsfähigkeit, Bern.

Gehrig, Th. (1991), Competing Markets, WWZ-Discussion paper, forthcoming.

Kane, E.J. (1991), "Financial Regulation and Market Forces", in: Schweiz. Zeitschrift für Volkswirtschaft und Statistik, 127, 3.

Part II: The Swiss Banking Sector

The Swiss Banking Sector: Development and Outlook

Andreas Bossard, Matthias Wirth, Niklaus Blattner

I. Introduction

Time and again the Swiss banking sector is in the centre of public attention. The interest shown for this branch of the economy has various origins. On the one hand, there are economic aspects and on the other, the political implications of bank transactions in the small country of Switzerland. In the practical debate the economic and political arguments unavoidably merge into one another.

With this present report we do not wish, in the first place, to furnish a further contribution to the current controversial issues of economic policy. The debates are to be stimulated too, of course, but another concern is in the foreground: it is a question of obtaining an assessment of the strong and weak aspects of the Swiss banking sector as far as they can be derived from the developments of the last ten years and from international comparison. With the help of this report it should be easier to identify the opportunities and risks in the Swiss banking sector. A better basis permits more appropriate decisions.

The report begins with an elucidation of the banking sector's significance as component of the Swiss economy. Its importance is measured on the basis of value added, employment, net exports and tax contribution.

The banks' activities are analysed according to the classical separation of on-balance sheet and off-balance sheet business. A simultaneous analysis of the changes on all the relevant markets has been waived. The banks' income naturally depends on developments on the finance markets. But in this report it is not so much a matter of the markets themselves but more of what takes place on them and its consequences for the volume and structure of the activities of the banks in Switzerland.

Besides the changes in the structure of the banks' activities, it is also interesting to look at the changes in the structure of the banking industry, i.e. the shares of the various bank groups in the aggregate assets and the status and evolution of concentration.

A comparison of the Swiss banks to those of other important countries is also part of the survey. In all the comparisons, alongside the indications of extent of activity, there are always those of performance, i.e. profitability, efficiency and security.

Finally, on the basis of the various analytical elements of development during the period 1980 - 1989, an outlook is ventured into the Nineties. It does not consist of forecasts or prospects. It is more in the form of a short review of the parameters of the competitiveness and the prosperity of the Swiss banking sector, as seen from today.

The report is divided into a textual and a statistical section. As regards the statistics a few remarks are necessary. The main source of information is the bank statistics of the Swiss National Bank. In addition, other national and international data has been obtained and evaluated. Estimations have only been taken in cases of necessity. Consequently, the data evaluated is in the main accounting data.

The quality of the data varies. Although the reliability of the bank statistics, in comparison to other statistics, is over-average, they also have their problems. The principles of data capture are stipulated to a large extent by law and by the bank supervisory authorities. The legal rulings change and give rise to scope, this does not facilitate analysis. In this connection the constitution and releasing of hidden reserves is to be mentioned. An other problem emanates from the fact that the bank statistics are compiled from notifications from the individual bank institutions, i.e. the domestic offices and branches plus the legally non-independent branches abroad, instead of from the banks as groups, i.e. a group's own branches and subsidiaries, consolidated as they are effectively controlled economically, and separated between domestic and foreign activities.

But as a whole, in spite of these restrictions, the data should provide an accurate picture of developments in the Swiss banking sector.

II. Development 1980 - 1989

1. The banks as component of the Swiss economy

1.1 Value added, employment, net exports and taxes

The business activity of all the banks and finance companies domiciled in Switzerland (hereafter the "Swiss banks") has developed over-averagely over the past ten years. The real gross value added increased annually from 1980 to 1989 by more than 5.5 %. In comparison, the growth rate of the Gross Domestic Product (GDP), i.e. the gross value added of all domestic branches of the economy, amounted to only 2 %. The growth of Switzerland's other important sectors was also clearly surpassed by that of the banks (see **Chart 1** and **Table A 1** in the appendix). Logically, the banks' part in the GDP also increased from 6.5 % in 1980 to 8.8 % in 1989.

Employment in the banking sector also showed an over-average increase over the last ten years. Thanks to the growth rate of 4.2 % p.a., the number of bank employees in Switzerland's working population rose from 2.5 to 3.3 %. Employment at the end of 1989 totalled 117'000 persons. Thus the banking sector ranks as one of the major employers of the country. Noteworthy too, is the very steady evolution of the uptrend.

The increase in employment was less than that of the real value added. Productivity, i.e. the gross value added per employee, has risen. The expansion of the Eighties was accompanied by over-average productivity gains. In 1989, the value added per employee of the banking sector was more than two and a half times higher than the Swiss average. At 1985 prices, it amounted in 1989 to about Sfr. 194'000 (Swiss average: Sfr. 72'000).

The net exports are used to measure the banks' net service exports as contribution to the GDP (net exports = exports minus imports) (see **Table A 3**). There are no published statistics of the banks' net exports. Our estimation for 1989 is in excess of Sfr. 8 billion. Approximately every third franc in the banking sector is earned from services to foreigners or capital revenue from abroad. The banks' net exports are higher than that of other Swiss industries and are a decisive contribution to the financing of Swiss imports. In the course of the Eighties they probably grew over-proportionally in comparison to the GDP and proportionally to the banks' own gross value added.

Chart 1:

Value Added and Employment

real growth p.a. 1980-1989

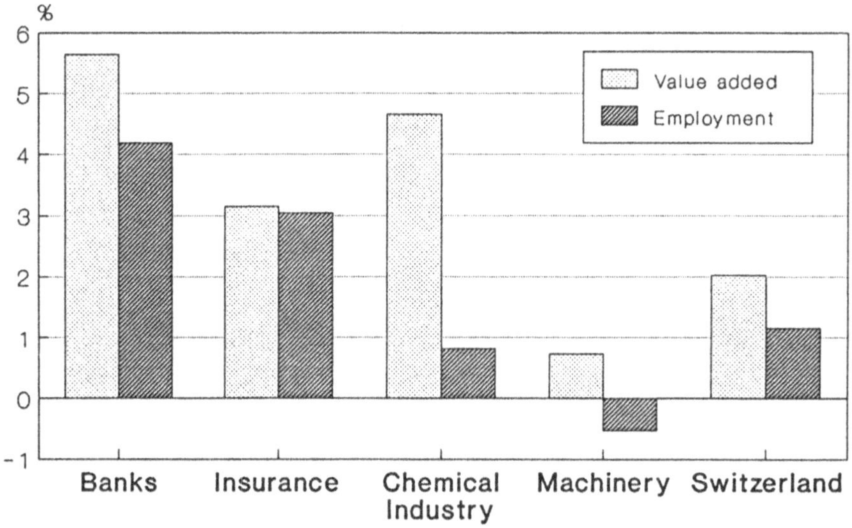

Sources: FOS, BBG

Swiss Banks 1980-1989 SBA 12/90

The importance of the Swiss banks as taxpayers also grew during the period 1980 to 1989 (see **Table A 4**). The direct taxes paid by the banks increased more (7.8 % p.a.) than the Confederation's fiscal revenue (6.7 % p.a.) and the taxes of all corporations (7.5 % p.a.). More important, however, is the aspect of indirect taxes in connection with financial services. The rates of increase of the Stamp Duty (14.6 % p.a.) and the Withholding Tax (8.8 % p.a.) are extraordinary. In spite of the weaker development since the stock exchange crash of 1987, the share in the Confederation's fiscal revenue, in 1989 too, was still around 19 %.

The strong expansion of the banking sector is attributed on the one hand to the favourable economic environment worldwide, i.e. the excellent level of activity in general, the boom in the issuing and securities markets as well as the declining rates of inflation and interest and, on the other, to the dynamic and innovatory development of bank services offered. Furthermore are to mention the investments in process and information technology and the efforts undertaken in connection with staff training.

In the Eighties, the banking sector caught up, at least in part, the under-average performance of the traditional providers of Swiss prosperity (see **Chart 1**), such as e.g. the machine industry. The slowing down of growth and the losses in employment in these sectors of the economy were compensated so that the necessary real adjustment process could be absorbed for the economy as a whole. In this process the banks contributed to the Swiss economy not only from the aspect of quantity but also - as is shown by the development in productivity - from the aspect of quality.

In addition to this, when one bears in mind that a prospering banking sector creates directly and indirectly - through its employees - considerable impulses for demand and growth in other sectors of the Swiss economy, it can be said generally that in the past ten years the banks were a central promoter of the overall economic growth and of Swiss prosperity. However, the banks' growth slowed down from the mid-Eighties. The reasons for this are above all the sharper international competition, declining importance in the comparative advantages of location in Switzerland, poor stock exchange climate (crashes in 1987 and 1989) and the new rise in interest and inflation rates since 1988.

1.2 Regional importance

Banking services are available over the whole of Switzerland. There is a dense network of branches. But owing to economic performance, a regional concentration can be observed which increased further between 1975 and 1985. There is a strong concentration of bank employees in the Cantons of Zurich and Geneva. Nearly 50 % of the total bank staff are employed in these two Cantons (see **Chart 2**). Canton Zurich is dominant in this respect employing about one third of bank staff in 1985 (31.7 % in 1975). Geneva (15.6 % in 1975 and 15.8 % in 1985) and Vaud (6.1 % in 1975 and 6.6 % in 1985) have as well increased their shares.

With regard to employment, the importance of the banking sector varies according to Canton (see **Table A 2**). In 1985, of the all-Swiss total of bank staff of 3.1 %, 7.7 % were employed in Geneva, 5.6 % in Tessin, 5.3 % in Zurich and 4.7 % in Basle. Since 1975 all these shares have increased.

2. Balance sheet and income statement

2.1 Review

In the period 1980 - 1989 the balance sheet total of the Swiss banks increased annually by 8.7 % (see **Tables A 5, A 6, A 7** and **Chart 3**). The on-balance sheet business in 1989 totalled Sfr. 1'036 billion and exceeded the trillion limit for the first time. The fiduciary transactions increased more strongly than the balance sheet total and in 1989 attained almost Sfr. 300 billion or 28.9 % of the balance sheet total. Gross income, which corresponds to the total of net revenue prior to deduction of expenses, reached the amount of Sfr. 29.7 billion in 1989. With an annual nominal growth rate of 10.7 %, it exceeded the balance sheet growth. This growth applies to the period 1981 - 1989, as the corresponding data for private banks has only been published since 1981. The lower balance sheet growth is due to the revaluation of the Swiss franc and to the expansion of off-balance sheet business.

In 1989 both performance figures, the cash flow, i.e. the total of net profit and value adjustments, and the net profit amounted to Sfr. 11.6 and Sfr. 6.0 billion respectively. On bank average they increased more strongly than both the balance

Chart 2:

Regional Structure of Total Employment in Banking Sector 1985*

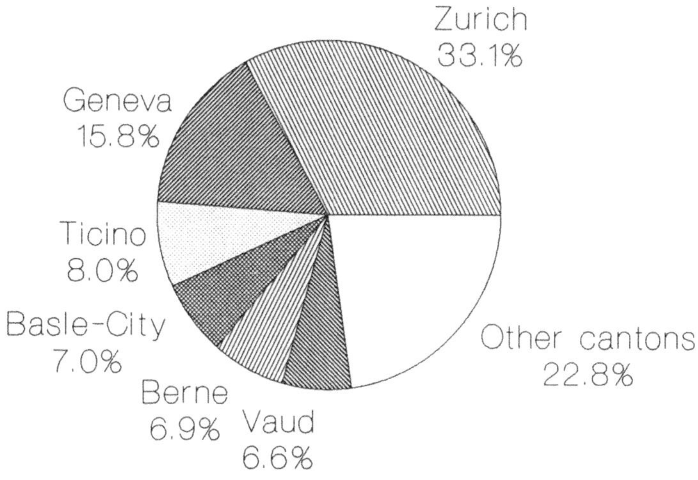

Quelle: FOS

*Employees of banks by cantons

Chart 3:

Balance Sheet and Income Statement

growth p.a. 1980-1989

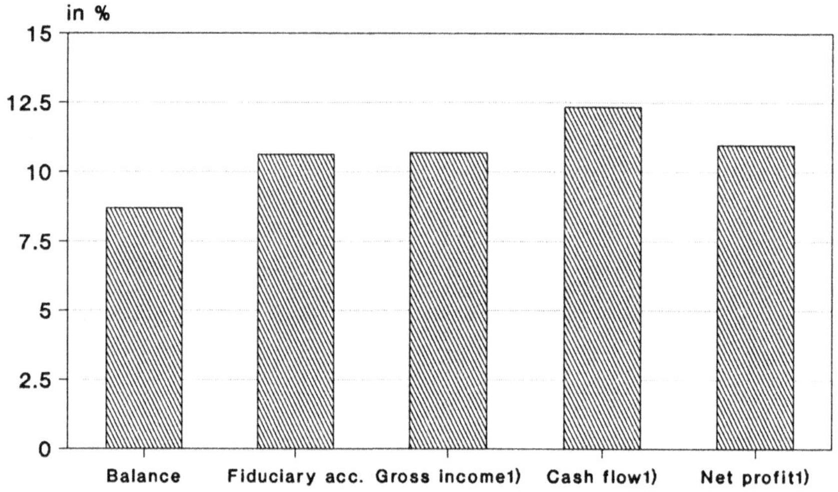

Sources: SNB, The Swiss Banking System

1) 1981-1989

Swiss Banks 1980-1989 SBA 12/90

sheet total and the gross income. Thus, as a whole, the available resources were used more and more efficiently. But the relative profitability ratios fluctuated considerably and since the mid-Eighties a stagnation can be observed. On the average, however, an improvement can be seen. There was an increase in the return on assets (ROA) from 0.71 % (1981) to 0.78 % (1989) and in the return on equity (ROE) from 10.47 % to 11.44 % (see **Table A 13**).

So the economic expansion was not only one of quantity but also of quality. Furthermore, it was not at the cost of security and solvency. According to the Swiss National Bank (SNB), the own and liquid funds were always clearly in excess of the legal requirements.

As from 1st January, 1990 new capital adequacy rules have been in force, which had to be met already as per 31st December, 1989. The new regulations constitute an assimilation to the recommendations issued in July 1988 by the Basle Committee for Bank Supervision (BIS capital adequacy recommendations). The own capital in the sense of the Banking Law, i.e. including eligible subordinate loans and eligible hidden reserves, amounted to Sfr. 81.8 billion at the end of 1989. The portion of own capital - as per Banking Law - in the balance sheet total was consequently 8.4 %. This does not take into consideration the non-eligible hidden reserves. The relationship between the available and the required own capital rose from 113 (1980) to 127 (1989).

Owing to the fundamentally new regulations effective as from 1st January, 1988, a comparison over ten years for the liquidity requirements is not possible. But, here too, it can be said that both up to 1987 and as from 1988 the legal requirements were clearly more than fulfilled. At the end of 1989 the banks disposed of liquid assets in the sense of the Banking Law, i.e. cash on hand and easily realizable assets, of Sfr. 75.8 billion. The required amount was Sfr. 53.3 billion.

But a differentiation must be made in this generally positive tendency. In some banks and bank groups, as well as in individual business fields development was very different. The fields of activity as well as the bank structure continued to change.

2.2 Change in field of activity

2.2.1 Balance sheet structure

In order to judge development of the balance sheet structure in the banking sector from 1980 - 1989, an analysis has been effected of the changes in the balance sheet shares. In **Chart 4** selected items of the assets and liabilities are shown. The following points are worthy of mention individually (see **Table A 5**):

1. The balance sheet item liquid assets (cash, giro and post office balances) decreased strongly. In 1989 it was clearly below that of 1980. The development of cash on hand was quite steady up to 1987. Subsequently it declined by half in only a year. Over the whole ten-year period, the cash in hand declined from Sfr. 27.6 billion in 1980 (3.9 % of the balance sheet total) to Sfr. 13.0 billion in 1989 (1.3 %). Measured as balance sheet share, this resulted in a reduction by 2.6 percentage points (see **Chart 4**). In the main, this reduction is due to the fundamental change in the liquidity requirements of 1st January, 1988 and to the introduction of Swiss Interbank Clearing (SIC). The new regulations and the more efficient cash management have strongly diminished the need for cash on hand. In addition, the reduction led to the halfing of the bank giro funds with the SNB, which had extensive effects on monetary policy.

2. The rapid increase in interbank business on both sides of the balance sheet in the Sixties and Seventies, a result of the internationalization of bank transactions and the lack of domestic investment possibilities for short-term surpluses of liquidity, slackened. Balances with other banks and of other banks even declined slightly as a whole measured as portions of the balance sheet to 22.2 % (1980 22.8 %) and 22.5 % (1980 23.2 %) respectively. It is remarkable here that up to 1988 the portion of interbank assets increased to 26.0 %. Between 1988 and 1989 the portion then decreased by 3.8 percentage points, which corresponded to a reduction of Sfr. 22 billion. It was first and foremost the deposits by banks abroad which were lowered. In addition, for the first time since 1982, funds due to banks are again higher than funds due from banks. This puts the Swiss banks in a net debtor position. They needed these funds to finance domestic credits due to the unfavourable evolution of savings deposits.

Chart 4:
Banking System: Variation of Balance Sheet Items 1980-1989

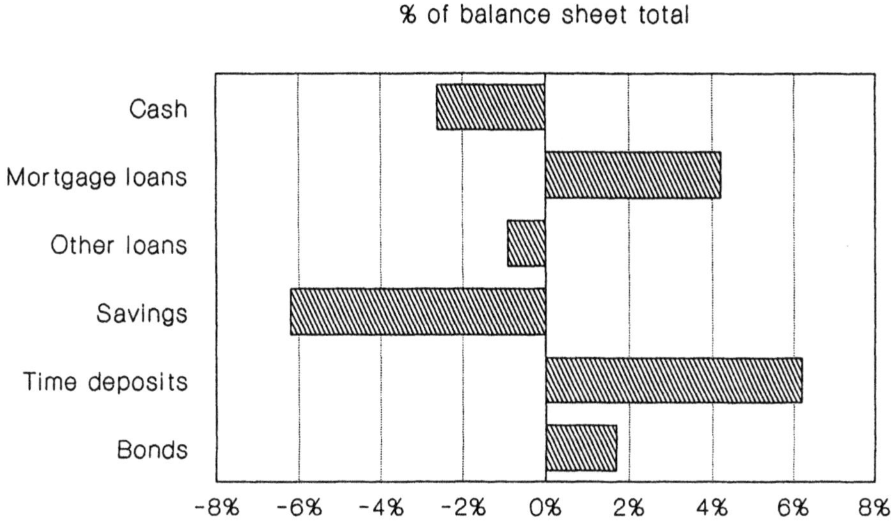

Source: SNB, The Swiss Banking System
Swiss Banks 1980-1989 SBA 12/90

3. Economic growth, strong demand in the building sector and the increasing property and land prices led to an over-proportional increase in mortgage loans (10.4 % p.a.). The share of all loans in the balance sheet total rose to 61.2 % (1980 57.9 % - an increase by 3.3 percentage points), that of mortgage loans to 32.9 % (1980 28.7 % - an increase by 4.2 percentage points). Therefore, a proportional decrease resulted in the other domestic and foreign credits, i.e. secured other than by mortgages. This is an indication of a shifting from commercial to the less costly mortgage credits. Consequently, mortgage loans increasingly became the most important form of credit for the Swiss banks and the Swiss economy in the period under review. According to the SNB, at the end of 1989 more than 90 % of the outstanding claims were within two thirds of the market value of the corresponding property. The collateral value of the mortgage credits seems to be very good.

4. As regards public funds (savings, demand and time deposits), the trend of the Seventies was intensified. There was a shifting of savings accounts to time deposits. The speed of the shifting depended on the interest rate and currency situation. A consequence of this process is that the relative balance sheet portions of savings and time deposits were completely reversed in the Eighties, i.e. for savings from 23.7 % (1980) to 17.4 % (1989) - a reduction by 6.3 percentage points - and for time deposits from 16.9 to 23.1 % - an increase by 6.2 percentage points. Assuming that balance sheet shares were constant, the dimension of the change corresponds to a shifting of about Sfr. 60 billion. In addition to this is the fact that the evolution of public funds as a whole took place under-proportionally.

5. Finally, it must be noted that more funds have been raised in the capital market. Attractive share prices up to 1987 led to numerous equity-linked bond issues. On the other hand, the portion of cash bonds in the balance sheet increased only slightly.

Summarizing it can be said that during the strong balance sheet growth switching of means and shifting of refinancing took place to a large extent. Strong growth in credit business could not be financed sufficiently by public funds. In 1989 especially, other means, such as funds with banks abroad, had to be called in.

The change in the public funds, the switching from savings to time deposits, probably had structural causes. Part of the shifting was certainly due to rates of interest, but another part was due to a change in public attitude. First of all, owing to the compulsory saving stipulated by the state, the motivation for personal saving changed. While earlier on, providence for old age was a central motivation for saving on bank accounts, the situation today with the background of a guaranteed old-age provision (Old Age Pension and compulsory Second Pillar) has led to this motivation becoming less important. Savings which are in surplus of the compulsory deducted amounts can be invested at higher risk or spent. Performance oriented investments are more and more in the foreground for the private individual, which is detrimental to traditional saving with banks. Secondly, compulsory saving leads to a shifting of the relative importance of the individual investment groups. Institutional investors have become more important compared to private investors. In this way, the investors are, on the average, more professional, i.e. also more yield conscious. Thirdly, and in general, the change in preference and the professionalizing lead to higher flexibility. Investors react more flexibly and more rapidly to changes in interest rates. The market has accordingly become more efficient. It is very easy today to place funds in other forms of investment such as money market payment rights, securities, etc. The change in customer attitude has two consequences:

1. The higher flexibility of public funds forces the banks to adapt their interest rates more rapidly to market evolution if they wish to maintain their margin. However, this could not be carried out fully up to now, as the banks acted with reserve on political grounds especially in the mortgage field.

2. Savings with banks are losing their significance as favourable source of refinancing. Competition is fierce. An inversed interest rate structure, as has prevailed since 1988, makes the problem worse. For the banks the refinancing is more expensive and at the same time the risk of changes in interest rates increases.

Today's refinancing situation for mortgages shows the economic consequences very clearly. The traditional refinancing sources, i.e. savings accounts, deposits and investment books, have developed under-proportionally in the last few years (see

Chart 5). On the average for the sector, the portion of mortgages to savings fell from 82.5 % to 53.0 %. The accumulated financing deficit has to be made up from other funds which, in comparison to savings funds, are more expensive and volatile, i.e. above all from cash bonds and time deposits.

It would be wrong to conclude a lack of congruent refinancing or any mismanagement from this structural evolution. First of all it is a question of a structural change in customer attitude to which the banks on their side must react by structural changes, which, in turn, can only be implemented cautiously. Secondly, the inversed interest rate structure has aggravated the structural problem cyclically. And finally, congruent refinancing is just as much a question of managing the interest rate risk as one of refinancing sources.

2.2.2 On-balance sheet foreign business and fiduciary deposits

Foreign assets and liabilities together with fiduciary business, which is concluded to a large extent with customers domiciled abroad, is of major importance for the Swiss banks (see **Tables A 5** and **A 6**). The level of involvement abroad is exceptionally high. The Swiss banks assume the function of international financial turntable, i.e. they take in funds from foreign sources and invest then in their own name abroad. From the market point of view, they provide a transformation of risk. Foreign business is mainly handled by the big banks and the foreign banks.

In 1989, foreign assets (liabilities) amounted to Sfr. 382.2 (309.1) billion or 36.9 % (29.8 %) of the balance sheet total. Whereas the on-balance sheet foreign business grew very strongly in the Sixties and the Seventies, a relative stagnation has been observed in the last ten years. Growth rates of both the foreign assets with 8.6 % p.a. and liabilities with 9.0 % p.a. corresponded only with balance sheet growth (8.7 % p.a.). The net foreign balance of the balance sheet (foreign assets minus foreign liabilities) was always positive. As balance sheet portion, however, it declined from 8.3 % (1980) to 7.1 % (1989), a consequence of the absolute decrease between 1987 and 1989 by Sfr. 16.2 billion to Sfr. 73.1 billion.

In contrast to this, the fiduciary transactions at 10.6 % p.a. exceeded the growth of the balance sheet also in the Eighties. They benefitted from the inversed interest

Chart 5:
Development of Mortgage Loans and Savings 1980-1989

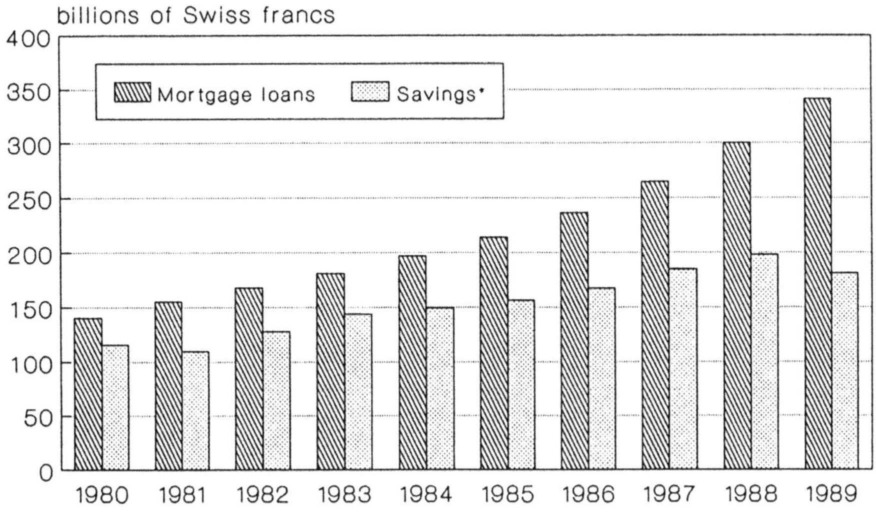

*Savings deposits + other deposits

Swiss Banks 1980-1989 SBA 12/90

rate structure at the end of the ten-year period. Between 1987 and 1989 there was an increase of almost 60 %, i.e. Sfr. 111 billion.

That the foreign transactions, unlike the domestic investments, are subject to additional non-economic risks, viz. political and transfer risks, clearly recalled the international debt crisis of the Eighties. The Swiss banks were also affected by that crisis, which reached its climax following the second oil crisis in 1979, at the beginning of the ten-year period (1980 Poland, 1982 Mexico). Since then, higher provision requirements have been in force - in Switzerland as from 1980 - and a more cautious approach on the part of the banks towards solvency when granting international credit facilities can be observed. The Swiss banks have extensive provisions. The expenditure item value adjustment, under which among other things provisions for loans are held, increased from Sfr. 1.3 billion in 1980 to Sfr. 5.6 billion in 1989. Today, the Swiss banks are in a comparatively comfortable position in this respect. In 1984, for the 135 institutes furnishing figures, there was still 6.7 % of all foreign assets (Sfr. 17.5 billion) in the 17 highly indebted countries (according to World Bank definition). In 1989 it was only 3.3 % or Sfr. 11.0 billion.

According to the separation of foreign assets registered by the 135 notifying institutes, by far the most debtor domiciles are in BIS countries. Furthermore, their portion has increased from under 70 % to almost 80 %. Since 1989 the USA is again the most important debtor land, followed by the United Kingdom and Japan.

Thus, in the ten years from 1980 to 1989 on one side fiduciary transcations developed very well. On the other side, the former strong growth element of foreign on-balance sheet business was disappointing. Yet, Swiss Banks have a low exposure to the third world debt crisis.

2.2.3 Income statement

The income statement permits the reviewal of the cost and income evolution of all bank transactions. On the income side we have to distinguish between the classical interest margin business (interest income) and the non-credit or off-balance sheet business (non-interest income) (see **Table A 7**). The income from non-credit business, i.e. brokerage, custodian charges, portfolio management, issue and fiduciary commissions, income from trading in foreign exchange and precious metal, etc., developed better than the net interest income, i.e. among other things income from the deposit and credit business. The portion of non-credit business in the gross income increased from 48.7 % (1981) to 52.4 % (1989). The non-interest income (NII) increased nominally by 11.7 %, about 2 percentage points faster than the net interest income (II) and about 3.3 percentage points faster than the balance sheet total (see **Chart 6**).

The development of the net interest income was below average, although the interest margin (net interest income in % of the average balance sheet total) was increased from 1.29 % in 1981 to 1.41 % in 1989. However, the interest margin fluctuated depending on interest and currency evolution and in international comparison continues to be very low (see **Table 2** and **A 13**).

The shift in emphasis from interest margin to non-credit business can be observed world-wide. It had already started in the Seventies. The main reasons are the professionalization of investors, the institutionalization of savings as well as securitization. Furthermore, reference must be made to the increasing need for hedging transactions as a result of higher interest and exchange rate risks and to the new issue and stock exchange boom of the Eighties.

The higher significance of the non-credit services causes the cyclical risks to increase. With high fixed costs, income is strongly dependent on the momentary favour of the interest, stock exchange and issuing situation. Just how volatile this income can be was shown following the decline on the stock exchange market in 1987 and 1989, when tight trading capacity was transformed into over capacity practically overnight. Abroad, especially in London and New York, such cyclical fluctuation led to losses in employment and in real assets.

On the expenditure side the over-proportional increase in value adjustments (VA), i.e. depreciation, provisions and losses, are most prominent (see **Chart 6**). The adjustments increased nominally from 1981 to 1989 by 14.0 % p.a., not only more strongly than all the other expense items but also faster than the gross income (10.7 % p.a.). At Sfr. 5.6 billion in 1989, they almost attained the level of office

Chart 6:
Banking System: Income Statement
growth p.a. 1981-1989

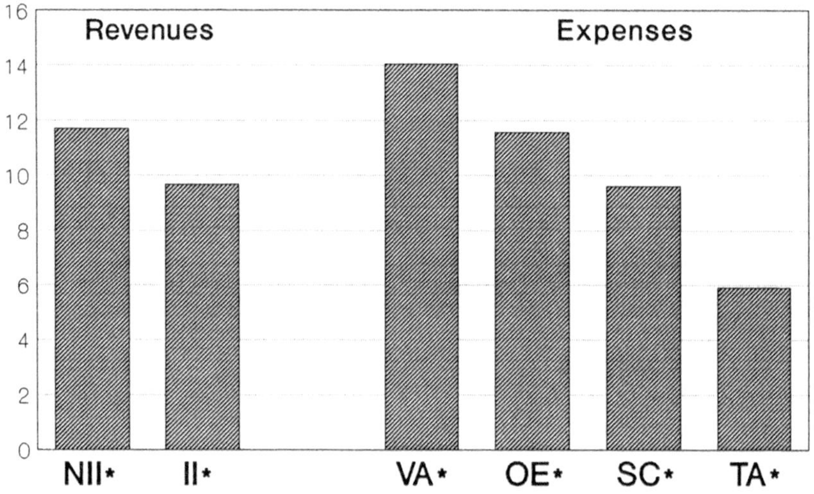

Source: SNB, The Swiss Banking System

* For abbreviations see paper

Swiss Banks 1980-1989 SBA 12/90

expenses (OE) of Sfr. 5.7 billion, although the latter's rate of growth was over-average as well (11.6 % p.a.). The higher electronic data processing (EDP) and rationalization investments increased the need for depreciation. Parallel to this, the higher provisions in connection with credits to problem countries also play a role. Contrary to widespread opinion and in spite of the increase in employment and the drained employment market, the increase in staff costs (SC), the highest cost item of all, was only under-average (9.6 % p.a.); measured against gross income, its portion diminished from 39.0 % (1981) to 36.0 % (1989). Also under-average is the increase in direct taxes (TA).

Cost efficiency measured on the basis of unit costs (portion of the staff and office expenses in % of gross income), improved (see **Table 2** and **A 13**). The unit costs decreased very strongly at first from 56.8 % (1981) to 52.3 % (1985). Since then, in connection with weaker demand, a re-increase to 55.1 % can be seen. In spite of salary increases, expensive EDP investments and high rents, one can say that costs were kept under control. It must be mentioned here, however, that in general costs increased faster than the inflation rate. At least partly the success in the control of costs was a consequence of technical progress. The expensive production factor "labour" in comparison to the less expensive "capital" is being used more economically. Examples of this are the substitution of bank cashiers by automatic teller machines, the partial electronification of stock exchange dealing, cashless payments systems and finally electronic home banking. The bank-to-customer relationship, especially in retail banking, is characterized increasingly by standard products and services.

2.3 Change in bank structure

2.3.1 Market shares

The change in the field of activity has not left bank structure unaffected. To understand this, the main business elements of the bank groups, as they are defined in the Swiss National Bank (SNB) statistics, must firstly be analysed. In doing so, in the main, the SNB classification has been adopted. An exception to this is the creation of a bank group "Foreign Banks" from the foreign-controlled banks and branches of foreign banks. As a consequence, contrary to the SNB statistics, the group "Other Swiss Banks" no longer contains the foreign-controlled banks. Reference is made to the SNB for the composition of bank groups.

Although, as a rule, the Swiss banks are full service banks, the individual bank groups are characterized by specific main activities. The bank groups can be classified on the basis of foreign integration and the volume of non-credit business (see **Table A 10** and **Chart 7** - the lines correspond to the average for all banks). The banks active especially domestically and in the traditional interest rate margin field are the Credit Cooperatives and Raiffeisen Banks (CR), the Regional and Savings Banks (RS) and the Cantonal Banks (CB). Their activities are usually subject to regional restrictions by virtue of their Articles of Association or for legal reasons. Their counterparts are the Foreign Banks (FB), which are primarily engaged in non-credit business and, as is the case of the Finance Companies (FC), are highly active abroad. The banks concentrating on non-credit business, above all in securities transactions, which do not dispose of an over-average share of foreign business in their balance sheets, are the Other Swiss Banks (OB) and the Private Banks (PB). By virtue of their size, the Big Banks (BB) are in the close vicinity of the all-Swiss average.

Table 1 shows the development in the market shares of the individual bank groups. A correction has been made for 1989 in the gross income data. In 1989, the TDB American Express Bank distributed an exceptional dividend of Sfr. 465 million. Although no allowance has been made for this special dividend in the tables annexed, the size of the dividend calls for an appropriate correction in the data for the following discussion on market share development.

Measured in relation to the balance sheet total and to the gross income, the market share of the big banks in 1989 was 49.2 % and 46.7 % respectively (see **Table** 1). With regard to the balance sheet total, the Cantonal Banks rank second (18.8 %) and the Foreign Banks third (12.1 %). In the case of gross income, which in view of the shifting towards non-credit business increasingly reflects market development better, the Foreign Banks are in second place (18.7 %), followed by the Other Swiss Banks, in the main commercial and brokerage banks (11.5 %).

The Foreign Banks and the Finance Companies were able to increase their share of the market in relation to both balance sheet total and gross income. As a result of their convertion to joint stock companies, certain Private Banks were transferred from the Private Bank group to Other Swiss Banks group (in particular Bank

Chart 7:
Banking Groups*: Main activities 1989

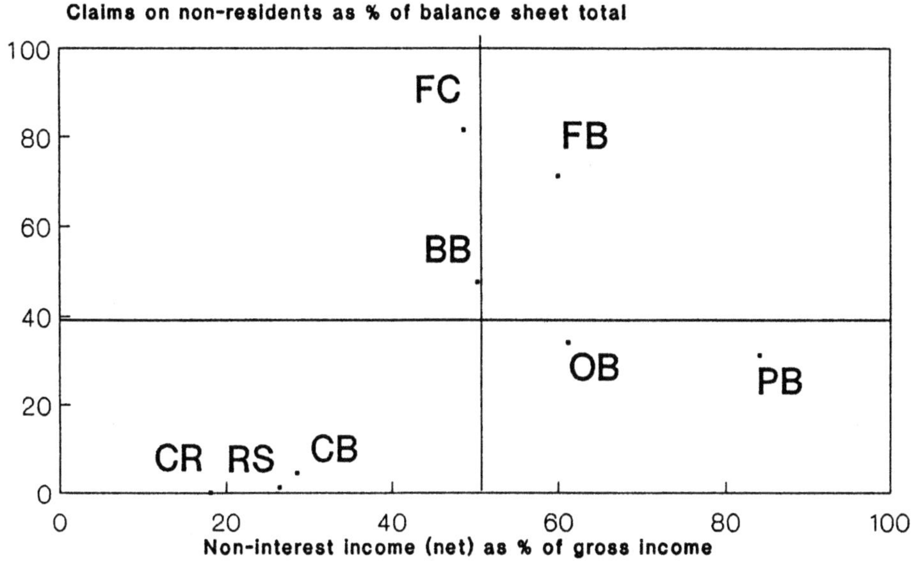

Source: SNB, The Swiss Banking System

*For abbreviations see paper

Swiss Banks 1980-1989 SBA 12/90

Table 1: Market shares of the bank groups[1)]
(all figures in %)

	Balance Sheet Total		Gross Income	
	1980	1989	1981	1989[2)]
Cantonal Banks	20.7	18.8	11.5	10.1
Big Banks	48.9	49.2	47.7	46.7
Regional and Savings Banks	9.4	8.5	5.9	4.8
Credit Cooperatives and Raiffeisen Banks	2.7	3.0	1.2	1.2
Other Swiss Banks	4.4	5.4	9.3	11.5
Finance Companies	2.3	2.4	3.0	3.7
Foreign Banks	11.1	12.1	18.2	18.7
Private Banks	0.5	0.5	3.2	3.3

1) For definitions see SNB and Table A 10
2) Corrected for the amount of the special dividend of the TDB American Express Bank of Sfr. 465 million in 1989.

SBA

J. Vontobel & Co. AG), so that the data for these two groups is distorted. The gain in the market share of the Private Banks is under-estimated and that of the Other Swiss Banks over-estimated. However, the increase of the share in the gross income of the Other Swiss Banks from 9.3 % to 11.5 % is not only the result of the aforementioned artificial effect. All the other bank groups experienced losses in one or even in both items. It is clear that the development of an individual bank can be different to that of its bank group.

If one looks at selected aspects from balance sheets and income statements in the period under review (see **Table A 10**), the following points are worth noting in particular:

- the dissimilar development of interest rate margin and of non-credit business is reflected in the individual bank groups. The more active a bank group is in non-credit business, the better its growth and its results. Or: the more important the interest rate margin business is, the less favourable are the growth rates and the results. The differences in the return on equity (ROE) emphasizes this situation.

- considerable shifting of market shares can be seen in non-credit business. The Foreign Banks have progressed particularly strong in this respect. They increased their corrected market share by 2.9 percentage points to 23.4 %. This increase was above all to the detriment of the Big Banks, whose share fell from 51.4 % to 45.5 %. The lion's share was probably due to losses in securities business. But as this type of business is very cyclical, gains in market shares should not be over-interpreted, as they are possibly only of temporary nature. In these fields of activity, fast changes and restructuring is possible (see London, New York).

- in interest margin business the trend of the last decades continued. The Big Banks gained in market shares to the detriment of the Cantonal and Regional Banks. Considerable shifting can be seen particularly in the fields of mortgage credits and savings deposits. The market share of the Big Banks in mortgage business increased from 33.1 % (1980) to 39.0 % (1989), that of the Cantonal Banks declined from 38.9 % to 33.7 % and that of the Regional Banks from 19.1 % to 16.6 %. Although slightly more modest in extent, a similar shifting in market shares can be seen in savings business. The Credit Cooperatives and Raiffeisen Banks were able to avoid this trend. Their market shares increased in mortgage business (from 5.5 % to 6.2 %) and in savings (from 7.6 % to 9.2 %).

2.3.2 Concentration

In all, the net number of institutes increased between 1980 and 1989 by 74 to a total of 631 (see **Table A 8**). The increase is due above all to the Finance Companies (net increase by 53 institutes) and the Foreign Banks (36 institutes) (see **Chart 8**). The Regional Banks and the Other Swiss Banks show net decreases following takeovers, mergers and closures. The decrease in the case of the Private Banks is a result of the conversions into joint stock companies.

The increase in the number of legally dependent branches is attributed to all bank groups. The number of branches (excluding foreign subsidiaries) increased by 481 (of which 20 abroad) to 4'336 (of which 91 abroad). The strongest expansion in network was by the Big Banks (by 174) and by the Foreign Banks (81).

Thus net market accesses have taken place. As already shown, the market shares of the bank groups also changed. Market structures are consequently not rigid; they change continuously and do not move unilaterally in a specific direction. That concentration only increased marginally is shown by **Table A 11** and **Chart 9**, where a Lorenz curve based on the balance sheet total is shown. According to this, 10 % of all the banks accounted for 82.17 % of the aggregate balance sheet total in 1980 and 83.35 % in 1989. Concentration is very high but it showed only a slight change. And the figures change only marginally when economic interdependence is taken into consideration.

It can be shown that concentration practically stopped as from 1970. Just how far this can be said to be a temporary occurrence in the development of bank structure, remains to be seen. In retail banking, however, there are increased indications of economies of scale and scope with corresponding constraint towards concentration. Endeavours also exist in the field of Regional and Cantonal Banks towards an integration of basic services, in order to take advantage of synergies and economies of scale. In addition to this is the abolishing of private regulations and progressively stiff competition. It must be remembered that as recently as 1989 and 1990 mergers and takeovers have increased in the banking sector.

Chart 8

Swiss Banking: Market Access 1980-1989
Net Number of Institutes

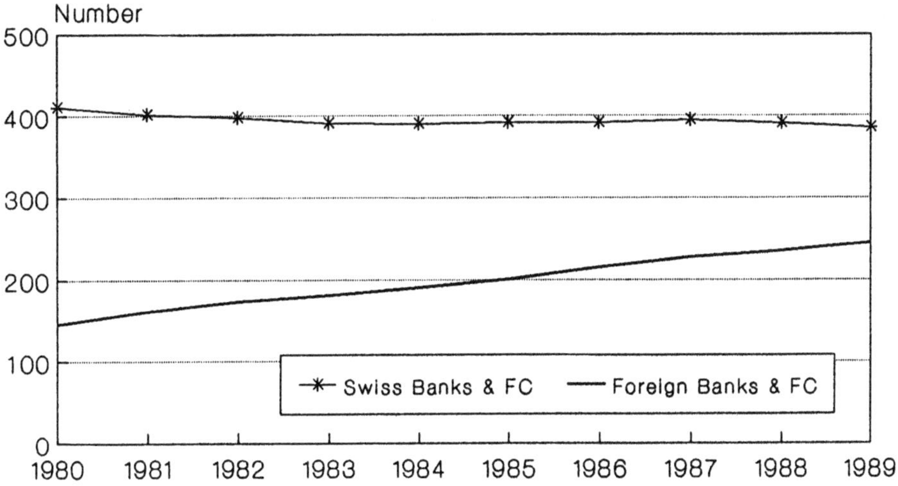

Source: SNB, The Swiss Banking System

Swiss Banks 1980-1989 SBA 12/90

Chart 9

Concentration of Swiss Banking: Lorenz curves 1980 and 1989

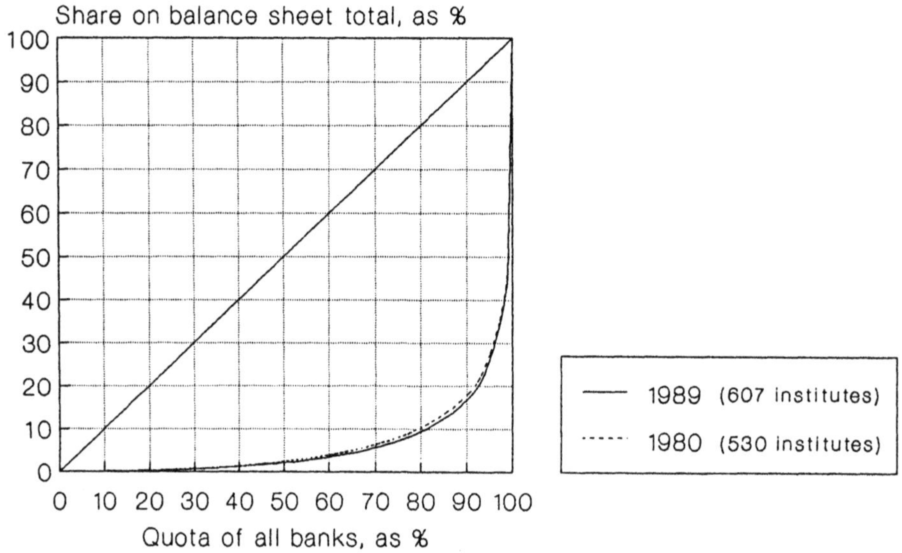

Source: SNB, The Swiss Banking System

3. International comparison

In the following chapter the Swiss bank system is to be compared to the foreign on an aggregate level (see **Tables A 12** to **A 16**). It must be said already at the outset that the results must be considered with some caution. The comparison of the data is critical owing to different regulations, accounting rules and bank systems. In addition, there could be distortion resulting from segmented and protected markets.

For data reasons and in view of the objective of worldwide comparison, the countries chosen are Germany, the USA and Japan. The basis is OECD data from 1980 - 1986, which has been updated up to 1989. This offers the advantage of accounting differences being corrected as far as possible. On the other hand, in part, the data does not include all banks of the corresponding countries. The degree of data collection fluctuates from country to country.

First of all, the size and income structure of the bank systems are compared. The size of a bank system depends on the size and the dynamics of the national real economy, as well as on the share in the international bank market. The Swiss banks have considerably more foreign assets and liabilities in percent of their balance sheet totals than the banks of the countries under comparison. With a share of foreign assets of just 30 % - on taking the fiduciary assets into consideration it would be more than 50 % - the Swiss banks are clearly higher than the USA (9.5 %), Japan (12.8 %) and Germany (16.2 %). This demonstrates that they are distinctly internationally oriented.

In addition, as export institutes Swiss Banks are compared with the own national economy relatively bigger, than the other more domestically oriented banking systems. The relationship between the aggregate balance sheet total and GNP is the highest for the Swiss banks at 2.36, whereby must be considered that the degree of data collection differs from country to country. But it can be said that in all countries the banking sector grew more rapidly than the GNP.

The non-interest income in percent of the gross income shows the importance of the non-credit business in comparison to the on-balance sheet business. Higher figures would have been expected for the universal bank systems. However, the American and the Japanese banks show a higher share of non-interest income than the German full-service banks. The share of the Swiss banks is clearly the highest.

The dissimilar growth rates of the individual banking systems is remarkable. In balance sheet total and foreign assets and liabilities as well as in non-interest income the Japanese banks developed very expansively with two digit growth rates. From the under-average development of their gross income (increase 8.2 % p.a.) it can be assumed that the growth in quantity was attained to the detriment of the interest rate margin. Whereas the growth in the balance sheet total and in gross income of the Swiss banks was comparatively good to very good, foreign assets and liabilities and non-interest income, in comparison, show poorer results. Overall, an average development results. The German banks show under-average growth rate in almost all these spheres. The only positive factor is the strong increase in the net foreign assets. The American banks evolved very differently. The remarkable aspect is that vis-à-vis foreign countries they transformed themselves from net creditors to net debtors.

The differences in development partly reflect the events of the real economy. Here, the Japanese banks naturally benefitted a great deal from the dynamic development of their national economy. Contrary to this, the development of the Swiss real economy is not amongst the leaders. Considered in this light, the average development of the banks can be viewed as successful.

Tables 2 and **A 13** show selected performance indicators. The return on assets and on equity measure the efficiency of resource allocation. The interest margin gives an indication of the cost of traditional banking, i.e. of deposit and credit business. The unit costs, understood as staff and office expenses in percent of the gross income, give indications as to cost efficiency. The level of depreciation and provisions effected is measured by way of value adjustments in percent of the balance sheet total. Further, the own capital ratio is shown, which, inter alia, shows the regulatory influence.

The profitability indicators give a mixed picture. In return on assets the Swiss banks come out well. Only the Americans, with 0.86 %, are better, whereby their ratio was the only one to fall between 1980 and 1989. The Swiss banks were the lowest, however, as to return on equity. This is certainly a result, at least partially, of the high capital requirements. Just how far the constitution of hidden reserves leads to distortion here cannot be ascertained. But the comparative countries show falling return on equity as from 1980 (USA), as from 1983 (Germany) and as from 1987 (Japan), whereas the Swiss ratio has remained quite stable.

Table 2: Performance of banking systems in comparison 1980 - 1989 (average values, all figures in %)

	USA	Japan	Germany	Switzerland*
Return on assets 1)	0.86	0.51	0.65	0.74
Return on equity 2)	13.86	19.68	17.39	11.25
Interest rate margin 3)	3.30	1.32	2.33	1.38
Unit costs 4)	67.56	66.30	63.05	54.86
Value adjustments 5)	0.61	0.03	0.43	0.49
Own capital ratio 6)	6.02	2.46	3.59	6.35

Remarks:

* Swiss average 1981 - 1989
1) Profit before taxes in % of average balance sheet total
2) Profit before taxes in % of equity
3) Net interest income in % of average balance sheet total
4) Staff and office expenses in % of gross income
5) Losses, depreciation and provisions in % of the average balance sheet total
6) Own capital in % of end-year balance sheet total

Source: see indications in Tables A 7, A 13, A 14, A 15 and A 16 in the appendix.

SBA

The Swiss banking system showed excellent results as regards both cost indicators. Financial intermediation was effected very favourably with an interest margin of only 1.38 % and the unit cost indicator, at 55 %, is below of all the comparative countries. Alongside the high own capital ratio, the lower interest rate margin could be an additional reason for the low return on equity. Japan's interest margin at 1.32 %, is even somewhat lower. It continued to fall from 1.61 % (1980) to 0.92 % (1989), which strengthens the assumption that the balance sheet and foreign assets and liabilities expansion was pursued to the detriment of the interest rate margin. On the other hand, the unit costs of the Japanese banks also dropped sharply from 76.8 % (1980) to 57.9 % (1989). The interest rate margin of the US banks averaged a full 3.3 %, which is more than double that of the Swiss and the Japanese.

As to value adjustments, strong fluctuation and big differences from country to country are apparent. Whereas the US banks, above all in the second half of the Eighties, effected large value adjustments (especially in 1987 when huge provisions were made for credits to third world countries), practically no value adjustments are shown in Japan. The Swiss banks made value adjustments to a slightly higher extent than the Germans.

Finally, the Swiss banks had the highest own capital ratio. The figure calculated is not based on the legal capital adequacy requirements but on the portion of the published own capital in the balance sheet total. This has been done as the regulatory differences are too big. As is already known, Switzerland has the most strict capital adequacy requirements worldwide, which is reflected in the highest own capital ratio. From the security angle, this is good thing. But special handicaps, which go beyond the BIS recommendations, render the Swiss banks' task more difficult when competing internationally with other banks.

All in all, it can be said that the relative position of the Swiss banks is excellent. Whereas their growth has been average, they have maintained or improved their position as regards the quality ratios. Thus, the performance of the Swiss banks in comparison to their competitors is over-average.

4. First conclusions

In the past decade the Swiss banks developed excellently. They benefitted from the strong growth of the economy, from a favourable stock exchange climate and from falling interest rates. In addition, the technical progress in the EDP and telecommunication fields brought rises in productivity. Both the classical credit as well as the non-credit business recorded high rates of growth. The Swiss banks have nothing to fear from an international performance comparison.

But in acknowledging the good evolution of business which was also cyclic, the fact must not be overlooked that the structural conditions in banking have changed further. Alongside the changes in structure in on-balance sheet business, above all with regard to refinancing, the shifting of emphasis towards non-credit business continued. The individual bank groups are affected by it very differently. The banks strongly active in non-credit business gained market shares to the detriment of the classical "domestic" banks.

The cost of the change in structure was obscured and hidden by the general positive trend. Slower growth in individual fields of activity or with individual banks or departments was compensated by over-proportional growth in other spheres. Necessary real adjustments could thus be carried out without high costs in the form of loss of employment, restructuration or closures. In the light of the weak development in demand today and in connection with the rapid abolition of conventions, with the technical progress, the further sharpening of international competition and the change in customer attitude, the costs of change will certainly be more apparent in the current decade than previously.

III. Outlook

The Eighties showed a Swiss banking system in full bloom. At the end of the decade, i.e. 1989, the banks announced balance sheet totals, income and net profits at levels never reached before. Never were so many of the working population employed by banks. The proportion of total salaries paid by banks attained record amounts. As source of demand in other sectors of the economy, from the building industry to the high-productivity services in the field of informatics and telecommunication, the banks became increasingly important over the years. Furthermore, the development in the banking sector was reflected in the increasing dependency of the state on the fiscal revenue from the finance centre.

As regards exports, too, the picture was one of success. At the end of the Eighties, the banks contributed considerably more to the surplus in the Swiss balance of payments than say the tourist industry. Contrary to this, the machine industry recorded a negative external contribution for several years.

At the end of the Eighties the following statement was consequently unavoidable: never before was Swiss prosperity so dependent on the banking sector. This by no means implies that events in the other sectors of the economy are to be neglected. But it would be a mistake to qualify the importance of prospering banks as insignificant.

In view of this development it is doubtlessly worthwhile to pursue the key factors of further evolution in the banking sector. What is the situation as seen today? What sort of outlook can be envisaged for the Nineties on the considerations made up to now?

On the demand side, it is first and foremost a question of the extent to which the worldwide economic uptrend of the last few years can continue. Financial services are characterized by a high degree of income elasticity. This is naturally valid for intermediation between saving and investing. It is valid to even a larger extent for financial services in the fields of portfolio management, stock exchange and corporate financing.

There are good reasons for allowing for further economic expansion. Already the classical economic theory looked on the integration of the markets as the key to rising productivity. The impulses firstly emanating from Western Europe could be increased further by the integration of the planned economy of the Eastern countries into a World trading system under free economy and could bring about sustained continuation of economic growth. Two premises must be named, however: first the GATT multilateral foreign trade system must survive the present crisis. Secondly, the Soviet Union must liberalize its economy successfully.

The Swiss banks are particularly well-equipped to confront present and future risks. The Swiss banks dispose of extensive equity, are shown by their high level of depreciation of outstanding credits as being very cautious and are comparatively less affected by the payment difficulties of the Third World Countries. In addition to this there are their comfortable hidden reserves. In times when higher risks prevail the soundness of the Swiss banks should be instrumental in attracting customers.

At the end of the Eighties the climbing inflation and interest rates already began to affect the Swiss banking sector unfavourably. The success of the Swiss National Bank in combatting inflation cannot be appraised as long as the worldwide political conditions risk being subjected to unprevisible changes. A restoration of the Swiss franc's "safe haven" function by way of subsequent revaluations could facilitate the efforts to limit the rise in the cost of living and at last allow the Swiss National Bank to let the short-term interest rates decline again. In view of the growth prospects which are beginning to show at medium and long term, not least of all in Europe including Eastern Europe, and in view of the continuous considerable savings deficit worldwide, the deficit of the US household in particular, rising real interest rates can by no means be excluded. In spite of this, the increasing successes in the combat against inflation should cause the short-term rates of interest to decline again in the coming years, thus correcting the inversed rate structure prevailing today.

On the political and regulatory side attention should be given to the following observations: when interest rates are rising the difficulties for the banks increase in proportion to their inability to keep pace on the asset side with the increases on the liability side. As in the past, it must be expected in future that the flexible reactions of investors will cause the rates on the liabilitiy side to rapidly follow international market evolution. In this respect the prospects for the banks in Switzerland at the beginning of the Nineties are rather dismal. State supervision of mortgage interest rates has already become a reality. A general supervision of interest rates is imminent. The political pressure exerted on the price controller as to what is expected of him is considerable. In times of rising rates, however, every postponement of adjustment involves a narrowing of margin. Supply shortages and waiting queues will be unavoidable. The quality of financial intermediation declines.

With regard to taxes, as a further important element of the Swiss finance centre's environment, today's view for the Nineties can only be expressed in the form of hopes. The total package of tax bills has been turned down by a recent public vote. Therefore, the revision of the Stamp Duty Act, which has been requested by the banking sector for years, has been rejected as well. But, a reform of the tax system is urgent and would clearly improve the conditions for a successful activity for all export oriented economic sectors in Switzerland.

Parallel to price control and fiscal policy, again and again bank supervision has an impeding effect on the further development of the Swiss banking sector. In the past, state policy on finance centre and bank matters, in all its dimensions and practically uncoordinated ramifications, was criticized again and again by the industry's leading exponents. Although it disturbs the banks now and again in their development, the Federal Banking Commission can nevertheless be credited with having also contributed over the years to the banks' reputation of sound institutions.

How the activity of the authorities will finally affect the attractiveness of Switzerland as an international financial services centre must remain unanswered for the time being. Fortunately, it is less possible than ever before for the political authorities to evade international developments. For the time being, the European integration has more of a liberalizing effect on market force. Regulations, which contradict this trend promply result in the loss of market share. In view of the already emphasized importance of the banking sector for the Swiss economy, corrections will be unavoidable even for the most resolute domestic oriented politicians. It would consequently be appreciated if the political authorities would now concentrate on obtaining as speedily as possible a sound place for finance centre Switzerland on the free market wing of integrated Europe.

On the market side, the described change in customer attitude seems to be irreversible. Banks have to take into consideration that even retail customers will be more professional and flexible and that the institutional savings will grow faster than private savings. Consequences of this process are more competition and customers being more performance and price conscious.

Further, the tendency towards non-credit business will certainly continue into the Nineties, although a certain calming down is perceptible chiefly due to various special factors. But at long term, the classical intermediation function of the banks may be increasingly assumed by the markets themselves. Technical progress, globalization, changing attitude of customers and product innovation are creating the prerequisites for it. As full-service banks, the Swiss institutes can contemplate further changes in structure towards non-credit business calmly. The resources available for investment, innovation and restructuring in the sector are considerable.

Investment ability, innovation capacity and readiness to restructure are finally dependent on human capital, a key success factor for banking. Human capital, like finance capital, is internationally mobile. The same principle is applicable for the internationally oriented banking sector as for the other Swiss sectors of the economy strongly oriented to foreign business. Business operations will continue to be run from Switzerland for as long as the Swiss location offers special advantages for the mobile production factors. The bankers must face the challenge in every case and in every country. Whether they attempt to do so from Switzerland depends on how far the Swiss location, for its part, will meet the challenges of the Nineties.

Appendix: Tables

Table A1:

GROSS VALUE ADDED, EMPLOYMENT, PRODUCTIVITY

	1980	1981	1982	1983	1984	1985	1986	1987	1988	1989	1980-1989
GROSS VALUE ADDED											growth p.a.
	billions of Swiss francs (1985 prices)										(as %) 1)
Banks 2)	13,8	14,4	15,6	16,5	17,7	19,3	20,3	21,0	21,8	22,6	5,6
Insurance	3,8	3,6	3,7	3,8	4,0	4,4	4,6	4,7	4,8	5,0	3,1
Chemical Industry 3)	6,6	6,9	6,7	7,1	7,6	8,0	8,3	8,5	9,3	10,0	4,7
Machinery 4)	20,4	19,7	18,5	17,7	17,6	19,1	20,6	19,9	20,9	21,8	0,7
Gross Domestic Product	213,2	216,3	213,8	215,3	219,0	228,0	234,4	239,1	246,8	255,5	2,0
	% of gross domestic product (GDP)										
Banks 2)	0,0	4,8	8,2	5,7	7,0	9,1	5,6	3,2	3,8	3,7	
Insurance	0,0	-4,6	2,2	2,3	6,5	9,2	5,0	1,9	2,6	3,8	
Chemical Industry 3)	0,0	3,6	-2,2	6,2	7,0	4,2	3,8	2,3	9,5	8,1	
Machinery 4)	0,0	-3,4	-6,1	-4,2	-1,1	8,9	7,9	-3,6	5,1	4,5	
EMPLOYMENT											
	1000										
Banks 2)	81	86	90	92	93	96	102	109	114	117	4,2
Insurance	43	45	47	48	48	49	50	52	55	56	3,0
Chemical Industry 3)	73	73	72	71	71	72	74	75	77	79	0,8
Machinery 4)	274	278	265	253	249	253	260	263	261	261	-0,5
TOTAL (Switzerland) 5)	3170	3211	3190	3149	3288	3352	3398	3438	3478	3518	1,2
	% of total employees										
Banks 2)	2,5	2,7	2,8	2,9	2,8	2,9	3,0	3,2	3,3	3,3	
Insurance	1,4	1,4	1,5	1,5	1,5	1,5	1,5	1,5	1,6	1,6	
Chemical Industry 3)	2,3	2,3	2,3	2,2	2,2	2,2	2,2	2,2	2,2	2,2	
Machinery 4)	8,6	8,7	8,3	8,0	7,6	7,5	7,7	7,6	7,5	7,4	
PRODUCTIVITY 6)											
	1000 Swiss francs (1985 prices)										
Banks 2)	170,8	168,6	174,0	179,7	189,3	200,0	198,8	191,9	191,2	193,6	1,4
Insurance	88,4	80,3	78,6	78,6	83,4	90,3	92,9	90,7	88,6	89,3	0,1
Chemical Industry 3)	90,9	94,9	93,6	101,2	107,7	110,2	111,9	112,5	120,3	127,2	3,8
Machinery 4)	74,7	71,1	70,0	70,1	70,6	75,6	79,2	75,8	80,1	83,8	1,3
TOTAL (Switzerland)	67,3	67,4	67,0	68,4	66,6	68,0	69,0	69,5	71,0	72,6	0,9
	% of country average										
Banks 2)	254	250	260	263	284	294	288	276	269	267	
Insurance	131	119	117	115	125	133	135	130	125	123	
Chemical Industry 3)	135	141	140	148	162	162	162	162	169	175	
Machinery 4)	111	106	104	103	106	111	115	109	113	115	
TOTAL (Switzerland)	100	100	100	100	100	100	100	100	100	100	SBA 12/90

Table A1 (continued):

Remarks:

1) Average annual growth rates
2) All banks and finance companies
3) Including refineries
4) Machines and vehicles, electrical engineering, electronics and optics
5) Including border crossers, without seasonal workers
6) Gross value added per head (gross value added as percentage of employment)

Sources:

Gross value added	Data on growth rates from Basle Business Cycle Research Group (BBG), converted to data on gross value added by sector for 1985 from Swiss federal office of statistics (FOS)
Employment	
Total Switzerland	Federal office of statistics
Banks	Swiss National Bank "The Swiss Banking System" (SNB, The Swiss Banking System), yearly averages
Other industries 1980-1986	Federal office of statistics
Other industries 1987-1989	Basle Business Cycle Research Group (yearly averages)

SBA 12/90

Table A2:

REGIONAL STRUCTURE OF EMPLOYMENT

Employees of banks by cantons:

	1975			1985		
	total	% of total employment (canton)	% of total employment (banking sector)	total	% of total employment (canton)	% of total employment (banking sector)
Zurich	25148	4,09	31,72	36456	5,31	33,07
Geneva	12357	6,59	15,58	17371	7,71	15,76
Ticino	6466	4,71	8,15	8765	5,59	7,95
Basle-City	6154	3,86	7,76	7686	4,73	6,97
Berne	5666	1,23	7,15	7621	1,53	6,91
Vaud	4820	1,96	6,08	7235	2,57	6,56
Other cantons	18679	1,31	23,56	25099	1,59	22,77
Switzerland (total)	79290	2,45	100,00	110233	3,07	100,00

Source:

Federal office of statistics

SBA 12/90

Table A3:

NET EXPORTS

	1980	1981	1982	1983	1984	1985	1986	1987	1988	1989
	billions of Swiss francs									
NET EXPORTS 1)										
Banks (estimation) 2)	3,4	2,9	3,9	4,6	5,8	7,2	7,7	8,2	8,3	8,2
Insurance	0,5	0,5	0,5	0,7	0,6	0,6	0,7	0,8	1,1	1,2
Tourism	1,9	2,6	2,4	2,7	3,0	2,8	2,4	2,2	1,7	2,0
Chemical Industry	3,2	4,1	4,3	4,5	4,9	5,2	5,8	6,3	6,5	7,1
Machinery 3)	2,2	2,4	2,9	1,8	2,3	2,7	1,5	-0,2	-1,2	-2,2
	billions of Swiss francs									
CURRENT ACCOUNT (balance)	-0,9	5,4	8,0	8,1	10,3	12,4	12,3	11,3	13,2	12,2
CAPITAL INCOME OF NON-BANKS (balance) (estimation) 4)	6,9	10,7	10,4	11,0	13,0	13,1	11,6	11,6	15,2	17,5

Remarks:

1) Net exports = exports ./. imports
2) Net interest income and non-interest income (net) [net capital income, commissions, etc] of banks
3) Machines, appliances, electronics, vehicles and precision instruments (optics and precision engineering)
4) Total capital income (net) ./. net interest income of banks (estimation)

Sources:

Commission for Economic Affairs (Balance of Payments)
Federal customs authorities
Own calculations

SBA 12/90

Table A4:

TAXES

	1980	1981	1982	1983	1984	1985	1986	1987	1988	1989	1980-1989
	millions of Swiss francs										growth p.a. (as %) *)
Direct taxes of banks	911	1130	1196	1341	1422	1700	1807	1803	1677	1788	7,78
Stamp duties	696	877	948	1233	1447	1874	2228	2267	2096	2379	14,63
Withholding taxes 1)	1249	1746	2150	1472	2034	1822	2542	1961	2758	2667	8,79
Total fiscal revenues (Confederation)	14619	15745	17382	18000	19863	20559	23426	23315	25957	26287	6,74
Direct taxes of all corporations	3870	4225	4650	4900	5130	5535	6385	6570	7250	7390	7,45

Remarks:

* Average annual growth rates 1980-1989
1) Net earnings

Sources:

SNB (The Swiss Banking System)
SNB (monthly report no. 11, november 1990) SBA 12/90

Table A5:

BANKING SYSTEM: BALANCE SHEET

	1980	1981	1982	1983	1984	1985	1986	1987	1988	1989	1980-1989
	billions of Swiss francs										growth p.a. (as %) 1)
ASSETS											
1 Cash	19,1	18,4	19,5	20,8	22,7	24,8	26,1	27,6	13,0	13,0	-4,2
2 Interbank deposits	111,5	131,0	151,0	158,2	180,4	197,7	226,9	235,4	251,8	229,8	8,4
3 Loans	283,4	309,3	327,9	347,6	385,8	415,4	443,9	484,7	553,5	634,1	9,4
of which											
Mortgage loans	140,4	155,6	167,8	180,9	196,9	214,4	236,8	264,8	300,1	341,1	10,4
4 Securities	54,5	59,6	63,4	75,5	79,8	90,0	100,7	103,1	98,6	106,5	7,7
5 Other assets	20,8	41,5	49,7	54,5	54,1	49,8	50,3	51,5	50,8	53,2	11,0
LIABILITIES											
6 Equity	32,6	35,7	38,2	40,2	43,2	48,4	54,1	58,6	62,6	67,9	8,5
7 Interbank deposits	113,5	133,1	128,8	134,8	143,5	167,3	197,9	207,9	216,9	233,3	8,3
8 Non-bank deposits	247,7	279,6	319,1	350,1	389,2	396,3	414,4	441,3	476,9	505,1	8,2
of which											
Savings	115,9	110,1	127,9	143,7	149,3	156,3	167,4	184,7	198,0	180,9	5,1
Time deposits	82,8	107,7	114,5	125,1	153,1	155,3	159,8	161,0	188,9	239,2	12,5
9 Bonds	69,6	82,2	93,3	96,5	104,9	117,7	130,7	140,6	151,3	164,4	10,0
10 Other liabilities	25,8	29,3	32,1	34,9	42,0	48,0	50,6	53,8	59,9	65,7	11,0
BALANCE SHEET TOTAL											
End year total	489,2	559,9	611,5	656,6	722,8	777,7	847,8	902,2	967,6	1036,5	8,7
Claims on non-residents	182,5	203,9	229,4	250,5	289,0	308,7	337,3	349,7	375,9	382,2	8,6
Liabilities to non-residents	141,9	172,7	195,3	210,9	230,3	238,6	259,7	260,4	289,1	309,1	9,0
	% of end-year balance sheet total										
ASSETS											
1 Cash	3,9	3,3	3,2	3,2	3,1	3,2	3,1	3,1	1,3	1,3	
2 Interbank deposits	22,8	23,4	24,7	24,1	25,0	25,4	26,8	26,1	26,0	22,2	
3 Loans	57,9	55,2	53,6	52,9	53,4	53,4	52,4	53,7	57,2	61,2	
of which											
Mortgage loans	28,7	27,8	27,4	27,6	27,2	27,6	27,9	29,4	31,0	32,9	
4 Securities	11,1	10,7	10,4	11,5	11,0	11,6	11,9	11,4	10,2	10,3	
5 Other assets	4,2	7,4	8,1	8,3	7,5	6,4	5,9	5,7	5,2	5,1	
LIABILITIES											
6 Equity	6,7	6,4	6,2	6,1	6,0	6,2	6,4	6,5	6,5	6,6	
7 Interbank deposits	23,2	23,8	21,1	20,5	19,9	21,5	23,3	23,0	22,4	22,5	
8 Non-bank deposits	50,6	49,9	52,2	53,3	53,8	51,0	48,9	48,9	49,3	48,7	
of which											
Savings	23,7	19,7	20,9	21,9	20,6	20,1	19,7	20,5	20,5	17,4	
Time deposits	16,9	19,2	18,7	19,1	21,2	20,0	18,9	17,8	19,5	23,1	
9 Bonds	14,2	14,7	15,3	14,7	14,5	15,1	15,4	15,6	15,6	15,9	
10 Other liabilities	5,3	5,2	5,3	5,3	5,8	6,2	6,0	6,0	6,2	6,3	
TOTAL ASSETS/LIABILITIES	100,0	100,0	100,0	100,0	100,0	100,0	100,0	100,0	100,0	100,0	
Claims on non-residents	37,3	36,4	37,5	38,1	40,0	39,7	39,8	38,8	38,8	36,9	
Liabilities to non-residents	29,0	30,8	31,9	32,1	31,9	30,7	30,6	28,9	29,9	29,8	SBA 12/90

Table A5 (continued):

Remarks:

*) Average annual growth rates 1980-1989

1 Cash on hand, giro-account deposits with National Bank and deposits with the Post Office

2 Balances with other banks on sight + Balances with other banks on time

3 Loans =
Current account loans (secured and unsecured) +
Fixed loans and advances (secured and unsecured) +
Current account advances and loans to public authorities +
Mortgages
Mortgage loans =
Fixed loans and advances, secured by mortgage +
Mortgages

4 Bills and money market papers +
Securities +
Permanent participations

5 Real estate +
Other assets +
Capital non paid in +
Balances of the profit and loss statement

6 Capital and reserves (statuory and other)

7 Balances of other banks on sight +
Balances of other banks on time

8 Non-bank deposits =
Deposits on sight +
Time deposits +
Savings deposits +
Deposits on deposits books and investment books
Savings =
Savings deposits +
Deposits on deposits books and investment books

9 Medium-term notes and cash bonds +
Bonds +
Mortgage bond loans (Pfandbriefe)

10 Acceptances and promissary +
Mortgages on bank-owned real estate +
Other liabilities +
Balances of the profit and loss statement

Sources:

SNB, The Swiss Banking System

SBA 12/90

Table A6:

BANKING SYSTEM: FIDUCIARY ACCOUNTS

	1980	1981	1982	1983	1984	1985	1986	1987	1988	1989	1980-1989
	billions of Swiss francs										growth p.a. (as %) *
1 Fiduciary accounts (assets)	120,7	158,4	166,4	182,8	232,0	215,0	187,3	188,0	226,5	299,2	10,61
of which claims on											
a residents	1,3	2,2	2,0	2,5	3,0	2,4	2,3	2,8	2,5	2,4	7,02
b non-residents	119,4	156,1	164,5	180,3	229,0	212,6	185,0	185,2	224,0	296,8	10,65
2 Fiduciary accounts (liabilities)	120,7	158,4	166,4	182,8	232,0	215,0	187,3	188,0	226,5	299,2	10,61
of which liabilities on											
a residents	17,5	24,0	19,3	18,5	36,6	38,8	37,0	39,7	49,2	71,5	16,92
b non-residents	103,2	134,4	147,1	164,3	195,4	176,2	150,3	148,3	177,3	227,7	9,19
	% of fiduciary accounts total										
1 Fiduciary accounts (assets)	100,0	100,0	100,0	100,0	100,0	100,0	100,0	100,0	100,0	100,0	
of which claims on											
a residents	1,1	1,4	1,2	1,4	1,3	1,1	1,2	1,5	1,1	0,8	
b non-residents	98,9	98,6	98,8	98,6	98,7	98,9	98,8	98,5	98,9	99,2	
2 Fiduciary accounts (liabilities)	100,0	100,0	100,0	100,0	100,0	100,0	100,0	100,0	100,0	100,0	
of which liabilities on											
a residents	14,5	15,1	11,6	10,1	15,8	18,1	19,8	21,1	21,7	23,9	
b non-residents	85,5	84,9	88,4	89,9	84,2	81,9	80,2	78,9	78,3	76,1	

Remarks:

*) Average annual growth rates 1980-1989

Sources:

SNB, The Swiss Banking System

SBA 12/90

Table A7:

BANKING SYSTEM: INCOME STATEMENT

	1980*	1981	1982	1983	1984	1985	1986	1987	1988	1989	1981-1989 growth p.a. (as %) °
	billions of Swiss francs										
REVENUES											
1 Interest income	28,5	39,1	41,5	36,3	42,0	42,6	41,9	44,2	49,0	64,9	6,5
2 Interest expense	22,7	32,4	33,3	27,6	32,4	31,9	30,5	32,7	35,9	50,7	5,8
3 Net interest income	5,8	6,8	8,2	8,7	9,6	10,7	11,4	11,5	13,1	14,1	9,7
4 Non-interest income (net)	5,3	6,4	6,9	8,0	8,5	10,3	12,0	13,4	12,5	15,6	11,7
GROSS INCOME	11,1	13,2	15,2	16,6	18,1	21,0	23,4	24,9	25,5	29,7	10,7
EXPENSES											
5 Staff costs	4,4	5,1	5,7	6,1	6,6	7,3	8,2	9,0	9,7	10,7	9,6
6 Office expenses	2,1	2,4	2,7	2,9	3,2	3,7	4,2	4,7	5,0	5,7	11,6
7 Provisions	1,3	2,0	2,7	3,1	3,3	4,0	4,4	4,7	4,4	5,6	14,0
8 Income taxes	0,9	1,1	1,2	1,3	1,4	1,7	1,8	1,8	1,7	1,8	5,9
NET PROFIT	2,3	2,6	2,9	3,2	3,6	4,3	4,8	4,7	4,8	6,0	11,0
BALANCE SHEET											
Average total	461,2	524,6	585,7	634,1	689,7	750,3	812,8	875,0	934,9	1002,0	8,4
	% of gross income										
REVENUES											
3 Net interest income	52,0	51,3	54,4	52,2	53,0	50,9	48,7	46,3	51,2	47,6	
4 Non-interest income (net)	48,0	48,7	45,6	47,8	47,0	49,1	51,3	53,7	48,8	52,4	
EXPENSES											
5 Staff costs	39,8	39,0	37,8	36,8	36,2	34,8	34,9	36,2	37,9	36,0	
6 Office expenses	18,9	17,8	17,8	17,4	17,7	17,5	18,1	18,9	19,7	19,0	
7 Provisions	12,2	14,8	17,6	18,6	18,4	19,2	18,8	19,0	17,2	18,8	
8 Income taxes	8,2	8,6	7,9	8,1	7,8	8,1	7,7	7,2	6,6	6,0	
NET PROFIT	20,9	19,8	18,9	19,2	19,8	20,4	20,4	18,7	18,6	20,1	
	% of balance sheet total										
REVENUES											
1 Interest income	6,18	7,46	7,09	5,72	6,09	5,67	5,15	5,05	5,24	6,47	
2 Interest expense	4,93	6,17	5,68	4,35	4,69	4,25	3,75	3,73	3,84	5,06	
3 Net interest income	1,25	1,29	1,41	1,37	1,39	1,43	1,40	1,32	1,40	1,41	
4 Non-interest income (net)	1,15	1,23	1,18	1,25	1,24	1,37	1,47	1,53	1,33	1,55	
GROSS INCOME	2,40	2,51	2,59	2,63	2,63	2,80	2,87	2,84	2,73	2,97	
EXPENSES											
5 Staff costs	0,96	0,98	0,98	0,97	0,95	0,97	1,00	1,03	1,04	1,07	
6 Office expenses	0,45	0,45	0,46	0,46	0,47	0,49	0,52	0,54	0,54	0,56	
7 Provisions	0,29	0,37	0,46	0,49	0,48	0,54	0,54	0,54	0,47	0,56	
8 Income taxes	0,20	0,22	0,20	0,21	0,21	0,23	0,22	0,21	0,18	0,18	
NET PROFIT	0,50	0,50	0,49	0,50	0,52	0,57	0,59	0,53	0,51	0,60	SBA 12/90

Table A7 (continued):

Remarks:

* Without private banks
°) Average annual growth rates 1981-1989

1 Interest receivable +
Net income from bills and money
market papers +
Net income from securities +
Income from permanent participations
2 Interest payable
4 Net commissions +
Income from trading in foreign exchange
and precious metals +
Miscellaneous +
Net loss

5 Bank directors and staff +
Contribution to staff welfare funds
6 Rents and maintenance for office premises
7 Losses, depreciations and provisions

Source:

SNB, The Swiss Banking System SBA 12/90

Table A8:

NUMBER OF INSTITUTIONS AND BRANCHES

	1980	1981	1982	1983	1984	1985	1986	1987	1988	1989
NUMBER OF INSTITUTIONS										
1 Cantonal Banks	29	29	29	29	29	29	29	29	29	29
2 Big Banks	5	5	5	5	5	5	5	5	5	5
3 Regional and Savings Banks	220	219	218	217	217	216	215	214	213	210
4 Credit Co-operatives and Raiffeisenbanks 1)	2	2	2	2	2	2	2	2	2	2
5 Other Swiss Banks 2)	93	87	86	82	82	85	88	91	89	91
6 Finance Companies	84	90	95	100	103	112	119	130	133	137
7 Foreign Banks 3)	99	107	112	113	119	120	125	128	133	135
8 Private Banks	25	25	25	25	24	24	24	23	22	22
TOTAL (banking system)	557	564	572	573	581	593	607	622	626	631
NUMBER OF BRANCHES 4)										
1 Cantonal Banks	719	733	749	741	659	687	709	722	741	755
2 Big Banks	759	777	800	811	821	853	876	889	901	933
of which abroad	29	30	31	32	32	36	36	38	38	39
3 Regional and Savings Banks	609	625	640	653	616	617	640	658	672	664
4 Credit Co-operatives and Raiffeisenbanks 1)	1214	1220	1226	1227	1232	1237	1243	1242	1241	1229
5 Other Swiss Banks 2)	241	233	234	232	249	257	266	273	287	301
of which abroad	2	2	3	4	6	6	7	9	8	9
6 Finance Companies	88	95	98	106	112	122	131	142	144	148
of which abroad	0	0	0	0	1	2	1	1	2	2
7 Foreign Banks 3)	199	209	219	223	237	239	245	251	273	280
of which abroad	40	38	38	39	38	37	36	37	39	41
8 Private Banks	26	26	27	27	25	26	25	25	27	26
TOTAL (banking system)	3855	3918	3993	4020	3951	4038	4135	4202	4286	4336
of which abroad	71	70	72	75	77	81	80	85	87	91
NUMBER OF RECEIPT OFFICES, REPRESENTATIVE OFFICES, ETC.										
TOTAL (banking system)	1103	1151	1148	1147	1396	1439	1444	1469	1466	1423
of which abroad	0	0	0	0	86	98	104	100	110	117
TOTAL NUMBER OF AGENCIES 5)										
TOTAL (banking system)	4958	5069	5141	5167	5347	5477	5579	5671	5752	5759
of which abroad	71	70	72	75	163	179	184	185	197	208

Remarks:

1) Number of federations
2) Other banks without foreign-controlled banks
3) Foreign-controlled banks and branches of foreign banks
4) Places of business, branches, agencies and branch-offices, without receipt offices, representative offices, etc.
5) Places of business, branches, agencies and branch-offices, including receipt offices, representative offices, etc.

Source:

SNB, The Swiss Banking System

Table A9:

EMPLOYMENT 1)

	1980	1981	1982	1983	1984	1985	1986	1987	1988	1989	1980-1989
	1000										growth p.a. (in %) *)
1 Cantonal Banks	12,9	13,5	14,0	14,4	14,7	15,3	16,1	16,9	17,3	18,0	3,78
2 Big Banks	47,0	49,7	50,6	50,3	50,5	52,7	56,6	59,9	60,8	62,9	3,28
3 Regional and Savings Banks	6,0	6,6	6,7	6,9	7,1	7,4	7,7	8,0	8,2	8,4	3,68
4 Credit Co-operatives and Raiffeisenbanks	1,8	1,8	2,1	2,2	2,3	2,4	2,6	2,7	2,8	3,0	6,24
5 Other Swiss Banks 2)	6,4	6,7	7,1	7,3	8,0	8,8	10,1	11,2	11,2	11,8	7,05
6 Finance Companies	0,5	0,7	0,7	0,8	0,9	1,1	1,4	1,7	1,9	2,0	15,55
7 Foreign Banks 3)	10,0	11,2	12,2	12,8	13,0	13,7	14,6	16,2	17,0	17,3	6,31
8 Private Banks	1,9	2,0	2,1	2,2	1,9	2,1	2,3	2,4	2,5	2,7	3,62
TOTAL (banking system)	86,6	92,2	95,4	96,9	98,5	103,5	111,4	119,0	121,8	126,0	4,26
of which abroad	3,5	3,8	4,2	4,2	4,5	4,9	5,4	6,0	6,7	7,8	9,22
	share, as % of total employment (banking system)										
1 Cantonal Banks	14,9	14,6	14,6	14,8	14,9	14,8	14,5	14,2	14,2	14,3	
2 Big Banks	54,3	53,9	53,0	51,9	51,3	51,0	50,8	50,4	49,9	49,9	
3 Regional and Savings Banks	7,0	7,2	7,0	7,1	7,2	7,1	6,9	6,7	6,8	6,6	
4 Credit Co-operatives and Raiffeisenbanks	2,0	2,0	2,2	2,3	2,4	2,4	2,3	2,2	2,3	2,4	
5 Other Swiss Banks 2)	7,4	7,2	7,4	7,6	8,1	8,5	9,1	9,4	9,2	9,4	
6 Finance Companies	0,6	0,7	0,7	0,9	0,9	1,1	1,3	1,4	1,5	1,6	
7 Foreign Banks 3)	11,5	12,2	12,8	13,2	13,2	13,2	13,1	13,6	14,0	13,7	
8 Private Banks	2,2	2,2	2,2	2,2	1,9	2,0	2,0	2,0	2,1	2,1	
TOTAL (banking system)	100,0	100,0	100,0	100,0	100,0	100,0	100,0	100,0	100,0	100,0	
of which abroad	4,1	4,1	4,4	4,4	4,6	4,8	4,9	5,1	5,5	6,2	

Remarks:

*) Average annual growth rates 1980-1989

1) Number of bank employees, end-year total
2) Other banks without foreign-controlled banks
3) Foreign-controlled banks and branches of foreign banks

Source:

SNB, The Swiss Banking System

SBA 12/90

Table A10:

BANKING GROUPS: SELECTED ASPECTS FROM INCOME STATEMENTS AND BALANCE SHEETS

	1980	1985	1989	1980	1985	1989	1980-1989
	billions of Swiss francs			share, as %			growth p.a. (as %) *)
BALANCE SHEET TOTAL							
1 Cantonal Banks	101,2	144,0	195,2	20,7	18,5	18,8	7,6
2 Big Banks	239,4	394,6	509,7	48,9	50,7	49,2	8,8
3 Regional and Savings Banks	45,8	64,4	88,6	9,4	8,3	8,5	7,6
4 Credit Co-operatives and Raiffeisenbanks	13,2	20,7	31,2	2,7	2,7	3,0	10,0
5 Other Swiss Banks 1)	21,7	37,5	55,9	4,4	4,8	5,4	11,1
6 Finance Companies	11,1	19,4	25,1	2,3	2,5	2,4	9,5
7 Foreign Banks 2)	54,3	92,8	125,2	11,1	11,9	12,1	9,7
8 Private Banks	2,6	4,2	5,6	0,5	0,5	0,5	8,8
TOTAL (banking system)	489,2	777,7	1036,5	100,0	100,0	100,0	8,7

	1980	1985	1989	1980	1985	1989	1980	1985	1989	1980-1989
	billions of Swiss francs			share, as %			% of balance sheet total			growth p.a. (as %) *)
MORTGAGE LOANS 3)										
1 Cantonal Banks	54,7	79,3	114,8	38,9	37,0	33,7	54,0	55,1	58,8	8,6
2 Big Banks	46,5	75,2	132,9	33,1	35,1	39,0	19,4	19,1	26,1	12,4
3 Regional and Savings Banks	26,9	38,7	56,6	19,1	18,0	16,6	58,7	60,1	63,9	8,6
4 Credit Co-operatives and Raiffeisenbanks	7,8	13,4	21,1	5,5	6,2	6,2	58,7	64,5	67,6	11,8
5 Other Swiss Banks 1)	3,6	6,2	11,9	2,6	2,9	3,5	16,8	16,5	21,3	14,1
6 Finance Companies	0,2	0,2	0,4	0,1	0,1	0,1	1,4	1,0	1,8	11,9
7 Foreign Banks 2)	0,8	1,4	3,3	0,6	0,6	1,0	1,5	1,5	2,6	16,6
8 Private Banks	0,0	0,0	0,1	0,0	0,0	0,0	1,6	1,0	1,5	7,5
TOTAL (banking system)	140,4	214,4	341,1	100,0	100,0	100,0	28,7	27,6	32,9	10,4

	1980	1985	1989	1980	1985	1989	1980	1985	1989	1980-1989
	billions of Swiss francs			share, as %			% of balance sheet total			growth p.a. (as %) *)
SAVINGS 4)										
1 Cantonal Banks	42,3	54,1	60,3	36,5	34,6	33,3	41,8	37,6	30,9	4,0
2 Big Banks	36,1	53,1	63,6	31,1	33,9	35,2	15,1	13,4	12,5	6,5
3 Regional and Savings Banks	22,4	27,6	30,3	19,3	17,7	16,7	49,0	42,9	34,2	3,4
4 Credit Co-operatives and Raiffeisenbanks	8,9	12,6	16,6	7,6	8,0	9,2	67,0	60,6	53,0	7,2
5 Other Swiss Banks 1)	4,7	7,0	8,7	4,1	4,5	4,8	21,8	18,7	15,5	7,0
6 Finance Companies	0,0	0,0	0,0	0,0	0,0	0,0	0,0	0,0	0,0	0,0
7 Foreign Banks 2)	1,4	1,7	1,3	1,2	1,1	0,7	2,6	1,9	1,1	-0,7
8 Private Banks	0,2	0,2	0,2	0,1	0,1	0,1	6,2	3,7	2,8	-0,2
TOTAL (banking system)	115,9	156,3	180,9	100,0	100,0	100,0	23,7	20,1	17,4	5,1

SBA 12/90

Table A10 (continued 1):

	1980	1985	1989	1980	1985	1989	1980	1985	1989	1980-1989
	billions of Swiss francs			share, as %			% of balance sheet total			growth p.a. (as %) *)
FOREIGN BUSINESS 5)										
1 Cantonal Banks	5,1	6,3	8,6	2,8	2,0	2,3	5,0	4,3	4,4	6,0
2 Big Banks	120,9	205,1	242,3	66,2	66,5	63,4	50,5	52,0	47,5	8,0
3 Regional and Savings Banks	0,7	1,0	1,0	0,4	0,3	0,3	1,5	1,6	1,1	4,7
4 Credit Co-operatives and Raiffeisenbanks	0,0	0,0	0,0	0,0	0,0	0,0	0,0	0,0	0,0	0,0
5 Other Swiss Banks 1)	7,1	11,9	19,0	3,9	3,8	5,0	32,9	31,7	34,0	11,5
6 Finance Companies	8,3	17,0	20,4	4,6	5,5	5,3	75,2	87,8	81,5	10,5
7 Foreign Banks 2)	39,5	66,0	89,0	21,6	21,4	23,3	72,7	71,1	71,1	9,5
8 Private Banks	0,9	1,4	1,8	0,5	0,4	0,5	33,3	32,0	31,1	8,0
TOTAL (banking system)	182,5	308,7	382,2	100,0	100,0	100,0	37,3	39,7	36,9	8,6

	1980	1985	1989	1980	1985	1989	1980	1985	1989	1980-1989
	billions of Swiss francs			share, as %			% of balance sheet total			growth p.a. (as %) *)
FIDUCIARY ACCOUNTS										
1 Cantonal Banks	2,0	3,1	5,9	1,6	1,4	2,0	2,0	2,2	3,0	12,9
2 Big Banks	47,4	76,9	103,8	39,3	35,8	34,7	19,8	19,5	20,4	9,1
3 Regional and Savings Banks	0,5	0,7	1,7	0,4	0,3	0,6	1,0	1,1	2,0	16,2
4 Credit Co-operatives and Raiffeisenbanks	0,0	0,0	0,0	0,0	0,0	0,0	0,0	0,0	0,0	0,0
5 Other Swiss Banks 1)	14,5	23,1	38,0	12,0	10,7	12,7	66,8	61,5	67,9	11,3
6 Finance Companies	3,8	5,2	3,5	3,2	2,4	1,2	34,6	26,6	13,9	-1,1
7 Foreign Banks 2)	48,1	98,4	129,6	39,8	45,8	43,3	88,6	106,0	103,5	11,6
8 Private Banks	4,4	7,6	16,7	3,7	3,5	5,6	167,8	180,3	297,0	15,9
TOTAL (banking system)	120,7	215,0	299,2	100,0	100,0	100,0	24,7	27,6	28,9	10,6

	1981	1985	1989	1981	1985	1989	1981-1989
	millions of Swiss francs			share, as %			growth p.a. (as %) *)
GROSS INCOME 6)							
1 Cantonal Banks	1522	2204	2963	11,5	10,5	10,0	8,7
2 Big Banks	6289	10143	13681	47,7	48,3	46,0	10,2
3 Regional and Savings Banks	772	1040	1401	5,9	5,0	4,7	7,7
4 Credit Co-operatives and Raiffeisenbanks	157	238	348	1,2	1,1	1,2	10,5
5 Other Swiss Banks 1)	1233	2158	3376	9,3	10,3	11,4	13,4
6 Finance Companies	390	689	1077	3,0	3,3	3,6	13,5
7 Foreign Banks 2)	2404	3807	5904	18,2	18,1	19,9	11,9
8 Private Banks	421	711	980	3,2	3,4	3,3	11,1
TOTAL (banking system)	13189	20990	29729	100,0	100,0	100,0	10,7

Table A10 (continued 2):

	1981	1985	1989	1981	1985	1989	1981	1985	1989	1981-1989
	millions of Swiss francs			share, as %			% of gross income			growth p.a. (as %) *)
NON-INTEREST INCOME 7)										
1 Cantonal Banks	419	626	845	6,5	6,1	5,4	27,5	28,4	28,5	9,2
2 Big Banks	3306	4885	6879	51,4	47,4	44,2	52,6	48,2	50,3	9,6
3 Regional and Savings Banks	178	272	370	2,8	2,6	2,4	23,1	26,2	26,4	9,6
4 Credit Co-operatives and Raiffeisenbanks	21	40	63	0,3	0,4	0,4	13,3	16,7	18,1	14,8
5 Other Swiss Banks 1)	683	1334	2063	10,6	13,0	13,2	55,4	61,8	61,1	14,8
6 Finance Companies	184	317	525	2,9	3,1	3,4	47,2	46,1	48,7	14,0
7 Foreign Banks 2)	1316	2225	4009	20,5	21,6	25,7	54,8	58,5	67,9	14,9
8 Private Banks	321	597	824	5,0	5,8	5,3	76,1	84,0	84,1	12,5
TOTAL (banking system)	6429	10296	15579	100,0	100,0	100,0	48,0	49,1	52,4	11,7

	1981	1985	1989
	%		
RETURN ON EQUITY (ROE) 8)			
1 Cantonal Banks	7,7	8,0	8,0
2 Big Banks	9,8	12,0	10,2
3 Regional and Savings Banks	8,7	9,2	8,2
4 Credit Co-operatives and Raiffeisenbanks	10,1	8,0	6,4
5 Other Swiss Banks 1)	12,5	14,4	13,7
6 Finance Companies	10,2	12,7	10,3
7 Foreign Banks 2)	12,5	14,1	15,8
8 Private Banks	39,3	68,4	56,7
TOTAL (banking system)	10,5	12,3	11,4

Remarks:

*) Average annual growth rates

1) Other banks without foreign-controlled banks
2) Foreign-controlled banks and branches of foreign banks
3) Fixed loans and advances, secured by mortgage + Mortgages
4) Savings deposits + Deposits on deposit books and investment books
5) Claims on non-residents
7) Commissions (balance) + Income from trading in foreign exchange and precious metals + Miscellaneous + Net loss
8) Net profit + taxes, as % of capital resources

Source:

SNB, The Swiss Banking System

Table A11:

CONCENTRATION OF SWISS BANKING SYSTEM:
SHARES IN BALANCE SHEET TOTAL ABSORBED BY THE LARGEST BANKS

Number of largest institutions	1970	1980	1988	1989
	Market share in balance sheet total of the banking system, as % *)			
3	43,68	43,97	44,86	44,02
5	51,47	51,46	52,04	51,54
10	58,84	58,07	58,22	57,57
20	68,30	66,52	65,87	65,51
50	81,79	78,89	78,03	78,34
100	90,18	86,27	85,38	85,55

Largest banks as % of all banks	Market share in balance sheet total of the banking system, as % *)			
1%	51,92	53,59	55,44	54,90
2%	59,43	60,62	62,12	61,70
5%	72,29	72,70	73,81	74,00
10%	82,39	82,17	82,85	83,35
20%	90,69	89,73	90,31	90,62
50%	97,91	97,59	97,83	97,88

Remarks:

*) Without credit co-operatives and raiffeisenbanks and without private banks

	Number of institutions
1970	525
1980	530
1988	602
1989	607

Source:

SNB, The Swiss Banking System SBA 12/90

Table A12:

STRUCTURAL COEFFICIENTS OF BANKING SYSTEMS IN INTERNATIONAL COMPARISON

	1980	1981	1982	1983	1984	1985	1986	1987	1988	1989	growth p.a. (as %) 3)
BALANCE SHEET TOTAL 1)	billions of national currency 2)										
USA	1465	1594	1748	1879	1986	2206	2425	2602	2788	3015	8,35
Japan	2572	2809	3037	3317	3596	4003	4454	5009	5648	6358	10,58
Germany	1714	1865	1978	2100	2248	2418	2564	2678	2858	3098	6,80
Switzerland	337	365	430	461	496	543	575	624	666	719	8,77
CLAIMS ON NON-RESIDENTS 1)	% of balance sheet total										
USA	13,1	13,9	15,1	13,7	9,5	8,6	8,2	8,8	8,5	9,5	
Japan	4,2	4,6	4,7	5,2	5,0	6,3	8,1	9,7	11,3	12,8	
Germany	9,7	10,2	9,8	9,7	10,5	11,5	13,5	13,7	14,3	16,2	
Switzerland	34,7	34,8	32,2	32,3	32,4	32,6	32,8	32,5	31,8	28,6	
LIABILITIES TO NON-RESIDENTS 1)	% of balance sheet total										
USA	9,9	10,8	9,4	9,4	7,8	8,1	8,6	10,1	10,2	11,6	
Japan	7,3	7,5	7,7	7,7	8,4	10,2	13,4	16,0	17,2	18,3	
Germany	8,2	8,1	7,8	7,5	8,2	7,7	7,7	7,8	8,2	8,8	
Switzerland	25,1	28,9	26,1	25,8	25,6	24,2	23,3	22,5	23,2	23,7	
GROSS INCOME 4)	billions of national currency 2)										
USA	70	78	88	96	107	123	134	140	149	159	9,53
Japan	40	44	51	55	57	58	66	76	85	82	8,21
Germany	45	52	61	68	70	75	78	80	82	90	8,10
Switzerland	NA	13	15	17	18	21	23	25	26	30	10,69
NON-INTEREST INCOME 4)	% of gross income										
USA	22,1	24,0	24,6	26,5	24,7	26,6	29,8	30,1	30,0	31,1	
Japan	11,4	17,8	13,9	14,7	17,7	21,1	19,7	25,7	26,2	28,5	
Germany	20,4	19,1	17,9	16,7	18,0	20,6	20,4	20,1	18,9	25,6	
Switzerland	NA	48,7	45,6	47,8	47,0	49,1	51,3	53,7	48,8	52,4	
BALANCE SHEET TOTAL / GNP 1)											
USA	0,54	0,52	0,55	0,55	0,53	0,55	0,57	0,58	0,57	0,58	
Japan	1,07	1,09	1,13	1,18	1,20	1,26	1,34	1,43	1,51	1,59	
Germany	1,15	1,21	1,24	1,25	1,27	1,31	1,32	1,33	1,35	1,37	
Switzerland	1,90	1,88	2,09	2,15	2,19	2,25	2,26	2,35	2,35	2,36	

Remarks:

NA Data not available

1) USA: Commercial Banks (according to IMF);
Japan, Germany, Switzerland: Deposit Money Banks (according to IMF)
2) Japan: in 100 milliards of Yen
3) Average annual growth rates
4) Banking systems according to tables A14, A15, A16; Switzerland: All banks and finance companies

Sources:

Foreign business:	IMF (International Financial Statistics)
Non-interest income:	See tables A7, A14, A15, A16
Balance sheet total / Gross national product (GNP):	IMF (International Financial Statistics)

SBA 12/90

Table A13

PERFORMANCE OF BANKING SYSTEMS:
COEFFICIENTS IN INTERNATIONAL COMPARISON 1)

	1980	1981	1982	1983	1984	1985	1986	1987	1988	1989	
	%										average
RETURN ON ASSETS 2)											
USA	1,07	1,00	0,88	0,84	0,84	0,90	0,80	0,29	1,17	0,81	0,86
Japan	0,41	0,45	0,50	0,54	0,49	0,46	0,52	0,62	0,63	0,49	0,51
Germany	0,52	0,56	0,70	0,77	0,76	0,72	0,69	0,59	0,66	0,53	0,65
Switzerland	NA	0,71	0,69	0,72	0,73	0,80	0,81	0,74	0,69	0,78	0,74
RETURN ON EQUITY 3)											
USA	17,67	16,36	14,36	13,61	13,15	14,01	12,50	4,84	19,20	12,93	13,86
Japan	15,50	17,24	20,31	21,90	20,60	19,04	21,52	23,71	21,49	15,45	19,68
Germany	15,00	16,22	20,05	21,79	21,12	19,14	17,37	14,80	16,08	12,39	17,39
Switzerland	NA	10,47	10,63	11,27	11,62	12,35	12,15	11,02	10,27	11,44	11,25
INTEREST RATE MARGINS 4)											
USA	3,08	3,06	3,16	3,13	3,35	3,47	3,34	3,40	3,53	3,51	3,30
Japan	1,61	1,46	1,55	1,50	1,36	1,22	1,27	1,20	1,16	0,92	1,32
Germany	2,03	2,22	2,48	2,64	2,50	2,41	2,35	2,26	2,25	2,12	2,33
Switzerland	NA	1,29	1,41	1,37	1,39	1,43	1,40	1,32	1,40	1,41	1,38
UNIT COSTS 5)											
USA	66,51	68,69	69,55	69,14	68,41	66,53	66,79	67,90	66,07	65,97	67,56
Japan	76,78	74,02	69,11	67,45	68,08	69,01	64,44	59,32	56,91	57,90	66,30
Germany	69,47	64,08	58,71	56,92	59,29	60,55	62,66	66,13	68,08	64,56	63,05
Switzerland	NA	56,85	55,60	54,20	53,94	52,30	53,06	55,08	57,63	55,05	54,86
PROVISIONS 6)											
USA	0,25	0,26	0,40	0,47	0,57	0,67	0,78	1,27	0,54	0,93	0,61
Japan	0,01	0,01	0,06	0,04	0,04	0,02	0,04	0,03	0,05	0,04	0,03
Germany	0,26	0,43	0,55	0,60	0,48	0,48	0,41	0,37	0,23	0,49	0,43
Switzerland	NA	0,37	0,46	0,49	0,48	0,54	0,54	0,54	0,47	0,56	0,49
EQUITY 7)											
USA	5,79	5,83	5,87	6,00	6,14	6,20	6,19	6,12	5,89	6,18	6,02
Japan	2,56	2,39	2,34	2,34	2,24	2,34	2,29	2,48	2,73	2,93	2,46
Germany	3,27	3,27	3,34	3,36	3,39	3,56	3,69	3,98	3,95	4,08	3,59
Switzerland	6,67	6,38	6,25	6,13	5,97	6,23	6,38	6,49	6,47	6,56	6,35

Remarks:

NA Data not available

1) Banking systems according to tables A14, A15 and A16; Switzerland: All banks and finance companies
2) Profit before tax in % of average balance sheet total
3) Profit before tax in % of equity (capital and reserves)
4) Net interest income in % of average balance sheet total
5) Staff costs and office expenses in % of gross income
6) Losses, depreciations and provisions in % of average balance sheet total
7) Equity in % of end-year balance sheet total

Sources: See tables A5, A7, A14, A15, A16

Table A14:

USA: THE BANKING SYSTEM 1)

	1980	1981	1982	1983	1984	1985	1986	1987	1988	1989
	billions of US dollars									
INCOME STATEMENT										
REVENUES										
1 Interest income	174,4	228,8	235,6	214,2	249,3	247,0	236,3	240,5	265,0	308,7
2 Interest expenses	119,9	169,5	169,0	143,4	168,5	156,7	142,0	142,6	160,5	199,3
3 Net interest income	54,5	59,3	66,6	70,8	80,9	90,4	94,3	97,9	104,5	109,3
4 Non-interest income (net)	15,5	18,7	21,8	25,6	26,5	32,7	39,9	42,2	44,7	49,4
GROSS INCOME	70,0	78,0	88,4	96,3	107,4	123,1	134,2	140,1	149,2	158,8
EXPENSES										
6 Staff costs	24,6	28,0	31,4	33,7	36,7	39,8	42,6	44,5	45,6	48,1
7 Office expenses	21,9	25,6	30,1	32,9	36,8	42,1	47,0	50,7	53,0	56,6
8 Provisions	4,5	5,1	8,5	10,7	13,8	17,6	21,9	36,5	16,0	28,8
9 Taxes	5,0	4,6	3,6	4,1	4,7	5,6	5,3	5,3	9,9	9,5
NET PROFIT	13,9	14,7	14,8	15,0	15,5	18,0	17,4	3,2	24,8	15,7
BALANCE SHEET TOTAL										
End-year total	1851,9	2024,8	2189,2	2333,0	2498,8	2718,5	2924,6	2853,5	3064,5	3159,5
Average total	1770,3	1938,4	2107,0	2261,1	2415,9	2608,6	2821,5	2883,0	2959,0	3112,0
EQUITY	107,3	118,0	128,4	140,0	153,5	168,5	181,1	174,7	180,5	195,1
NUMBER OF INSTITUTIONS	14423	14402	14437	14454	14460	14357	14130	13273	12691	12323

Remarks:

1) All insured commercial banks (FDIC insured banks)

Sources:

OECD "Bank Profitability, Financial Statements of Banks 1980-1984", Paris, 1987
OECD "Bank Profitability (Statistical Supplement), Financial Statements of Banks 1981-1985", Paris, 1987
OECD "Bank Profitability (Statistical Supplement), Financial Statements of Banks 1982-1986", Paris, 1988
Federal Reserve Board "Profitability of Commercial Banks", Washington, July 1990

Table A15:

JAPAN: THE BANKING SYSTEM 1)

	1980	1981	1982	1983	1984	1985	1986	1987	1988	1989
	billions of Yen									
INCOME STATEMENT										
REVENUES										
1 Interest income	15888	18990	19457	19131	22665	21279	20550	22524	27252	35603
2 Interest expenses	12322	15336	15066	14476	17956	16663	15251	16860	20952	29750
3 Net interest income	3566	3655	4391	4655	4709	4616	5299	5665	6300	5852
4 Non-interest income (net)	458	790	711	801	1012	1231	1299	1954	2236	2331
GROSS INCOME	4024	4445	5103	5456	5720	5847	6598	7619	8537	8183
EXPENSES										
6 Staff costs	1884	1981	2093	2158	2242	2303	2360	2378	2420	2519
7 Office expenses	1205	1309	1434	1522	1652	1732	1892	2143	2437	2220
8 Provisions	18	37	170	118	126	72	160	154	268	283
9 Taxes	471	593	819	910	936	921	1177	1563	1842	1414
NET PROFIT	445	525	587	748	764	819	1010	1383	1569	1748
BALANCE SHEET TOTAL										
End-year total	230802	271435	295924	323147	368666	390205	443637	501022	581778	697282
Average total	221712	251119	283680	309535	345907	379436	416921	472330	541400	639530
EQUITY	5915	6484	6926	7568	8250	9134	10161	12420	15874	20464
NUMBER OF INSTITUTIONS	76	76	76	76	77	77	77	77	77	77

Remarks:

1) All Ordinary Banks (City Banks and Regional Banks)

Sources:

OECD "Bank Profitability, Financial Statements of Banks 1980-1984", Paris, 1987
OECD "Bank Profitability (Statistical Supplement), Financial Statements of Banks 1981-1985", Paris, 1987
OECD "Bank Profitability (Statistical Supplement), Financial Statements of Banks 1982-1986", Paris, 1988
Federation of Bankers Associations of Japan "Analysis of Financial Statements of All Banks", Tokyo 1989 and 1990

Table A16:

GERMANY: THE BANKING SYSTEM 1)

	1980	1981	1982	1983	1984	1985	1986	1987	1988	1989
	billions of DM									
INCOME STATEMENT										
REVENUES										
1 Interest income	138,4	173,2	181,9	166,9	175,3	180,5	177,4	182,2	191,8	224,8
2 Interest expenses	103,0	131,1	131,7	110,1	118,4	120,7	115,0	117,9	125,6	157,9
3 Net interest income	35,5	42,0	50,2	56,8	57,0	59,8	62,4	64,3	66,2	66,9
4 Non-interest income (net)	9,1	9,9	10,9	11,4	12,5	15,5	15,9	16,1	15,4	23,0
GROSS INCOME	44,6	52,0	61,1	68,2	69,5	75,4	78,3	80,4	81,7	89,8
EXPENSES										
6 Staff costs	21,1	22,5	23,8	25,6	26,8	29,4	31,5	34,2	35,8	37,0
7 Office expenses	9,8	10,8	12,1	13,2	14,4	16,2	17,6	19,0	19,8	21,0
8 Provisions	4,5	8,1	11,1	12,8	10,9	12,0	11,0	10,5	6,8	15,3
9 Taxes	5,0	6,5	9,2	11,0	11,1	11,4	11,4	10,3	12,0	9,3
NET PROFIT	4,1	4,1	5,0	5,5	6,3	6,4	6,8	6,4	7,3	7,3
BALANCE SHEET TOTAL										
End-year total	1852,6	1991,9	2116,7	2257,4	2427,3	2609,3	2843,2	2847,9	3029,0	3268,3
Average total	1745,4	1891,4	2023,5	2154,3	2281,1	2481,8	2654,9	2845,6	2938,5	3148,6
EQUITY	60,6	65,2	70,6	75,8	82,2	92,8	105,0	113,3	119,8	133,5
NUMBER OF INSTITUTIONS	3087	3072	3061	3039	3025	4439	4465	4326	4215	4080

Remarks:

1) All universal banks (big banks, regional banks and other commercial banks, private bankers, regional giro institutions, savings banks, regional institutions of credit co-operatives, and credit co-operatives)

Sources:

OECD "Bank Profitability, Financial Statements of Banks 1980-1984", Paris, 1987
OECD "Bank Profitability (Statistical Supplement), Financial Statements of Banks 1981-1985", Paris, 1987
OECD "Bank Profitability (Statistical Supplement), Financial Statements of Banks 1982-1986", Paris, 1988
Monthly report of the Deutsche Bundesbank ("Die Ertragslage der deutschen Kreditinstitute im Jahre 1989"), No. 8, 1990

SBA 12/90

Comment on

Andreas Bossard, Matthias Wirth, Niklaus Blattner: "The Swiss Banking Sector: Development and Outlook

John Noorlander

Working for one of the banks you just heard about, I would be unwise to do other than support the view Bosshard et al. have just presented. After all, they represent our lobby. Furthermore, there results are very flattering: Yes, we have done very well and we are very competitive internationally.

Two points strike me as being particularly important:

1. **Above average growth in employment, value added and productivity**. Value added per person is now more than 2 1/2 times higher than the Swiss average.

   This rises the question of the political economy of the treatment of the banking sector in Switzerland. In an economy with (almost) the highest levels of real income and wages worldwide, where it is a political aim to preserve this high living standard, it would seem essential to care about the development of those sectors that provide the highest value added. It is not merely self-pity of bankers to claim that this is not exactly what is happening in Switzerland.

   Proponents of public choice theory would of course argue that this is typical: Politicians tend to support the lagging industries, with usually below-average value-added and where employment is in danger. European examples are agriculture, the mining, steel and shipbuilding industries. True this may be. However, several European countries (where the banking sector provides an above-average value added, too) have promoted their financial sector very much: Britain, France and the Netherlands are important examples, and tax incentives have been an important parameter in this often footlose industry - let me remind that up to 33% of Swiss equities are traded in London.

2. Swiss banks are an export industry and as such seem to have contributed more to the current account surplus than most of the other industries in Switzerland.

Of course, this is nothing new to this audience - it is indeed part of the research project we are talking about these two days. But I do not think politicians are always fully aware of this issue. There is a widespread view that the financial sector, providing no benefits by its own, should be subservient to the needs of the "real" economy. This view is held in other countries - there has always been this debate in the UK - and in Switzerland, too.

Our finance minister, for example, expressed concern that the Swiss financial sector has grown beyond the needs of our domestic economy. I have never heard of any concern that Switzerland produces more watches than it could ever absorb domestically, but then everybody understands the Swiss watch industry as being a typical export industry. The laws of the international division of labour would definitely single out the Swiss banking sector as a prime export industry in high-wage Switzerland. The paper shows the high value added of Swiss banks and their ability to compete internationally. In this sense the banking sector could hardly be too large for Switzerland.

However, the very positive image portrayed in the paper by Bossard et al. seems to contradict feelings that abound in the market. Sentiment can probably best be measured in stock prices: Swiss bank shares have clearly underperformed the index for most of the Eighties, in contrast to the evidence in this paper. Bank stocks have underperformed in other countries too, but less persistently than in Switzerland. An explanation could be that the return on equity is low in international comparison and has also lagged behind its development in other sectors of Swiss industry - again in contrast to the figures we just heard on the value added of Swiss banks.

Another contrast to the rather bullish evidence presented here, is a recent study published by the EFTA[1]. Based on the methodology used in the Cecchini Report, it implies that, except for Austria, Switzerland has the highest prices for a typical set of banking products among all EC and EFTA countries. This seems very surprising,

---

1 E.P.M. Gardener and J.L. Teppett: The Impact of 1992 on the Financial Services Sectors of EFTA Countries. EFTA Occasional Paper No. 33

after we hear that productivity growth has been strong and unit costs are low in international comparison, and yet our margins and returns are relatively small.

Usually, a supplier of an expensive good will retort, that the high price is due to its high quality. In the case of Swiss banks (and if our prices really are high), this claim has some justification: We are "safe and sound" in the widest sense due to prudent bank management and high capital requirements. Given that banks in several European countries will struggle as they have to fulfil the EC's directives on capital adequacy, prices may just as well rise in our direction rather than downward, once European banking markets are fully integrated. Price competition has always been intense on the international markets, and Swiss banks, like others, have found it hard to sustain the constant pressure on margins as our lack of profitability of some of our foreign operations show. Maybe, the world is about to change. There is a tendency of corporations to get away from "shopping around" their 100 or more bank relations and instead concentrate on a core of banks. There is an increasing desire for a relationship to banks that are likely to remain loyal in times of financial distress, for which the client is prepared to pay. The issue has become more important in an economic environment where the risk implied by increased debt/equity ratios has become more apparent. Such a rebirth of the "Hausbank" is likely to constrain the development of the "anonymous capital market" - i.e. securitisation. Swiss banks have a good potential to be among such a core group of international "Hausbanks".

On the domestic scene, competition has undoubtedly played in the past - the change in market structure, the improvement of productivity and costs would seem unplausible in the absence of competitive pressures. However, the use of the price parameter has been limited, and this is likely to change. But if we consider our relatively feeble return on equity, it is doubtful whether a significant downward movement in prices or margins for banking products would be sustainable in the long-run.

Finally, there are the political threats to supervise our prices and margins. Beyond the institution of the "price supervisor" there is general pressure by the public and the media. Many find it hard to understand that, for example, banks reported increasing interest margins in the first quarter, and did not immediately reduce (old) mortgage rates. There is a lobby from usually market-oriented quarters and even within the banks calling for improved, product-related cost-accounting that should be revealed publicly to justify interest rate changes. There is nothing to be said against improvements of the banks' cost-accounting, but to promote it to a tool of price policy does make no sense economically, certainly not from a viewpoint of competition policy. Therefore, if my argument is correct, it would be nice to obtain support from the academic world!

I have been talking about some of the problems confronting banks in Switzerland. It would be unfair to assume that there are no problems for banks abroad.

By closing, I want to cite from a recent speech by Anthony M. Salomon[2], former president of the Fed in New York, who thought that (not specifically mentioning Switzerland) European banks would be in a fine competitive position in the Nineties, as American banks are stuck with bad loans, Japanese banks with the need to raise equity, and German banks will be fully absorbed in rebuilding East Germany.

2 At the European Finance Convention in Rome, 16 October 1990

Part III: Determinants of Trade in Banking Services

Regulation and Technology as Determinants of International Trade in Banking Services

Thomas Helbling[1]

1. Introduction

Regulation and deregulation of financial markets, including the banking industry, was traditionally a topic of national rather than international concern because these markets were submitted to numerous regulatory measures and their linkage with other markets abroad was weak. However, after the liberalization of capital account transactions and the deregulation of national financial markets in the beginning of the eighties, regulation and deregulation became a topic of international concern. As the links between national markets became closer, shocks in one country were transmitted faster to other countries. Also, the competitiveness of a country's financial service industry was at least indirectly affected by such deregulations. Two items on the agenda in international economic policy, namely the Basle accord on capital adequacy requirements of July 1988 and the second banking directive of the Commission of the European Community (EC), have or will have even a direct influence on the competitiveness of national financial markets and industries[2]. The present paper discusses three elements of special interest from the second banking directive:

a) the permission to supply financial services across intra-EC borders,

b) the authorization to set up branches and subsidiaries in all the EC countries, and

c) the principle of home country control rather than host country control for intra-European operations of EC financial intermediaries.

The propositions of the second EC banking directive are likely to improve the efficiency of financial markets and thus to ameliorate welfare. Nevertheless, they are also a reason for concern: Regulatory differentials between countries may induce shifts in a member country's banking industry structure that are undesirable.

---

1 The author thanks Ernst Baltensperger, Hans Genberg, Alexander Swoboda, the conference participants and the members of the research team for their helpful comments.

2 See Dermine (1990) and Walter (1990) on the second EC banking directive.

This paper examines the impacts of regulatory differentials and liberalization of cross-border transactions on trade patterns in banking services from a theoretical point of view. This question is of interest not only for EC member countries, but also for the neighbouring countries. It has always been acknowledged in the literature that regulatory differentials are likely to create incentives for trade in financial services and for the establishment of financial centers (cf. Niehans (1984), chap. 9, Freedman (1977), p. 175 or Aliber (1984), p. 668). Recently, Grilli (1989) evaluated the competitive position of financial centers in Europe after the liberalization of financial markets and the implication it could have on various products. By referring to the concepts of external increasing returns to scale because of thick market externalities and of consumer switching costs, he showed that the impact of trade liberalization in financial markets would not be as straightforward as a model of perfect competition would suggest. Grilli's argument is without a doubt relevant for most subindustries in financial markets. However, he does not take into account the specific nature of the banking firm nor does he refer to specific regulatory measures. For example, the thick market externalities were assumed to result from search costs that induce specialized production of information services etc. Nevertheless, as soon as these information services which may be considered as intermediate input become tradable, the external returns to scale will become international rather than national (cf. Ethier (1982)).

In this paper a model of the banking firm is applied to the theory of international trade in order to gain insight regarding the effects of regulatory differentials on trade patterns and their interaction with other determinants of trade[3]. The theory of the banking firm emphasizes the significance of risk transformation and transaction costs as determinants which explain the existence of financial intermediaries[4]. This study relies heavily on the real resource cost model of the banking firm which was developped by Baltensperger (1980) and Baltensperger, Milde (1987). Because the cost of risk and the balance sheet constraint are taken into account, this approach allows one to analyze the impacts of risk and operating costs and their dependence on technology and regulation. It can be conveniently used with concepts of international trade theory also. The method is rather ecclectic because the analysis is restricted to partial equilibria and different specifications of market structure, technology and demand are used to derive

---

3 See Niehans (1984, chap. 7) for a graphical representation of a similar approach.

4 Baltensperger (1980) or Santomero (1984) provide surveys in which the different approaches are presented.

conclusions about the effects and the importance of regulatory differentials. The set of regulatory measures explicitly analyzed includes only those dealing with the asset transformation function of the banking firm and market access; however, it is also shown that the approach allows one to deal with other regulatory distortions such as taxes or transaction restrictions.

In contrast with the bulk of the existing literature on international banking which stresses the importance of multinational banks and their foreign branches, this analysis focuses primarily on national or industry specific supply side issues. Aliber in his 1984 survey identifies the "industrial organisation issue, [that] centers on the patterns of expansion of foreign branches and subsidiaries of banks headquartered in the United States, Great Britain, Japan, and a few other industrial countries and on the nature of the advantage that these branches and subsidiaries have in relation to their host-country competitors" (p. 661) to be one of two sets of issues involved in the analysis of international banking. He proposes that "the follow-the-leader" explanation is the most frequently used explanation to illustrate the advantages that branches of foreign banks have compared to host country banks: branches of foreign banks can better serve their home country clients' needs in the host country than domestic banks can , or the "modified version", is that the foreign banks have to offer these services to their clients who consider the global linkages of a bank to be one differentiated product. Sapir (1990) uses M.E. Porter's type 3 competition in services to explain the prevalence of direct foreign investment in international trade in services. Because of the 'close and frequent interaction between buyers and sellers' such explanantions have been dominant in the literature. This paper takes the view that the traditional theory of international trade can help to gain some insight into the determinants of trade in financial services even if it does not incorporate elements of the buyer-seller relationship emphasized in other approaches. There are three main arguments for this. First, technological progress is likely to reduce the importance of the interaction between buyers and sellers , thus direct foreign investment may become less important relative to international trade. Second, concentration on firm-specific advantages makes it difficult to explain the systematic comparative advantage that some countries seem to have[5]. Thirdly, recentdevelopments in trade theory can explain the existence of multinational corporation via fundamental variables such as differences in factor endowments. Compared with other existing work, this paper neglects the currency denomination of

[5]. This argument was made by John D. Murray in a comment on Aliber's (1984) paper in the same issue of the journal.

banking services. There is no stringent relation between the location of production and the currency denomination if currencies are convertible[6]. The criterion to classify transaction of banking services as international trade is the location of producers and buyers.

The paper is organized as follows: Section 2 discusses some aspects of the theory of the banking firm which are crucial for the subsequent analysis of trade patterns and their dependence on technology and regulation presented in sections 3 and 4.

2. A Simultaneous Model of the Determination of a Banking Firm's Balance Sheet Structure and Balance Sheet Size

This section takes up the resource cost model of the banking firm as it was developped by Baltensperger, Milde (1987, chap. 5). Their approach is slightly modified in order to capture the effects of regulations in the banking industry and to evaluate the impact of different technology specifications on the behaviour of the banking firm.

2.1. Set-up of the model

There exist two types of assets for a bank, credits C and non-interest bearing cash reserves R, and two types of liabilities, deposits D and equity capital E. The corresponding balance sheet constraint is:

(1) $C + R - D - E = 0.$

The total volume of credits and deposits depends only on the number of clients as both the size of a credit and of a deposit account are assumed to be standardized at C_0 and D_0. Thus, total credits C and total deposits D are given by:

(2a) $C = mC_0,$

(2b) $D = nD_0,$

where m denotes the number of credit accounts and n the number of deposit accounts. The production of both credits and deposits requires labour L and capital K as

---

6 Camen (1990), for example, shows that a major part of foreign assets and liabilities of Swiss banks is denominated in foreign currencies. The currency denomination of banking services may also be modelled by using differentiated products.

input factors. It is assumed that the production processes of both balance sheet items are independent of each other and that the production functions are of the form:

(3a) $m = f_1(L_m, K_m)$ and

(3b) $n = f_2(L_n, K_n)$.

The banking firm is a price- taker in the factor markets and must pay W and V as compensation to the owners of L and K. This implies that two cost functions c_m and c_n of the form:

(4a) $c_m = c_1(V, W, m)$ and

(4b) $c_n = c_2(V, W, n)$

can be used in the analysis of the banking firm's decision problem.

Besides outlays for factors of production, the bank has also to cope with liquidity costs that stem from the uncertain amount of deposit withdrawals per period[7]. This uncertainty requires a bank to hold a positive amount of non-interest bearing cash reserves as long as a shortage of reserves is costly for the bank. For the present purpose, it is furthermore assumed that the bank is forced by a supervising authority to hold some reserves . Let v_j denote the withdrawal per deposit account j and suppose that it is normally distributed with mean 0 and variance d^2 and that it is uncorrelated with any other v_i $(i = j)$. The end-of-period minimum reserve requirement is violated if

(5) $R - v < \tau(nD_0 - v)$,

where $v = \Sigma v_j$ and where τ denotes the minimum reserve requirement factor[8]. The bank will be charged a penalty δ if it does not fulfill the reserve requirements. In the appendix, it is shown that this set up leads to an expected liquidity cost function

(6) $X(R, n, \delta, \tau, d)$

with the partial derivatives

---

7 It is assumed that a period consists of two subperiods. Deposit holders are allowed to withdraw amounts up to the deposit size D_0 within the second subperiod.

8 This is the formulation chosen by Baltensperger, Milde (1987, pp. 70).

$X_R < 0, X_{RR} > 0, X_n > 0$ and $X_{nn} < 0$[9].

An increase in reserves decreases the expected liquidity costs because the probability of a costly violation of the minimum reserve requirement is reduced. An increase in the number of deposit accounts augments the expected liquidity costs as the variance of v will become larger. Expected liquidity costs, however, will grow disproportionally lower relative to deposits as the variance has a negative second order derivative with respect to n. The second-order effects of changes in the regulatory environment are the following:

$X_{R\tau} < 0$, $X_{R\delta} < 0$, $X_{n\tau} > 0$ and $X_{n\delta} > 0$.

An increase in the minimum reserve requirement rate τ augments the probability of an end-of-period cash reserve shortage, therefore the marginal liquidity costs for the last deposit account are increasing in τ, whereas the marginal reduction in liquidity costs for the last reserve unit is decreasing in τ. The same kind of argument can be applied to an increase in the penalty rate δ for a violation of the minimum reserve requirements.

Insolvency cost is another fundamental cost component for the banking firm. As the return on credits is a stochastic variable there exists a positive probability that the market valuation of the end-of-period assets of the bank may not cover the liabilities by their full amount. Equity capital can be used as a buffer to prevent insolvency. The latter state is assumed to be costly for the bank, otherwise depositors would have no incentive to hold parts of their assets as deposits in a bank. If expected insolvency costs are positive, the bank will generally hold a positive amount of equity capital. For the present study, it is furthermore assumed that there is a capital adequacy requirement imposed upon the bank by a supervising authority[10]. The authority calculates the end-of-period equity capital as:

---

9 The analytic derivation of these partial derivatives can be found in Baltensperger, Milde (op. cit., chap. 2).

10 Baltensperger, Milde (op. cit.) develop their model with some proportional insolvency cost which is a necessary condition to prevent default from being a viable option for the banking firm. The penalty imposed in case of a violated capital adequacy requirement fulfills the same function in the present model. The correspondance between the two formulations is already noted in Baltensperger, Milde (op. cit., p. 187), and has the advantage of allowing for a comparison between countries in which the regulatory environment differs. For the derivation of the expected capital requirement cost function it is also assumed that the bank is never liquidated in case of a default but merely reorganised. By this assumption, the problem becomes tractable.

(7) $\quad E_{t+1} = (1+r)mC_0 + (R-v) - \Omega(m,n,W,V) - (1+z)nD_0,$

where r denotes the exogeneous stochastic return on total credits, z the contract rate paid on deposits and Ω the expenditures on factors of production. It is assumed that the expected rate of return on deposits μ^t is a given parameter for the bank. The contract rate z on deposit accounts is therefore determined endogeneously so that the expected rate of return on deposits which reflects the implied insolvency risk of the chosen balance sheet structure will be equal to the required rate. Suppose that the capital adequacy requirement is formulated in terms of an end-of-period requirement

(8) $\quad E_{t+1} = \varepsilon mC_0,$

ε denotes the capital adequacy requirement rate. This requirement is violated if

(9) $\quad (1+r)mC_0 + (R-v) - \Omega(m,n,V,W) - (1+z)nD_0 < \varepsilon mC_0.$

The bank is charged by the penalty rate φ per unit violation of the requirement. In the appendix, it is shown that this set up leads to an expected capital adequacy requirement cost function

(10) $\quad Y(m,n,R,\varepsilon,\varphi)$

with the partial derivatives

$$Y_m > 0,\ Y_{mm} = 0,\ Y_n > 0,\ Y_{nn} > 0,\ Y_{mn} < 0 \text{ and } Y_{nm} < 0\,.$$

By assumption, an increase in m reduces σ_r^2, the variance of the bank's rate of return on credits, but it increases the variance of total returns $C^2\sigma_r^2$, so that expected insolvency costs grow. An increase in n augments the probability of a violation of the capital adequacy requirement which in turn raises expected insolvency costs. A similar argument applies to the second-order partial derivative Y_{mn}. Changes in the regulatory environment have the following effects on the marginal capital adequacy requirement cost:

$$Y_{m\varepsilon} > 0,\ Y_{m\varphi} > 0,\ Y_{n\varepsilon} > 0 \text{ and } Y_{n\varphi} > 0.$$

An increase in ε raises the probability that the capital adequacy requirement rate will be violated, so that this marginal cost element for m and n will increase. An increase in the penalty rate φ augments the expected cost of a capital adequacy requirement violation which in turn will increase the corresponding marginal risk costs for m and n.

The bank is assumed to maximize its expected end-of-period profit[11] which is given by:

(11) $E[\Pi]= \mu^r mC_0-\mu^t nD_0-X-Y-c_1-c_2-V_E R,$

where V_E denotes the rate of return on equity capital. By using the balance sheet constraint, this equation can be rewritten as:

(11a) $E[\Pi]=(\mu^r-V_E)mC_0-(\mu^t-V_E)nD_0-X-Y-c_1-c_2-V_E R.$

2.2. Optimality Conditions

The bank has not only to decide on the balance sheet volume by choosing the optimal amounts of factor inputs, but also on the optimal balance sheet structure. Its choice variables are m, n and R. The given parameters are the expected rate of return on credit μ^r, the expected rate μ^t on deposits, the wage rate W, the rate of return on capital V, and the rate on equity capital V_E, the minimum reserve penalty cost δ, the minimum reserve requirement rate τ, the capital adequacy requirement rate ε and the penalty rate φ. This set-up corresponds to the usual case of the profit maximizing firm being a price-taker in all markets.

The first-order conditions for a maximum are:

(12a) $\Pi_m = (\mu^r-V_E)C_0 - X_m - Y_m - c_{1m} = 0$

(12b) $\Pi_n = (\mu^t-V_E)D_0 - X_n - Y_n - c_{2n} = 0$

(12c) $\Pi_R = -V_E - X_R - Y_R= 0$

Equations (12a) and (12b) state the usual conditions that the marginal revenues of both a credit and a deposit account must be equal to their marginal costs. Equation (12c) states that the marginal reduction in risk cost because of reserve holdings must match its opportunity costs. The second-order conditions are discussed in the appendix.

---

11 Santomero (1984) discusses the problem of risk aversion for the determination of a banking firm's behaviour. Risk neutrality is assumed for simplicity as the different degrees of risk aversion of banks will not fundamentally change forthcoming results. In any case, the variance of the stochastic variables will influence the results as they are part of the expected liquidity cost and the expected capital adequacy requirement cost function.

2.3. Comparative statics

The comparative static properties of the model are summarized in **Table 1**. Only in some cases are the results clearcut. A question mark indicates uncertainty about the sign of the comparative static effect; the signs in parenthesis show what sign is assumed for further analysis. (Normally, these signs result from the assumption made about the elements of the hessian matrix (A9)). B denotes the balance sheet volume.

Table 1

	μ^r	μ^t	V_E	ε	φ	τ	δ
m	+	-	-	-	-	-	-
n	+	-	?(+)	-	-	-	-
R	+	-	?(-)	?(-)	?(-)	?(-)	?(-)
B	+	-	?(-)	?(-)	?(-)	?(-)	?(-)

An increase in μ^r, the expected return on credits, will augment the balance sheet volume as well as the number of credit and deposit accounts. The rise in the difference (μ^r-V_E) raises the marginal revenue of a credit expansion which in turn induces banks to increase production of deposit accounts as their marginal costs decrease with the higher number of credit accounts.

An increase in μ^t, the expected rate of return on deposits, will decrease the balance sheet volume as well as the number of credit and deposit accounts. The lower marginal revenue per deposit account forces the bank to reduce the number of deposits. This reduction raises the expected marginal capital adequacy requirement cost per credit account and diminishes its reserve holdings as the expected savings in expected capital adequacy requirement cost goes down.

Counteracting effects prevent an increase in V_E from yielding clearcut results. The lower marginal revenue per credit account will induce a decrease in the number of credit accounts, a movement that via increases (decreases) in marginal risk costs (savings) has a negative impact on the number of deposit accounts and reserve holdings. In addition, the increase in V_E also raises the opportunity costs of reserve holdings and equity capital, respectively. However, the increase in V_E will augment the marginal revenues per deposit account, thus the bank will tend to produce more deposit accounts, and will reduce the expected marginal capital adequacy requirement cost which tends to increase the number of credit accounts and reserve holdings. For the signs in paranthesis it was assumed that the negative impact on credit accounts because of the reduction in marginal revenues and the augmentation of opportunity costs on equity capital as well as on reserves, is stronger than the positive impact due to the improved marginal revenues on deposit accounts.

An increase in ε, the capital adequacy requirement rate, will tend to reduce the balance sheet volume as well as the number of credit and deposit accounts. The higher ε increases the marginal costs of credit and deposit production as the increased probability of a violation of the capital adequacy requirement raises the expected marginal capital adequacy requirement cost. The indirect effects of this tendency to reduce m and n will reinforce the direct effects because a lower value of m will decrease the expected marginal capital adequacy requirement cost for n (and vice versa). The increase in ε will also increase the marginal savings in the expected capital adequacy requirement cost of a reserve unit which tends to augment reserve holdings and, via indirect effects, the number of credit and deposit accounts. But this effect is assumed to be weak compared with those mentioned previously. The same arguments also apply for the case of an increase in φ, the penalty rate for a violation of the capital adequacy requirement.

An increase in τ, the minimum reserve requirement rate, decreases the balance sheet volume as well as reduces the number of credit and deposit accounts. As before, this statement relies on the assumption made about the relative importance of direct and indirect effects. The higher value of τ raises the probability of a violation of the minimum reserve requirement and thus the expected liquidity costs. This tends to augment the marginal cost of deposit production and to indirectly diminish the production of credits. But the increase in τ also tends to increase reserve holdings which influence the incentives to raise credits and deposits positively. The same comparative static effects result from an increase in δ, the corresponding penalty rate.

3. Perfect Competition and Trade Patterns in Banking Services

The perfect-competion model of sections 2.1. to 2.3. can be used to analyze trade patterns in banking services. The two marginal cost conditions (17a') and (17b') and equation (17c) determine simultaneously the expected rate of return on credits, and the expected rate on deposits and the probability of a reserve deficit [12].

Of course, the pricing equations form only the supply side of the industry equilibrium, and even this part is not complete if factor markets are not specified. The demand for banking services is not modelled explicitly, but is assumed to react to interest rate changes in the standard way. There are no information or transaction costs for buyers of banking services. Transactions of economic units with a bank are not restricted by regulation. Confidence, security or other more psychological factors that are important in practice are neglected. The market structure is that of perfect competition, the firm is a price-taker in factor markets. If trade in banking services is allowed, the rates of returns on credits and deposits are equalized between countries. In this section, the focus is on the interaction between regulation and factor endowments as determinants of trade patterns in banking services[13]. In order to isolate those determinants of trade, it is assumed that both countries have access to the same technology and that the economies have the same structures concerning the riskiness of deposit withdrawals and rates of return on credits (the last assumption is relaxed in section 3.4). But instead of making rather arbitrary assumptions about the relative factor endowment of the two countries and about the relative capital intensity in the banking industry along the lines of traditional trade theory, the distinction is made between homogeneous and specific factors of production. Two different scenarios are possible:

> (a) the first assumes homogeneous labour and capital in the economy. It is also assumed that the industry's behaviour has no feedback effect on the rest of the economy, so that V and W are given parameters for banks.
>
> (b) the second assumes banking-specific factors for which factor prices are determined by the activites of the industry.

---

[12] Some of the difficulties to establish an industry equilibrium are discussed in section 3.1.

[13] It has to be assumed that regulation is binding in the sense that the minimum reserve requirement parameter and the capital adequacy requirement parameter are so high that holdings of reserves and of equity capital are higher than they would have been in a market solution without the two regulatory measures.

Both scenarios shall be analyzed in this section. Trade patterns are determined by comparing the autarky interest rates with those established in case of free trade. As interest rates are now endogeneous variables, there remains the question of the trade-off between risk and return. In the analysis of the banking firm's behaviour, a constant expected rate of return and a variance only being dependent on the number of accounts were assumed. With endogeneous rates of returns, the assumption of a constant variance loses some of its appeal. Unfortunately, however, incorporating this trade-off has the cost of impeding analytical tractability, so that the same constant variance per deposit and per credit account is assumed for the rest of the study.

3.1. Industry equilibrium and equations of change

The following 11 conditions describe the general specification of an equilibrium for the banking industry:

(13a) $\mu^r - V_E = c^M(Y_m, c_m)$

(13b) $V_E - \mu^t = c^N(X_n, Y_n, c_n)$

(13c) $V_E = c^R(X, Y)$

(13d) $a_{LM}(V,W)M + a_{LN}(V,W)N = L$

(13e) $a_{KM}(V,W)M + a_{KN}(V,W)N = K$

(13f) $M^D = M^D(\mu^r, V_E)$

(13g) $N^D = N^D(V_E, \mu^t)$

(13h) $M^S = qm$

(13i) $N^S = qn$

(13k) $M^S = M^D$

(13l) $N^S = N^D$

The first three equations are the marginal cost conditions of section 2.2 (C_0 and D_0 are assumed to be normalized at unity). The next two equations fix equilibrium in the factor market. M and N denote the total amount of credit and deposit accounts in the economy, while a_{iL} and a_{iK} denote the input requirement per unit of output i (i=m,n). Demand for credits and deposits are represented by equations (13f) and (13g). Equations (13h) and (13i) require the total supply of accounts to equal the optimal number per firm times the number of banking firms q in the economy. The market equilibrium for credits and deposits is illustrated by equations (13k) and (13l). The supply of equity capital is assumed to be infinitely elastic at the given rate of return V_E. The amount of cash reserves that banks wish to hold is not subjected to any restriction.

With those 11 equations, the model can be solved for 9 endogeneous variables. The model has, however, 10 endogeneous variables. Thus, an additional restriction or assumption is needed in order to solve the model: Two benchmark cases will be distinguished lateron. For one benchmark case, it is assumed that the analysis starts from a long-run equilibrium in which the number of firms in equilibrium q is supposed to be constant. It is furthermore assumed that there are industry specific increasing marginal risk costs. As soon as it is assumed that there are linear homogeneous production functions at the industry level, as it is done here, it is not clear from the analysis in section 2 how the marginal cost behave.Ymm and Xnn are decreasing in m and n, whereas Ynn is increasing in n. These partial derivatives suggest that there are rather constant or decreasing marginal cost than increasing marginal at the firm level as long as the magnitude of each partial derivative is not specified. In order to ensure increasing marginal cost at the industry level, it is assumed that the production decision of individual banks has negative spillover effects on the risk costs of other banks. The risk on credit and on deposits accounts is therefore not determined by a random variable that follows a univariate normal distribution, but one that follows a multivariate distribution, so that the covariance terms become important determinants of the risk costs.Because of this assumption, Xnn, Ymm and Ynn are now increasing in m and n. Another problem is the simultaneous structure: With V_E being the exogenous interest rate of the economy, the interest rates μ^r and μ^t are determined simultaneously with the total number of accounts M and N, and this being the source of the difficulty with m and n. Therefore, the optimal firm size is an endogenous variable in equilibrium; and an easy and intuitive illustration of the model's comparative static properties is impossible. By reducing the degree of simultaneity, the model can be solved easily for the interesting variables M,N, m,n, μ^r, and μ^t. This can be done by setting the second-order partial derivatives Y_{mR}, Y_{nR}, Y_{mn}, Y_{Rm} and Y_{Rn} equal to zero (for the graphical representations $Y_{m\mu(t)}$ is also set equal to zero).

Increasing marginal risk costs played an important role in the determination of the comparative static results in section 2.3. In order to contrast the results obtained there with the assumption of constant marginal risk costs with respect to m,n, and R, the latter assumption is made in some parts of the following analysis[14]. This is the second

---

14 By assuming constant marginal risk costs some of the substance of sections 2.1 to 2.3 is neglected. Nevertheless, this assumption may not be too strong. Taking the total differential of (13a) and (13b) shows that the changes of c^M and c^N with respect to m and n are second-order small and may therefore be negligible when evaluated at the optimal firm size.

benchmark case. With linear homogeneous production functions, this yields a model with the usual format in international trade theory in which constant returns to scale are generated on a industry level. This assumption is also convenient for parts of the analysis in section 4.

With the assumptions made about the second order partial derivatives Y_{mR}, Y_{nR}, Y_{mn}, Y_{Rm} and Y_{Rn}, the interest rates μ^r and μ^t are now determined endogeneously by the two marginal cost conditions (13a) and (13b) and the demand equations (13f) and (13g). For the analysis of an equilibrium's comparative static properties, it is useful to rewrite the total differential of equations (13a) to (13b) in elasticity form by using the results of section 2.3 (cf. Jones (1965)). Equations (13a) and (13b) yield the following equations for the equilibrium interest differential:

$$(14a)\quad \hat{\mu}^r - \theta_{mY} e(Y_m,\mu^t)\hat{\mu}^t = \theta_{mY} e(Ym,\mu)\hat{M} + \theta_{mV}\hat{V}_E + \theta_{mY} e(Ym,\varepsilon)\hat{\varepsilon} + \theta_{mY} e(Ym,\varphi)\hat{\varphi} + \theta_{mK}\hat{V} + \theta_{mL}\hat{W}$$

$$(14b)\quad -(1 + \theta_{nY} e(Y_n,\mu^t))\hat{\mu}^t = \theta_{nY} e(Yn,\nu)\hat{N} + \theta_{nV}\hat{V}_E + \theta_{nY} e(Ym,\varepsilon)\hat{\varepsilon} + q_{nY} e(Ym,\varphi)\hat{\varphi} + \theta_{nX}\varepsilon(X_n,\tau)\hat{\tau} + \theta_{nX} e(X_n,\delta)\hat{\delta} + \theta_{nK}\hat{V} + \theta_{nL}\hat{W}$$

where a hat on variables denotes a percentage change, θ_{ij} the share of marginal cost j (i=K,L,Y,X) in producing good i (i=m,n) and e(x,y) an elasticity of x with respect to y.

3.2. Homogeneous factors of production

For the first attempt to determine trade patterns in banking services between two countries, it is assumed that both countries have only homogeneous labour and capital as factors of production and that factor prices are equalized between the two countries. Furthermore, it is assumed that the banking sector is small relative to the whole economy, so that the supply of factors of production for this industry is infinitely elastic. This set up corresponds to a situation of an integrated equilibrium, an equilibrium in which the world is considered as an entity with perfectly mobile factors (cf. Helpman, Krugman (1985), Chap. 1) and allows one to concentrate only on the marginal cost conditions to derive the following results.

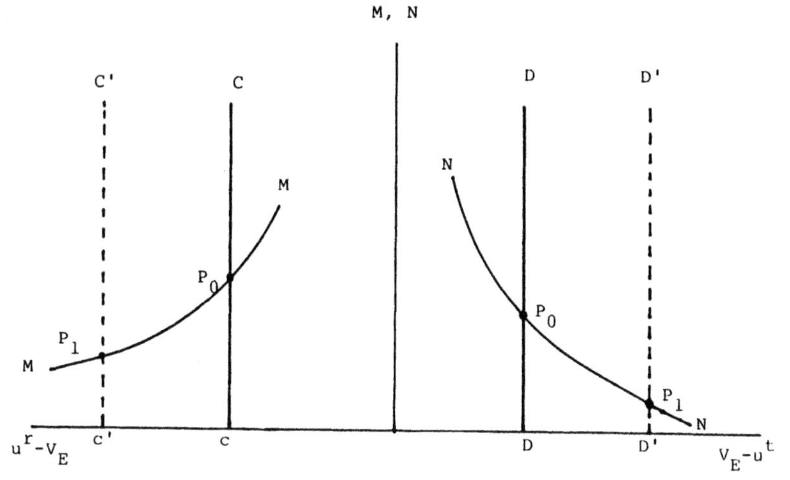

Figure 1

Proposition 1: If factor prices among countries are equalized, if the supply of factors of production for the banking sector is infinitely elastic, if marginal risk costs (Y_m, Y_n and X_n, respectively) are constant in m and n, and if trade in banking services between the two countries is allowed for, then the country with the tighter regulatory measures exports all deposits of its residents and imports all credits[15]. The other country becomes a financial center that produces all banking services.

Figure 1 demonstrates the foundation for this proposition that represents one of the two benchmark cases discussed in section 3.1. The CC-schedule in the left panel represents equation (13a). It is a vertical line because constant marginal risk costs are assumed. The positively sloped MM-schedule illustrates the total demand for credits M. The supply of deposits is given by the DD-schedule in the right panel. The NN-schedule in the right panel shows the deposit demand equation (13g). The initial equilibrium is denoted with P_0. In figure (1), the example of an increase in ε, the end-of-period capital adequacy requirement ratio, demonstrates the fundamental effects of tighter regulatory measures: Without exception, an increase in ε, φ, τ or δ leads to an increase in the interest differential (μ^r-μ^t) as the CC-schedule, and the DD-schedule both shift to the left or to the right, respectively. P_1 is the new equilibrium point. Now suppose that in autarky one of the two countries has tighter regulatory measures for the banking sector in the sense that at least one of the four parameter is bigger than in the other country

[15] The terminology corresponds to the one used in trade theory and thus to that of the current account in the balance of payments.

whereas the other ones are the same size. Then, for a constant V_E, the interest differential $(\mu^r-\mu^t)$ will become larger as it is demonstrated by the shift from P_0 to P_1 in both panels of **Figure 1**.

Proposition 1 demonstrates the possibility that financial centers may emerge merely because of regulatory differentials. An interesting aspect of the free trade equilibrium is the fact that the corresponding interest rate differential $(\mu^r-\mu^t)$ remains the same as it was in autarky in the country with the looser regulatory measures.

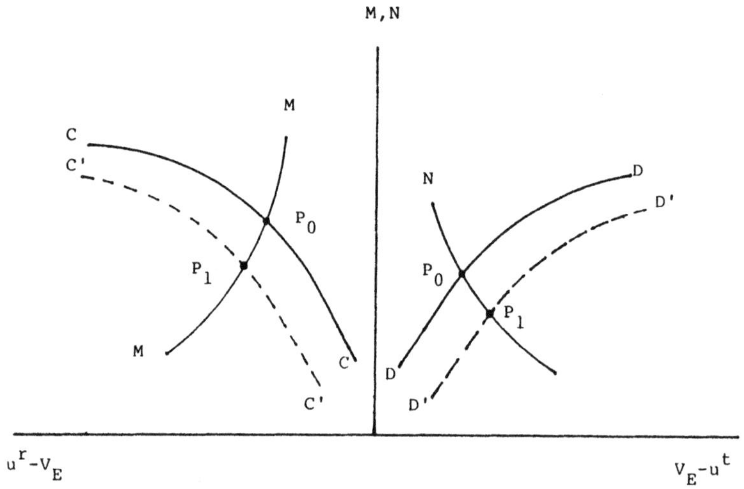

Figure 2

Inferences about the impact of regulation on the optimal firm size and market equilibrium cannot be drawn easily. To approach this question, suppose that there is an long-run autarky equilibrium in which the two countries do not trade any banking services at all because all exogeneous variables are the same. Suppose now that the number of banks is constant and that one country increases one or more of the four regulation parameters. This is likely to lead to a new autarky equilibrium in which the interest differential $(\mu^r-\mu^t)$ is higher than before and in which less total credit and deposit accounts M and N are produced and in which the optimal firm size as measured by m and n is smaller. This will create incentives for trade in banking services. With the assumption of increasing marginal risk cost, however, the interest differential $(\mu^r-\mu^t)$ will not remain constant but will be equalized between the two autarky values. This scenario is shown in **Figure 2**. P_0 denotes the initial autarky equilibrium in both countries. The new equilibrium point for the country with a comparative disadvantage in regulation is marked by P_1. The new free trade equilibrium will lead to an equilibrium between P_0P_1 on the MM and the NN-schedule, respectively. So the assumption of increasing marginal risk costs yields a weaker proposition about the specialization in banking services:

Proposition 2: Under the conditions of proposition 1, but with marginal risk costs that are increasing in m and n, free trade in banking services is likely to lead to an equilibrium in which the interest differential (μ^r-μ^t) is higher than the autarky differential in the country with a less restrictive banking regulation, in which the balance sheet volume of banks in the same country is higher than in autarky, and in which the same country becomes an exporter of credits and an importer of deposits. However, there will be no complete specialisation in the production of banking services as increasing marginal risk costs will limit the expansion of the banking sector in that country.

The difference in predictions about the degree of specialisation in proposition 1 and in proposition 2 leads to

Proposition 3: Variable marginal risk costs do not influence trade patterns, but they have an impact on the volume of trade in banking services. The higher the share of risk costs in marginal costs of credit and deposit production, the lower is the trade volume that will prevail in case of a regulatory differential.

The results of this section are in line with the literature explaining the existence and growth of Euromarkets[16]. The more banking products are standardized, the less significant are asset transformation costs relative to transaction costs (or production cost), hence the more regulation can be expected to lead to specialized financial centers. The set of regulatory measures, however, should be extended to include measures such as taxes or restrictions on transactions.

3.3. Specific factors of production

Homogeneous labour and capital as factors of production for the two economies and their infinitely elastic supply are a rather restrictive assumptions that allow the banking sector to expand without limits. As soon as the banking sector becomes large, however, it will be clearly inappropriate. Suppose now instead that labour is a banking-specific

---

16 See Freedman (1977) or Niehans (1984, chap. 9) and the references cited therein.

factor that is fixed in supply. Capital remains a homogeneous factor in the economy that is in infinitely elastic supply. Regarding the mobility of the specific factor, two alternatives will be analyzed in this section, the case of international mobility and the case of complete immobility.

If flexible wages for the immobile factor are assumed, the corresponding full employment condition (13d) has to be taken into account. The total differential of this equation yields:

$$(15)\quad (\alpha + \beta)(\hat{V}-\hat{W}) + \lambda_{Lm}\hat{M} + \lambda_{Ln}\hat{N} = \hat{L},$$

with

$$\alpha = \lambda_{Lm}\theta_{mK}\xi_m/(\theta_{mL} + \theta_{mK}) \text{ and } \beta = \lambda_{Ln}\theta_{nK}\xi_n/(\theta_{nL} + \theta_{nK}),$$

where λ_{Li} (i=m,n) denotes the share of labour employed in the production of i and ξ_i the elasticity of substitution between K and L in the production of i. Inserting (15) into (13a) and (13b) yields the following two equations determining the interest rates:

$$(16a)\quad \hat{\mu}^r - \theta_{mY}e(Y_m,\mu^t)\hat{\mu}^t = \theta_{mY}e(Ym,\mu)\hat{M} + \theta_{mV}\hat{V}_E + \theta_{mY}e(Ym,\varepsilon)\hat{\varepsilon} + \theta_{mY}e(Ym,\varphi)\hat{\varphi} + (\theta_{mK} + \theta_{mL})\hat{V} + (\theta_{mL}\lambda_{mL}/(\alpha+\beta))\hat{M} + (\theta_{mL}\lambda_{nL}/(\alpha+\beta))N - (\theta_{mL}/(\alpha+\beta))L$$

$$(16b)\quad -(1 + \theta_{nY}e(Y_n,\mu^t))\hat{\mu}^t = \theta_{nY}e(Ym,\nu)\hat{N} + \theta_{nV}\hat{V}_E + \theta_{nY}e(Ym,\varepsilon)\hat{\varepsilon} + \theta_{nY}e(Ym,\varphi)\hat{\varphi} + \theta_{nX}\varepsilon(X_n,\tau)\hat{\tau} + \theta_{nX}e(X_n,\delta)\hat{\delta} + (\theta_{nK}+\theta_{nL})\hat{V} + (\theta_{nL}\lambda_{mL}/(\alpha+\beta))\hat{M} + (\theta_{nL}\lambda_{nL}/(\alpha+\beta))\hat{N} - (\theta_{nL}/(\alpha+\beta))\hat{L}$$

With the assumption that the return on capital V_E continues to be equalized among the two countries and that the banking-specific factor is internationally immobile, the pre-trade endowment with the immobile factor is an important determinant for the trade patterns as a larger endowment implies lower wages and a smaller interest differential (μ^r-μ^t). In order to eliminate this reason for trade, it is assumed that both countries have the same endowment with banking-specific labour. Equations (16a) and (16b) show that a comparative advantage because of regulatory differentials still leads to a smaller interest differential. Free trade will thus ensure that a country with this advantage will become an exporter of credits and an importer of deposits. However, the specialisation is not complete. The increase in m and n will raise the marginal productivity of the banking-specific factor, a movement that will partially offset the comparative advantage because of the regulatory differential.

Proposition 4: If labour is a banking-specific, internationally immobile factor, if both countries have the same pre-trade endowment, and if marginal risk costs are constant in m and n, then the country with a less restrictive banking regulation becomes an exporter of credits and an importer of deposits after the allowance for free trade in banking services. The tendency to become a financial center is restricted by increasing costs for the specific factor. Compared with the case in proposition 1, specialisation will not be complete.

The banking-specific factor does not necessarily need to be internationally immobile, especially if one takes into account the wage differential in favour of the country with the comparative advantage in banking regulation. The possibility of internationally mobile banking-specific labour raises the following proposition:

Proposition 5: If labour is a banking-specific, internationally mobile factor and if both countries are endowed with the same quantitiy of it in autarky, the country with a less restrictive banking regulation will be an exporter of credits and an importer of deposits if one allows for free trade in banking services. Movements of the specific factor are complements to international trade in banking services and tend to increase the tendency towards towards financial center specialisation.

3.4. Risk diversification and regulation

Until now, the banking firm was assumed to deal only with one type of credits and one type of deposits. If, instead, it can produce several types of assets and liabilities, the question of specialisation or joint production arises. There are two reasons why the banking firm simultaneously produces several products. The first is risk diversification, the second is economies of scope. Only the first one is compatible with perfect competition, therefore the analysis is restricted to this case. The bank can now produce two types of credit, m_1 and m_2, and two types of deposit, n_1 and n_2. m_1 and n_1 are riskier in the sense that their standard deviations with respect to credit returns and deposit withdrawals are larger. This implies a higher expected rate of return for m_1 compared with m_2 and a lower interest rate on n_1 compared with n_2. The reason for the bank to produce all four product is their negative correlation: rates of return r_1 and r_2 as well as the deposit withdrawal rates v_1 and v_2 vary negatively with each other. If it is assumed that the variances of all four product decrease with the number of accounts, then a bank will hold more of the riskier products m_1 and n_1 as the balance sheet volume grows[17]. A different endowment with credit and deposit clients in two countries may therefore create incentives for trade in banking products as it may allow banks to reach the point of optimal diversification given the technology and regulation parameters.

In order to isolate the effects of regulation, assume now that both countries have the same relative demand for credit and deposit accounts. If, starting from an identical autarky equilibrium as in section 3.2, one country increases one of the four regulation parameters, then the country has a comparative advantage in banking regulation and its autarky interest differentials $(\mu^{r1}-\mu^{t1})$ and $(\mu^{r2}-\mu^{t2})$ will be lower provided that the regulation parameters are the same for all accounts. If free trade in banking services is allowed for, the following proposition can be established:

Proposition 6: If both countries have the same relative demand for risky credit and deposit accounts, if marginal risk costs are increasing in m and n and if free trade is allowed for, the country with a comparative advantage in regulation will produce relatively more of the riskier credit and deposit accounts and its banks will have larger balance sheet volumes.

Proposition 6 is an extension of proposition 2; it predicts that regulatory differentials will induce not only industry specialisation, but also product specialisation in the two countries.

4. Technology, Market Structure and Trade Patterns

The preceeding analysis of trade patterns in banking services in the presence of a regulatory differential has been rather restrictive in the sense that important characteristics of today's banking systems were not taken into account explicitly. A one-level banking system with no interaction between banks themselves, but only between clients and banks was assumed. Hence, characteristics like the linkages among banks through settlement systems (probably an important part of banking services), the considerable degree of intermediation within the banking system itself and information

17 Baltensperger stresses this point in his 1972a paper.

and/or switching costs that prevent some banking products from being traded internationally were neglected.

Two of these issues are analyzed in greater detail in this section. Linkages among banks may be introduced by treating them as intermediate inputs in the production process of the bank. The financial intermediation within the international banking system itself is difficult to explain in a model of a partial industry equilibrium with homogeneous units. On a national level, it would require a model that explains the specialization of different units (specialization on the level of the relationship between banks and non-banks) and their net asset position in the final product. On a international level, some information about a country's net asset postion would be necessary[18]. Those questions are beyond the scope of this paper and thus will not be pursued further. Consequences of switching costs can be taken into account if banking services are treated as non-traded goods. With the help of this concept of trade theory, aspects of the theory of multinational banks can be discussed.

4.1. Intermediate inputs and market size effects

A rather loose way of introducing linkages among banks in the model is to extend the production functions (3a) and (3b) by the total market size M and N, respectively, as arguments[19]. A larger market for the final goods credits and deposits sustains c.p. the production of more varieties of industry specific intermediate inputs at lower costs[20].This external market size effect increases the productivity of every firm producing the final goods. Consequently, external increasing returns to scale at the industry level that still allow for marginal cost pricing at the firm level emerge in the production of credit and deposit accounts. Helpman, Krugman (1985) have shown that an industry production function of the form:

(17) $m = f_1(K_m, L_m, M) = c(M)f_1(K_m, L_m)$

---

[18] See Thore (1984) for a spatial model of the Eurodollar market.

[19] See Ethier (1982) and Romer (1987).

[20] Another source for an external market size effect might be the investment decision of single banks if the total capital stock of the industry influences the productivity of a bank.

is a convenient shortcut to capture this idea. $f_1(.)$ is a linear homogenous function in K_m and L_m. c(M) is an increasing function in M, the total number of credit accounts in the economy, with an elasticity that is smaller than one. In their terminology, $f_1(.)$ is an index of factor inputs and c(.) a measure of productivity. The corresponding marginal cost function is

$$(17a) \quad c_m(V,W,M) = c(V,W)c(M).$$

Marginal cost pricing implies that the cost c(.) per unit of the factor input index equals its marginal revenue. The long-run zero profit condition requires that the revenues per credit and deposit account are equal to their average cost at the industry level. One problem with the production function (17) is, however, that the external effect is generated by the total number of credit accounts in the economy. There is no reason to separate linkages among banks with respect to credit and deposit production. By using a function of the form:

$$(18) \quad m = f_1(K_m, L_m, q) = c(q)f_1(K_m, L_m),$$

where q stands for the number of banking firms, the asset transformation function of the banking firm is taken into account. With respect to the marginal cost conditions (13a) and (13b) of the bank, it is important to recognize the distinction between the external effect resulting from the production function, and that which results from the risk costs functions X and Y. The overall size of credit and deposit markets should not influence marginal risk costs as the latter depend only on the probability distribution for the stochastic variables, the exogeneous regulation parameter and the balance sheet structure[21]. But if marginal risk costs are assumed to be constant, the banking industry will follow an average cost pricing rule. Thus, the marginal cost conditions can be rewritten as:

$$(19a) \quad (\mu^r - V_E)c(q) = Y_m\, c(q) + c_m(V,W)$$
$$(19b) \quad (V_E - \mu^t)c(q) = (X_m + Y_m)c(q) + c_n(V,W)$$

The corresponding equations of change now include the term $\theta_{mc}e(c(q),q)q$ and $\theta_{nc}e(c(q),q)q$, respectively, which enters with a negative sign. As a consequence of these external returns, the country size is relevant in autarky. A increase in q reduces the

---

21 There may exist an external effect on marginal risk costs through the influence of the market size on the probability of a deposit withdrawal.

interest differential (μ^r-μ^t). For the determination of trade patterns, international and national external returns to scale have to be distinguished[22]. National returns to scale are present if linkages among banks are restricted to happen between banks in the same country. If for simplicity, homogeneous factors of production in both countries are assumed, the following proposition can be derived:

Proposition 7: If there are non-traded intermediate inputs needed for the production of banking services, if there are homogeneous factors of production with factor prices being equalized among countries, then free trade will lead to a complete specialisation in banking services only if the the country that has a less restrictive banking regulation has also the same or a larger market size in autarky than the other country.

Proposition 7 demonstrates that a small country or a large county with small financial markets that wishes to become a financial center must relax its banking regulation measures considerably before it can succesfully specialize[23]. The tendency towards specialization can additionally be hampered by limitations in the endowments with a banking-specific factor or by risk considerations. The proposition shows that small countries can successfully specialize in domains in which risk costs are either very substantial or in which regulations such as taxes and/or restrictions on transactions outweigh the gains from external returns to scale.

However, if intermediate inputs are traded internationally, pre-trade information does not help in predicting trade patterns as the gains from external effects will be equalized internationally and proposition 7 changes to:

Proposition 8: If there are traded intermediate inputs needed for the production of banking services, and if there are homogeneous factors of production with factor prices being equalized among countries, free trade will lead to a complete specialisation in the country with a comparative advantage in banking regulation.

Similar arguments are relevant for the case in which the external effect is the result of the total capital stock available to process transactions among banks.

---

22 See Ethier (1982) and Helpman, Krugman (1985, chap.3).

23 This argument is in line with Grilli's (1989).

4.2. Non-traded banking services and market access

Until now, only regulatory measures that deal with the bank's risk transformation function were explicitly analyzed. But another important set of regulatory measures concerns the question of market access for branches and subsidiaries of foreign banks and their regulation. These measures become important as soon as some of the banking services are non-tradable goods that are not exchanged across national borders because information or transaction costs are too high. A second important distinction is that of home or host country regulation for branches and subsidiaries of foreign banks. If subsidiaries and branches of foreign banks are not allowed to access the domestic markets, and if banking services are non-traded goods, one might guess that the structure of the system of financial intermediation will change in the presence of regulatory differentials because economic agents will try to circumvent those restrictions unless the set of regulatory measures is very complete.

But assume now that branches and subsidiaries of foreign banks are submitted to home country regulation. This means that 'the control of the parent bank should apply to the entire worldwide consolidated bank, branches and subsidiaries included' (Baltensperger, Dermine (1987), p. 91). In a simple two-country framework with homogeneous products, there is no need to consolidate a bank's domestic and foreign activities. In order to illustrate the implications of the home country regulation principle in a simple model, assume that the production technology can be separated into an accounting processing unit for which marginal costs are denoted by c^{iP} and a client relation unit for which marginal costs are marked with c^{iC} (i=M,N). The accounting processing unit handles all operations that deal with the regulatory measures imposed upon the bank, the client relation units produce all services required by the clients. For both kind of operations, a linear-homogeneous technology is assumed. Then the marginal cost conditions (13a) and (13b) become:

$$\text{(20a)} \quad \mu^r - V_E = c^{MP}(Y,V,W) + c^{MC}(V,W)$$

$$\text{(20b)} \quad V_E - \mu^t = c^{NP}(X,Y,V,W) + c^{NC}(V,W)$$

The accounting processing unit must be located in the same country as the bank; the client processing units that should be considered as branches that can be located in both countries. The credits and deposits processed by the client relation units are attributed to the country where the accounting processing unit is located, whereas the value added created is attributed according to the location of the factors of production. If there are homogeneous factors of production with factor prices being equalized, the following proposition can be established:

Proposition 9: If banking services are non-traded goods, if the banking technology can be split into a two parts one of which is location specific, and if the client relation units are submitted to home country regulation, then the country with a comparative advantage in banking regulation will become the location of the accounting processing units. All banks will be located in that country. Measured by the share of value added created in the banking industry, the specialization will be incomplete.

Proposition 9 is another illustration of the consequences which occur when a specific factor, in this case the regulation parameters (risk costs may be considered as payments to factors of production), becomes internationally mobile.

The model used in this section, however, is rather special as different "endowments" with the specific factor regulation are the only reason to set up multinational banks. But the principle of home country control is hardly the only reason for the existence of multinational banks. In order to extend the analysis, a more general model of a multinational bank along the lines of Helpman, Krugman (1985) is used below.

Suppose now that credits and deposits are differentiated goods. Each bank has to choose one variety of credits and one variety of deposits. All varieties are produced with the same technology. The production of m and n includes three stages. The final production of the services uses a service production technology and is location specific, they must be produced in the country where they are sold. Thus, the locational advantage is introduced by assumption. The accounting processing unit deals with the management of the risk costs. Whether this stage of the production is location specific or not depends on the principle of regulation. The final production of m and n uses an intermediate input, headquarter services, that is firm-specific, but not location specific. By this assumption, a firm-specific fixed cost is introduced. The question is why the intermediate input is firm-specific and cannot be produced by another, independent firm. Grubel (1977) mentions firm-specific management and/or marketing know-how as reasons. Another reason might be information processing. Ethier (1986) argues that arm's length transactions 'become infeasible when the headquarter and plants must exchange a large volume of diverse information'. The service production functions for m and n are:

(21a) $m_s = f(K_m,L_m)f_1(h)$ and
(21b) $n_s = f(K_n,L_n)f_2(h)$,

where h denotes the intermediate input headquarter services. The production functions (21a) and (21b) are assumed to have economies of scale with respect to h and to be homothetic, thus $f(K_m, L_m)$ and $f(K_n, L_n)$ are linear homogeneous in K and L. Headquarter services can be used for the production for credit and deposit accounts, therefore they are a quasi-public input[24]. They are produced with a nondecreasing return to scale production function, $C^H(V,W,h)$ denotes its minimum cost function. The accounting processing units' cost functions are homothetic and have the form:

(21a) $C_{ma} = g(K_m,L_m,m)g_1(m,\varepsilon,\varphi,\delta,\tau)$ and
(21b) $C_{na} = g(K_n,L_n,n)g_2(n,\varepsilon,\varphi,\delta,\tau)$,

where g_1 and g_2 are supposed to capture the risk element in the production of m and n. Both functions g_1 and g_2 are assumed to have either constant or increasing costs in m and n. The regulation parameters $\varepsilon,\varphi,\delta,\tau$ are shift factors.

Thus, the integrated cost function for a bank is:

$$(22) \quad C(V,W,m,n,h,\varepsilon,\varphi,\delta,\tau) = \min_h[\, C_{ms}(V,W,h) + C_{ns}(V,W,h) + C_{ma}(V,W,m) + C_{na}(V,W,m) + C^H(V,W,h)\,].$$

This cost function exhibits economies of scope because the independent production processes m_s and n_s share a common input factor cost. Suppose now that m and n are generated by product specific economies of scale in the relevant range of output and that the market entry is not restricted. In that case, every variety of credits and deposits is produced by one bank at average cost. If branches and subsidiaries of foreign banks are submitted to home country regulation, the integrated cost function includes only one cost function C_{ma} for credits and C_{na} for deposits. If branches and subsidiaries of foreign banks are submitted to host country regulation, the integrated cost function includes cost functions C_{ma} for credits and C_{na} for deposits for every country the multinational bank has market access to.

What can be said about the impact of regulatory differentials and the question of market access? Without imposing further structure on the exogeneous variables and

---

24 See Panzar (1990) on economies of scope because of a common input in otherwise independent production processes.

demand, it is hard to derive precise propositions. Suppose now that there are two countries with factor prices being equalized between them, that the headquarter services are produced in the country in which the bank is located, that the different varieties are rather close substitutes, and that the relative demand for varieties is the same in both countries. If banks are free to set up subsidiaries and branches abroad, every variety will be produced by the same bank in both countries. It is also likely that this will decrease the interest differential (μ^r-μ^t) for every variety. In the case of home country control, the banks headquartered in the country with a comparative advantage in banking regulation will have a relative cost advantage. These assumptions imply:

Proposition 10: If banking services are non-traded differentiated goods, if there firm-specific economies of scope/scale, the authorization to set up branches and subsidiaries will lead to multinational banking networks. Trade in banking services is restricted to intrafirm trade in the intermediate good headquarter services. If branches and subsidiaries are submitted to home country control, then the country with a less restricitve banking regulation will produce relatively more of the headquarter services.

5. Conclusions

This paper identifies three major factors that determine whether a regulatory differential can lead to a complete specialisation in the production of banking services in one country:

> a) Specialisation in the production of banking services because of regulatory differentials is only likely for those products that are internationally tradable. If banking services are non-tradable, a less restrictive banking regulation in one country will lead to a specialisation in tradable intermediate inputs in that country on the one hand and to the establishment of branches and subsidiaries in the other country owned by banks headquartered in that country in that country (propositions 9 and 10).
>
> b) Specialisation in the production of banking services because of a comparative advantage in banking regulation is likely for products for which specific factors of production are internationally mobile or for which external effects are international (propositions 5 and 8).
>
> c) Specialisation in the production of banking services is only likely for banking services for which the share of risk costs is low and for which risk costs tend to be invariant with respect to the quantity produced (propositions 1 and 2).

To determine the relevance of regulatory differentials and liberalization of market access, it is crucial to know the relative share of traded banking services and the similarity of preferences in different countries. For the next decade, it will be interesting to observe whether technological progress in the area of information technology will diminish the need for direct interaction between buyers and sellers. The more likely this is to happen, the more trade in banking services will be generated by regulatory differentials.

With the approach used in the paper, some empirically testable implications of regulatory differentials were derived. However, the paper has several limitations: it deals only with some specific regulatory measures that affect either the risk transformation function of the bank, the question of market access, and the location of the supervisory authority. In practice, there may exist many other types of regulatory measures that affect trade patterns in banking services. Demand considerations or macroeconomic variables were not analyzed explicitly, hence some important determinants of trade patterns were not discussed. By focusing on the trade aspects of regulatory differentials, other important aspects that are probably even more important such as the safety of the international banking system or the effectiveness of regulation are neglected. It has always been assumed that a more restrictive banking regulation in one country does not change the quality of the banking services offered by banks located in that country. This must not necessarily be the case. Another limitation is the focus on the more traditional supply side considerations of trade theory. It would be desirable to incorporate aspects of the demand side and industrial organisation issues. The model used in this paper could be a first step in that direction.

Appendix

Derivation of the expected liquidity cost function

There exists a critical level of reserve withdrawals v_0 such that the minimum reserve requirement is matched exactly, it is given by:

(A1) $v_0 = (R - \tau n D_0)/(1-\tau)$.

The amount of violation can be derived to be

(A2) $(\tau n D_0 - \tau v - R + v) = (1-\tau)(v-v_0)$.

The standard deviation of v can be shown to be $\sigma^v = D_0 dn^{0.5}$. This implies that the variance of v is increasing with n, but at a decreasing rate. The standardization of v and v_0 to $u=v/\sigma^v$ and $u_0=v_0/\sigma^v$ allows one to write the expected liquidity costs as

(A3) $X(R,n,\tau,\delta) = \delta(1-\tau)\sigma_v \int (u-u_0)\phi(u)du$,

where $\phi(u)$ denotes the standard normal distribution. The partial derivatives depend crucially on the standard deviation σ^v which has the following partial derivatives :

(A4a) $\sigma^V{}_n = 0.5\sigma^V/n$
(A4b) $\sigma^V{}_{nn} = -0.25\sigma^V/n^2$.

The derivation of the expected liquidity cost function's partial derivatives can be found in Baltensperger and Milde (op. cit., chap. 2 and 5). Obviously, the level of credits cannot be assumed to remain constant for the present study as this was implicitly done in the previous derivations. But a variable level of credits will not change the signs of the partial derivatives of the expected liquidity cost functions as credits do not enter the calculation of the minimum reserve requirements. So, we will continue to work with the function $X(R,n,\delta,\tau)$.

Derivation of the expected capital adequacy requirement function

There exists a critical value for r such that the capital adequacy requirement is matched exactly, it is determined by

(A5) $r_0 = [(1+z)nD_0 + \Omega(m,n) + (\varepsilon-1)mC_0]/mC_0$[25].

Assuming r to be normally distributed with r_i $N(\mu^r,c^2)$ allows one to standardize r and r0 with $w=(r-\mu^r)/\sigma^r$ and $w_0=(r_0-\mu^r)/\sigma^r$ and to write expected capital adequacy requirement cost as

(A6) $Y(m,n,\varepsilon,\varphi)= \varphi mC_0\sigma^r\int(w0-w)\phi(w)dw$,

For the standard deviation of r, the total return on the credit portfolio can be shown to be $\sigma^r=cm^{(-1/2)}$ if individual returns on credit accounts are assumed to be independent. This implies that the standard deviation of r is decreasing with m, but at a decreasing rate:

(A7a) $\sigma^r_m = \sigma^r/2m$
(A7b) $\sigma^r_{mm} = -0.75\sigma^r/m^2$.

For the simultaneous determination of a bank's balance sheet volume and balance sheet structure, reserves have to be taken into account for the determination of the end-of-period equity capital. Then, according to the probability distribution of deposit withdrawals, the bank can be expected to hold reserves in excess of the required amount which should be included in the calculation of the expected capital adequacy requirement cost. For the rest of this paper it is assumed that Y has the form

(A8) $Y(m,n,R,\varepsilon,\varphi)$.

The signs of the partial derivatives remain the same as before; the partial derivative with respect to R is supposed to be negative as a c.p. increase in reserve holdings will decrease the expected capital adequacy requirement cost. The same sign is assumed for the second-order partial derivatives $Y_{R\varepsilon}$ and $Y_{R\varphi}$.

---

[25] The end-of-period reserves are neglected for the analytic derivation of the function.

Second-order conditions for a maximum

The hessian matrix for equations (12a) to (12c) is

$$(A9)\quad \Pi_h = \begin{bmatrix} \Pi_{mm} & \Pi_{mn} & \Pi_{mR} \\ \Pi_{nm} & \Pi_{nn} & \Pi_{nR} \\ \Pi_{Rm} & \Pi_{Rn} & \Pi_{RR} \end{bmatrix}$$

Its elements are given by:

$$\Pi_{mm} = -Y_{mm} \qquad \Pi_{mn} = -Y_{mn} \qquad \Pi_{mR} = -Y_{mR}$$
$$\Pi_{nm} = -Y_{nm} \qquad \Pi_{nn} = -(X_{nn} + Y_{nn})$$
$$\Pi_{nR} = -(X_{nR} + Y_{nR}) \qquad \Pi_{Rm} = -Y_{Rm}$$
$$\Pi_{Rn} = -(X_{Rn} + Y_{Rn}) \qquad \Pi_{RR} = -(X_{RR} + Y_{RR}).$$

Among others, the following second-order conditions are sufficient for a maximum:

$$\Pi_{mm} < 0$$
$$\Pi_{nn} < 0$$
$$\Pi_{RR} < 0$$
$$\Pi_{mm}\Pi_{nn} - \Pi_{mn}\Pi_{nm} > 0.$$

These four conditions alone are not sufficient to establish the existence of a maximum because the elements Π_{mn}, Π_{Rm} and Π_{Rn} of the hessian ˙h have a positive sign. Thus, we have to assume that the direct effects of an increase in m,n or R which will increase (reduce) the marginal costs (benefits) which are captured by Π_{mm}, Π_{nn} and Π_{RR} dominate the indirect effects which will generally save costs (augments benefits). The sufficient conditions for Π_{mm}, Π_{nn} and Π_{RR} are fulfilled if the marginal prodcution costs c_{1mm} and c_{2nn} increase faster than the marginal risk costs Y_{mm} and X_{nn} decrease.

Bibliography

Aliber, R. Z. (1984), International Banking, A Survey, Journal of Money, Credit and Banking 16, 661-678.

Baltensperger, E. (1980), Alternative Approaches to the Theory of the Banking Firm, Journal of Monetary Economics 6, 1-37.

Baltensperger, E. (1972a), Economies of Scale, Firm Size and Concentration in Banking, Journal of Money, Credit and Banking 4, 467-488.

Baltensperger, E. (1972b), Costs of Banking Activities - Interactions Between Risk and Operating Cost, Journal of Money, Credit and Banking 4, 595-611.

Baltensperger, E., and Dermine, J. (1987), Banking Deregulation, Economic Policy , 63-109.

Baltensperger, E., and Milde, H. (1987), Theorie des Bankenverhaltens, Berlin: Springer.

Bröker, G. (1989), Competition in Banking, Paris: OECD.

Camen, U. (1990), The Position of Swiss Banks in International Financial Markets: Their Balance Sheet Activites and Fiduciary Transactions, mimeo, I.U.H.E.I., Geneva.

Dermine, J. (1990), The Specialisation of Financial Institutions: the EC Model, Journal of Common Market Studies 28, 219-235.

Diamond, D. W. (1984), Financial Intermediation and Delegated Monitoring, Review of Economic Studies 51, 393-414.

Dixit A. and Norman, V. (1980), Theory of International Trade, Cambridge: Cambridge University Press.

Ethier, W. J. (1986), The Multinational Firm, Quarterly Journal of Economics 101 , 805-833.

Ethier, W. J. (1982), National and International Returns to Scale in the Modern Theory of International Trade, American Economic Review 72, 389 - 405.

Freedman, C. (1977), Micro Theory of International Financial Intermediation, American Economic Review, 67, PP, 172-179.

Grilli, V. (1989), Financial Markets, Economic Policy, 387-421.

Grubel, H. G. (1977), A Theory of Multinational Banking, Banca Nazionale del Lavoro Quarterly Review 123, 349-364.

Helpman, E., and Krugman, P. R. (1985), Market Structure and Foreign Trade, Cambridge (MA, USA): MIT Press.

Jones, R. W. (1965), The Structure of Simple General Equilibrium Models, Journal of Political Economy 73, 557-572.

Niehans, J. (1984), International Monetary Economics, Oxford: Phillip Allan.

Panzar, J. C. (1989), Technological Determinants of Firm and Industry Structure, in: Handbook of Industrial Economics, Vol. 1, ed. by. Schmalensee, R. E., and Willig, R., Amsterdam: North-Holland.

Romer, P. M. (1987), Growth Based on Increasing Returns Due to Specialisation, American Economic Review 77, PP, 56 - 62.

Santomero, A. M. (1984), Modelling the Banking Firm, Journal of Money, Credit and Banking 16, 576-602.

Sapir, A. (1990), The Structure of Services in Europe: A Conceptual Framework, Report prepared for the Commission of the European Communities.

Thore, S. (1984), Spatial Models of the Eurodollar Market, Journal of Banking and Finance 8, 51-65.

Varian, H. R. (1984), Microeconomic Analysis, 2nd Ed., New York: Norton.

Walter, I. (1990) , European Financial Integration and its Implications for the United States, INSEAD Working Paper, No. 90/22/Fin.

Comment on

Thomas Helbling: "Regulation and Technology as Determinants of International Trade in Banking Services"

Ernst Baltensperger

The paper by Helbling deals with the theory of international trade in banking services. Up to this time, not much of a formal theory of international trade in financial services exists. Consequently, this is a very welcome endeavor which deserves our applause. Helbling is especially interested in regulatory differences between countries as a source of comparative advantage and an influence on trade patterns. To some extent, he also considers other determinants of trade, such as the nature of technology or factor endowments. But his main motivation is to ask how changes in regulations (the creation of regulatory differences) affect trade and banking structures in the international economy, given these other elements. Still another group of factors which might affect comparative advantage and trade in the financial sector is left entirely in the background, such as political and monetary stability and reliability, differences in taxation, the geographical distribution of customers and the international nature of their activities (foreign trade, foreign investment), and the possible importance of customer relationships, to name a few.

This is legitimate; you have to confine the problem you are going to analyze somehow. It just constrains the conclusions you can draw from your analysis, and Helbling is well aware of that.

Helbling bases his analysis on an explicit model of the banking firm. Of course, I find this very recommendable. He uses this model to define an equilibrium for the banking industry and then interprets and employs the result in the context of and with the instruments of international trade theory. I believe this is a very sensible modelling strategy, and I find the paper and its results stimulating and refreshing.

Helbling disregards the currency denomination of financial services as a criterion for classifying transactions as international or domestic. Rather, the criterion he employs is the location (residence) of the customer relative to that of the financial intermediary. Again, this makes sense to me.

Let me begin with a few comments of a more general nature. I will add later on a number of remarks which are aimed more specifically at the model in the paper.

- The analysis is based on an asset transformation model of banking which concentrates on the "classical" banking products, loans and deposits. This is sensible, I believe. Nevertheless, in discussing trade issues in the financial sector, it might also be interesting to consider other types of banking services, such as the securities business (securities trading, the securities issuing business), portfolio management services, advisory services of various kinds, etc. Maybe these require a different type of banking model with different cost properties (one where risk costs play a different role than in the traditional banking business of borrowing short and lending long).

- As I said, the paper concentrates on the role of regulatory differences as an influence on trade in the financial sector. Characteristically, the paper asks how the tightening (or loosening) of one particular regulatory measure in one country affects trade, given an initial situation with either no trade (everything being equal in both countries) or with some trade caused by other factors (e.g. different endowments with a banking-specific factor of production).

  Now, it would be of interest to consider more systematically the interactions of regulation with other sources of trade in financial services, rather than just concentrate on the former. Admittedly, this is done to some extent in the paper, but I would like to see it explored more systematically.

  Furthermore, it might also be of interest to consider tradeoffs between different types of regulatory measures. That is, rather than just look at one marginal change in one country, consider the effects of combinations of different regulations. For practical applications, this would seem to be important, as regulation is not a one-dimensional affair.

- It would be of interest to investigate empirically the relative importance of different regulations (and other factors) as sources of international trade. Generally speaking, it would be worthwhile to try to test empirically the propositions developed in the paper.

- I consider the discussion of multinational banking and direct foreign investment in the financial sector and its interaction with international trade in banking services, which is developed along the lines of Helpman and Krugman (1985) in the last section of the paper, as very stimulating and interesting. I would like to see this pursued further.

- Maybe my most basic general comment on the paper refers to the nature and role of regulation in the model. In essence, regulation here just appears as a factor which raises banking costs (and therefore creates a comparative disadvantage, ceteris paribus), with no redeeming value. In many cases, I am inclined to believe that this is what regulations actually amount to. However, as a general assessment, this is probably not a maintainable position. A certain minimal amount of regulation can probably be economically justified. At least, this is a clear majority view prevailing today. Of course, it is difficult to know exactly what is justifiable in the field of regulation, as long as we don't have a full understanding of the workings and the functioning of financial markets. (Furthermore, regulation can also be a means of taxation or a substitute for cartel-type arrangements.)

  Now, if some amount of regulation is indeed justifiable, then abolishing (or loosening) these regulations will not necessarily result in a comparative advantage; instead, it might create a disadvantage. To express in different words what I mean: Regulation (and deregulation), at least in certain cases, can affect the quality (or, what is equally important, the customer's perception of the quality) of the financial services offered. Hence, it can indirectly affect the demand for these services. For example, by abolishing capital adequacy standards, the safety of bank deposits could be so much impaired that demand is reduced drastically. In a "deregulation race", it is not necessarily true that the winner will be the country with the most relaxed standards. Regulation then can be viewed as a sort of "public input". (The same idea can be expressed alternatively by saying that, in these cases, regulation can be viewed as a direct influence on the costs of producing services of a given quality level.)

  It seems to me that this is a serious issue in an analysis of the sort offered here, unless you assume that all regulation is redundant (in the sense that optimal behavior is guaranteed without it) or even damaging. So, your evaluation of the effects of deregulation on trade depend on your views of the function and justification of these regulations. Maybe one could say that what really matters for comparative advantage or disadvantage is not the level of regulation, but deviations from "optimal" regulation. Unfortunately, you can't really know these deviations without having a notion of what the optimal regulation looks like.

This raises another question (which, however, clearly goes beyond the aim of the present paper and thus is in no way meant as a criticism): To what extent is it justifiable to attempt to create comparative advantage through regulatory differences? Is this comparable to protectionism (through tariffs, quota and the like)? Or can it be viewed as a competitive process in the service of the search for the optimal regulatory system under uncertainty?

Let me now pass on to a few points which refer directly to the model in the paper:

- A first comment concerns the specification of equilibrium. In the paper, the analysis is restricted to the specification of industry equilibria for the financial sector, i.e. partial equilibria from the point of view of the economy as a whole (complemented with varying assumptions about the links of the financial sector to the rest of the system). This is clearly stated in the paper and legitimate; nevertheless, it is a limitation.

  In a sense, it seems essential to also consider the rest of the system (that is, to think in a general equilibrium framework) when discussing comparative advantage and trade, since the concept of comparative advantage does not only refer to another country, but also to other goods (sectors). No country can have a comparative advantage in every sector. Trade in financial services can, in principle, result from differences (advantages and disadvantages) between countries in other sectors, or from economies of scale in other sectors (suggesting the concentration of production of these other goods in one country) - even if technical and regulatory conditions in the financial sector in both countries are exactly alike. (This is taken into account to some extent by including sector-specific supplies of certain factors of production, but in a limited way only.)

- It could also be of interest to consider trade when factor prices are not equalized between countries.

- The possibility of increasing returns (e.g. along the lines of the argument in footnote 21 on p. 144) might make it worthwhile to think about the effects of increasing returns and of imperfect forms of competition on trade, e.g. along the lines of Helpman and Krugman (1985). (Of course, I realize that this creates considerable difficulties.)

- In the discussion on increasing marginal risk cost on p. 139 it is not clear whether these are firm- or industry-specific, and what is assumed about the interplay between firm size and number of firms. Is the latter (q) held constant? It seems so. Otherwise, one could simply have a larger number of firms in the country with the better regulation, as long as costs are firm-specific.

To conclude, let me emphasize once more that I have read this paper with interest, and that I have greatly enjoyed reading it.

Part IV: International Bank Deposits

The Swiss Position in the International Market for Non-Bank Deposits

Ulrich Camen[1]

1. Introduction

In recent studies Grilli (1989) analyzed the institutional determinants of external bank deposits by applying a cross-section approach. In this paper, the time series methodology is used to address the question which factors determine movements of the Swiss market share in the international market for non-bank deposits. Asset share equations are specified following the approach taken by Weale (1986), and Barr, Cuthbertson (1989, 1990) who derived asset share equations using the Almost Ideal Demand System (AIDS) as developed by Deaton, Muellbauer (1980) for consumer demand theory. Share equations are estimated for the case of Switzerland for the period 1975 to 1990.

The position of Swiss banks in international financial markets is of general interest for several reasons. Traditionally, the attractiveness of Swiss banks has been considered to be the result of specific institutional factors such as bank secrecy, and political stability which permitted Switzerland to play the role as a safe haven. The approach chosen in this study permits to investigates empirically which portion of the Swiss market share is explained by these factors. A second aspect of general interest to be is the impact on the Swiss market share of measures to stop capital inflows into Switzerland which were implemented in the Seventies.

2. Deposits of Non-Residents in Switzerland and the Potential Role of Capital Control Measures, Economic and Institutional Factors.

The focus of this paper is on non-bank deposits received by Swiss banks from non-residents. Interbank deposits are not considered because the market share of Swiss banks in the interbank market has been rather small, 1.7 percent in 1989, compared to about

1 I would like to thank Jean-Pierre Danthine, Alexander Swoboda and the members of the research team in Basel and Geneva for helpful comments and suggestions. This research was financially supported by a grant of the Swiss National Science Foundation.

15 percent in the market for cross-country non-bank deposits. Non-bank deposits of non-residents, as defined here, include fiduciary accounts. Series on non-bank deposits of Swiss banks, i.e. including subsidiaries of Swiss banks abroad, were used at several occasions instead of non-banks deposits of banks located in Switzerland due to data limitations. This section gives first a brief account of the evolution of external liabilities of Swiss banks to private non-residents, followed by a discussion of potential determinants of the Swiss market share in the international market for non-bank deposits.[2]

2.1 Stylized Facts

Figure 1 shows in the upper graph non-bank deposits of non-residents with banks located in Switzerland as share of external non-bank deposits of all countries and in the lower graph the growth rates of the respective stocks.[3] A first important feature of the Swiss market share has been its dramatic decline from about 30 percent in 1971 to below 17 percent in 1974. This drop of the Swiss market share was brought about by a decline in absolute terms of the stock of non-bank deposits by about 10 percent in 1972, and a growth rate of Swiss non-bank deposits that was lower than that of the world total in the two following years. In the period 1974 to 1990 the Swiss market share stayed, in contrast, rather stable. Till 1982, the share fluctuated in a narrow band between 15.9 and 17.5 percent, followed by a slight downward trend till 1988. Then, in the years 1989 and 1990 the Swiss market share moved upwards reaching 15.6 percent at mid-1990. Periods in which Swiss external liabilities declined in absolute terms included the years 1983, 1984, and 1988.

The decline of the Swiss market share in the early Seventies is even more dramatic when fiduciary accounts are not taken into account for computing the Swiss share in the market for non-bank deposits (**Figure 2**). The market share of non-fiduciary deposits dropped from 17 percent in 1971 to 3 percent in 1980 with the strongest decrease again in the years 1971 to 1974. Fiduciary accounts, instead, showed after an initial decrease

---

2 For a broader review of the external position of Swiss banks in international financial markets see Andrist, Schlup (1990), and Camen (1990).

3 The data for figure 1 and 2 are from the IFS tape of the IMF which reports non-bank deposits of banks located in Switzerland.

FIGURE 1

SWISS MARKET SHARE IN NON-BANK DEPOSITS, IN %

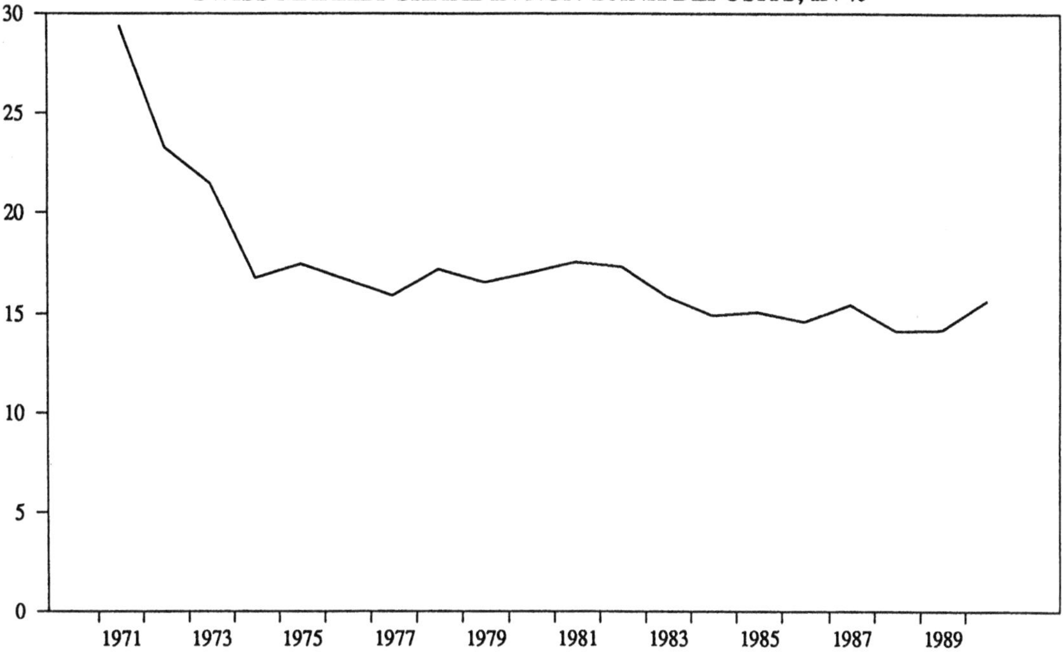

GROWTH RATES, IN %

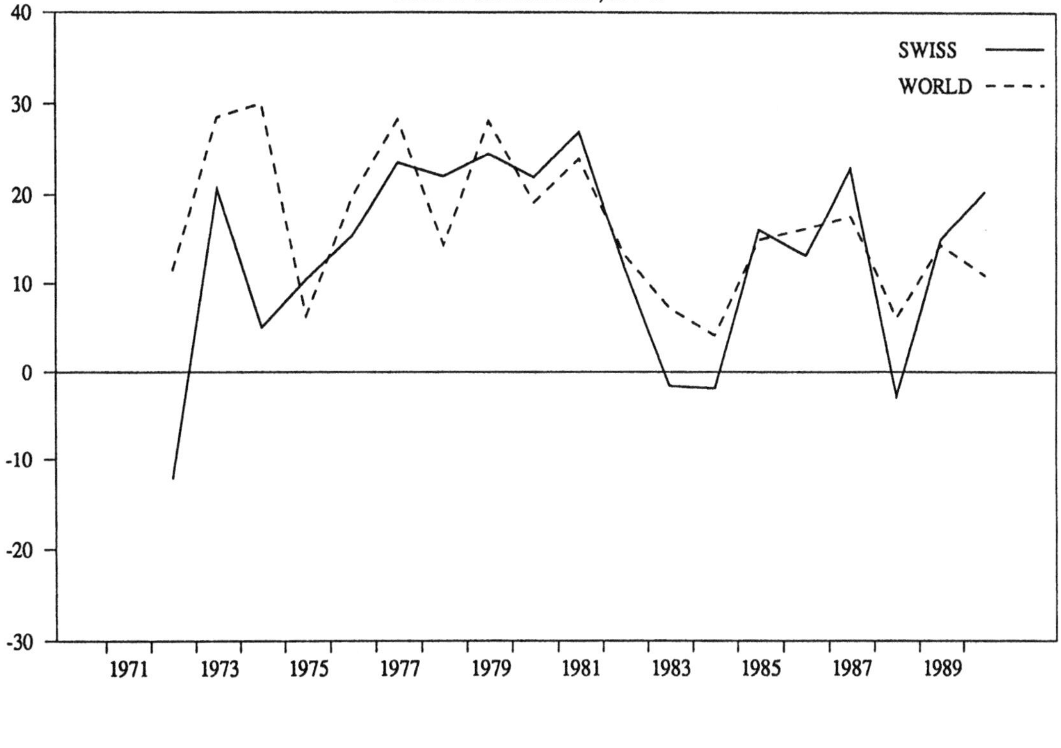

FIGURE 2

SWISS MARKET SHARE BY TYPE OF DEPOSIT

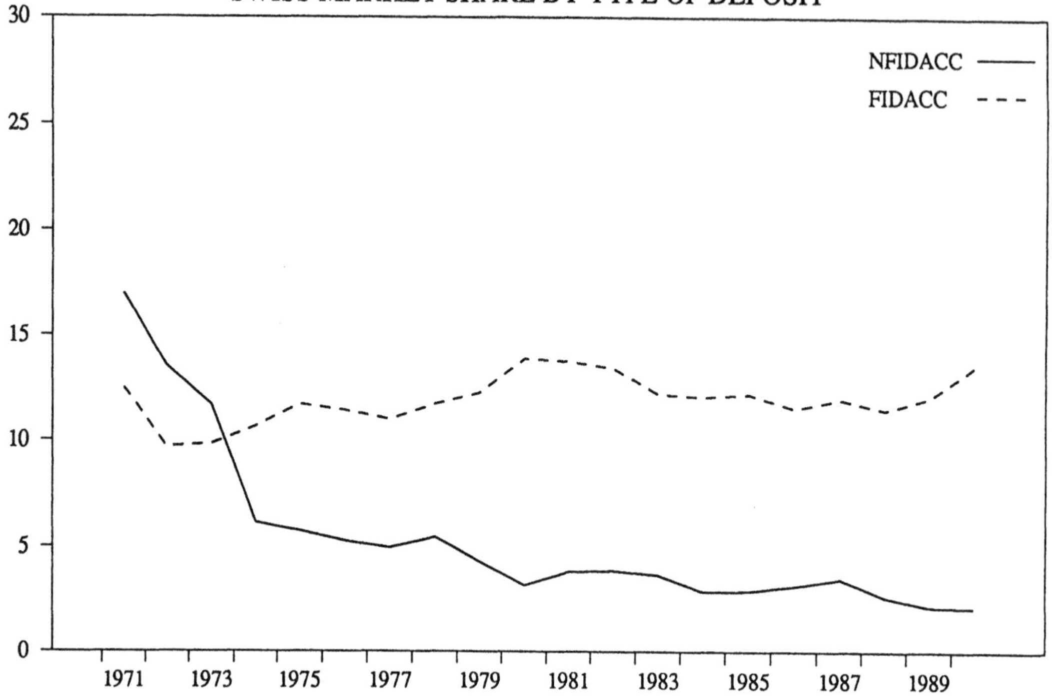

GROWTH RATES

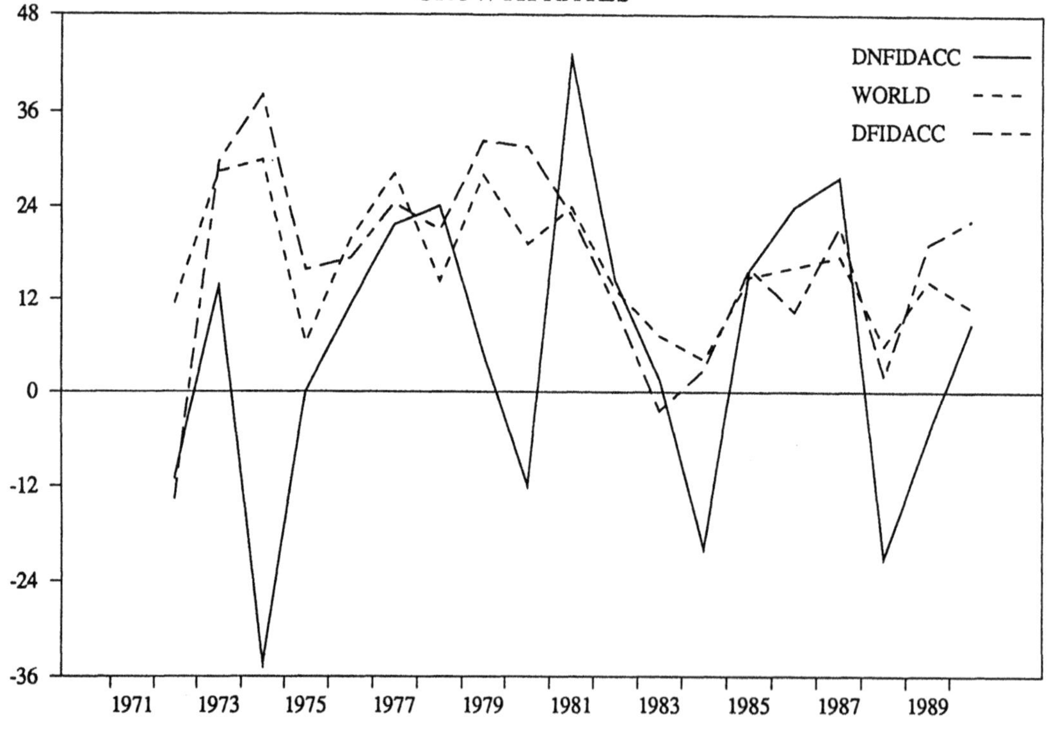

in 1971 an upward trend over the period till 1980, and a slight downward trend thereafter with a rebound in 1989 and 1990. This distinctly different evolution of the shares of fiduciary accounts and of non-fiduciary deposits is also reflected in their respective growth rates. Whereas the growth rate of fiduciary accounts tracks rather well the growth rate of total international non-bank liabilities, the growth rate of other types of non-bank deposits than fiduciary accounts has been negative in several years during the observed period with a decrease of more than 30 percent in 1974.

A second important characteristic of the Swiss position in the international market for non-bank deposits is the very high share of deposits in foreign currencies. Currently, about nine-tenth of non-bank deposits are held in currencies other than the Swiss franc (**Figure 3**, upper graph).[4] This share has been high since the early Seventies, when it increased from 68 percent in 1972 to 90 percent in 1976. With the exception of the years 1981 to 1983 when the share of non-bank deposits in foreign currencies fell to about 80 percent the share stayed close to 90 percent.

Further characteristics of Swiss banks' external non-bank liabilities relate to its composition by type of deposit. The largest portion of foreign deposits is invested in fiduciary accounts whose share accounts presently for slightly below 65 percent of external liabilities compared to 25 percent in 1972 (**Figure 3**, lower graph). This strong increase of the share of fiduciary accounts took place in two main phases. The share increased steeply from 25 percent to 57 percent in four years at the beginnings of the Seventies, and by about 10 percent in the period 1978 to 1980. Whereas the increase in the share of fiduciary accounts in the early Seventies resulted primarily from a strong increase in the share of fiduciary accounts held in foreign currencies, the increase at the end of the Seventies was brought about by an increase in the share of fiduciary accounts held in Swiss francs (**Figure 4**).

Summarizing the main stylized facts, three major changes can be identified with respect to non-bank external deposits in Switzerland. Firstly, the market share of Swiss banks in the market for non-bank deposits was about halved in the first half of the Seventies whereas it showed only a slight decline in the following 15 years till 1990. Secondly, the share of deposits held in foreign currencies increased strongly in the early Seventies. Thirdly, the share of fiduciary accounts more than doubled in the Seventies.

---

4 **Figures 3** and **4** use data from the 'Jahresendstatistik' published in the SNB publication "Das schweizerische Bankwesen". In this case external liabilities include non-bank deposits at subsidiaries of Swiss banks abroad.

FIGURE 3

EXTERNAL LIABILITIES TO NON-BANKS BY CURRENCY, IN %

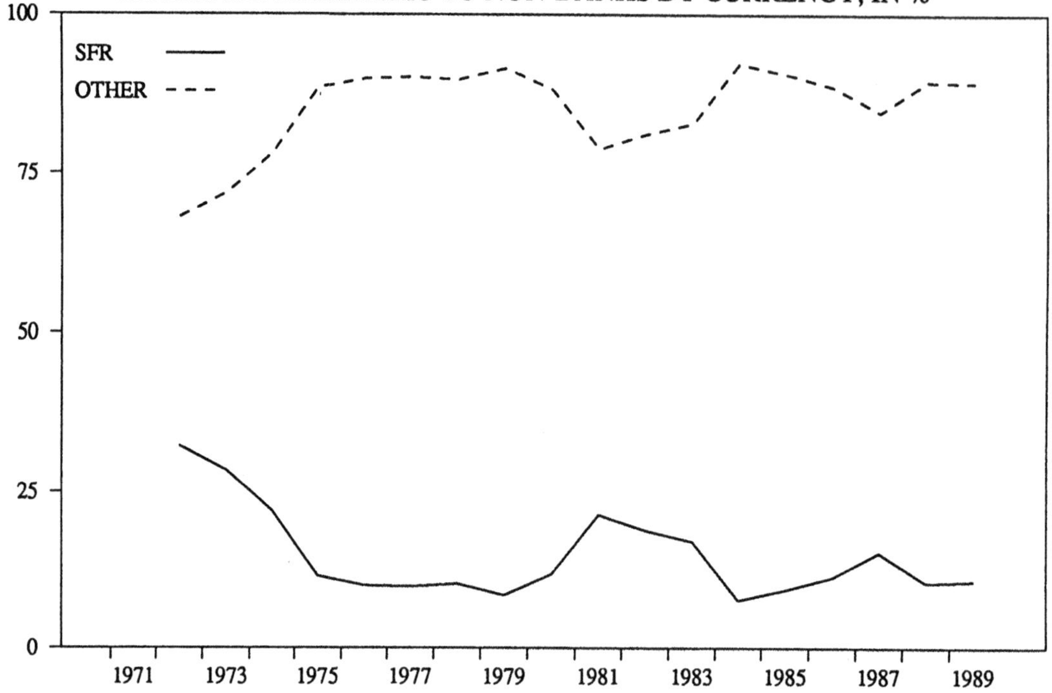

EXTERNAL LIABILITIES BY TYPE OF DEPOSIT, IN %

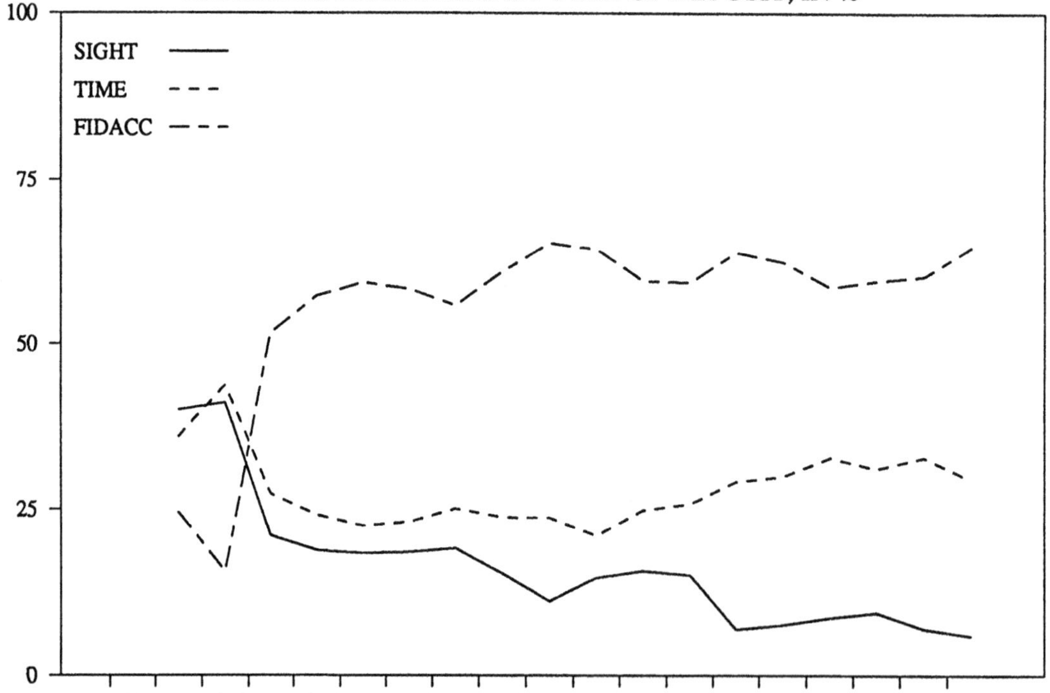

FIGURE 4

EXT. LIABILITIES IN SFR BY TYPE OF DEPOSIT, IN %

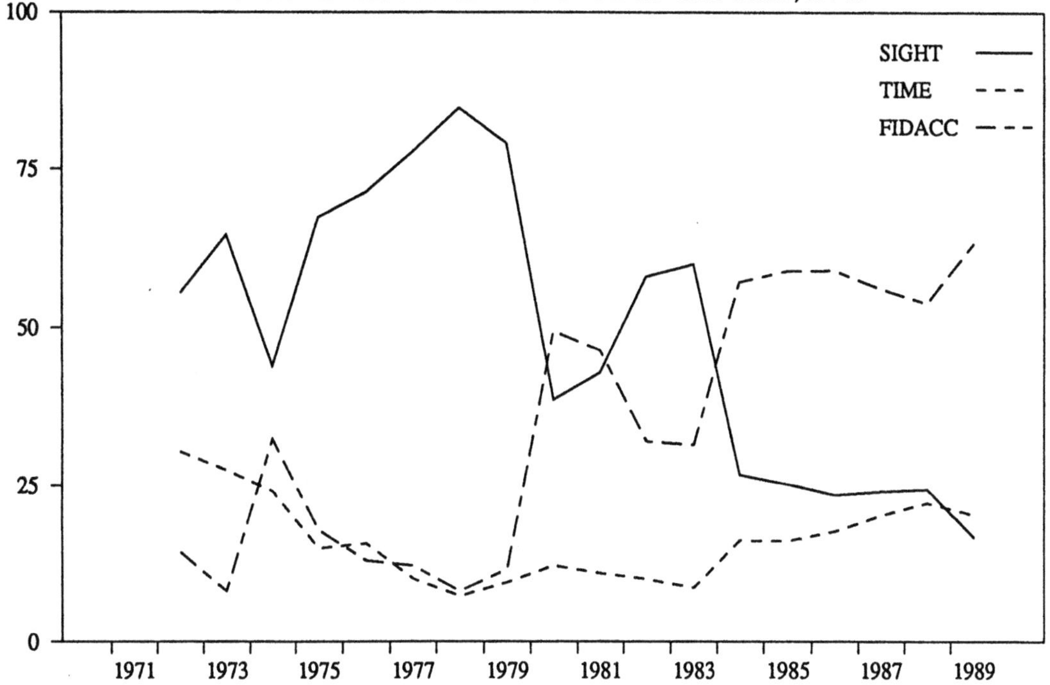

EXT. LIABILITIES IN FOREIGN CURR. BY TYPE OF DEPOSIT, IN %

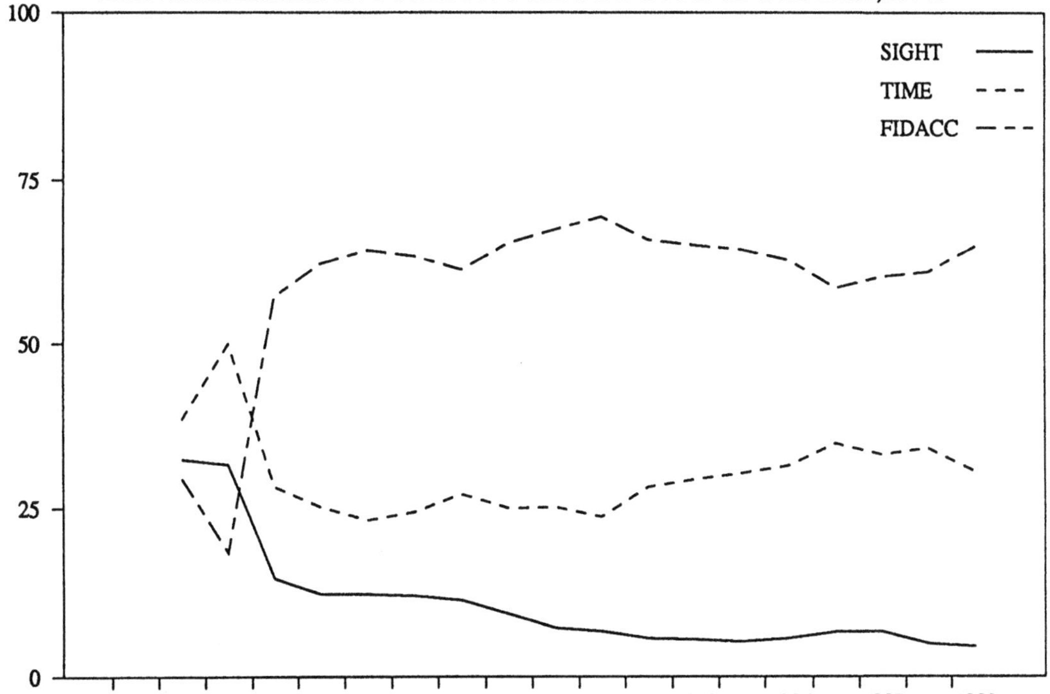

Currently, the main features of external non-bank liabilities of Swiss banks are that nine-tenth of the deposits are held in foreign currencies and about 65 percent of the deposits are fiduciary accounts.

2.2 The Potential Role of Capital Control Measures, Economic and Institutional Factors[5]

Determinants of the Swiss market share that are discussed in the literature include institutional, regulatory, and economic factors.[6] The main institutional factors that are generally thought to have created historically the attractiveness of the Swiss banking system include the high degree of bank secrecy, the safe haven function of Switzerland, the proven stability of the Swiss banking system, and the possibility to invest tax free in fiduciary accounts.[7]

Although bank secrecy is not unique to Switzerland it is more protective in Switzerland than in most countries. Generally, banks are obliged to provide information about clients' accounts only in cases where a criminal act as defined by Swiss law is investigated. This rule for providing information has been somewhat relaxed in recent years. In 1983, Swiss banks signed a convention according to which a request by the SEC for information on a bank's customer in connection with insider trading investigation will be considered by a specially appointed commission. The banks will provide information to the Commission on the customer's transactions, and if the case fulfills certain criteria, information will be forwarded to the SEC with the possibility of blocking the accounts in question. This convention is generally considered to have

---

5 The analysis in this section focuses on Swiss determinants of the market share disregarding potential foreign influences. The focus on domestic variables is mainly due to the fact that time series on international determinants are not readily available. Sheldon (1991) takes into account international determinants of market shares. Other factors than the Swiss one which potentially have an important impact on the Swiss market share include the relaxation of capital control measures in several countries.

6 For a discussion of these factors see Christensen (1986) and Hirszowicz (1987).

7 In addition to the factors mentioned here, Christensen (1986) considers political neutrality, a universal banking system, and Switzerland's geographic position in the heart of Europe as factors that have established confidence in its financial markets.

constituted a change in practice because a case of insider trading may lead to the lifting of bank secrecy although it is not a criminal act according to Swiss law.

Evidence supporting the argument that Switzerland is considered by investors in international financial markets as a safe haven is reported by Christensen (1986) for the years 1982 and 1983 after the second oil price shock. According to BIS statistics the Swiss bank's share of total BIS reporting banks' liabilities to Middle Eastern oil exporting countries rose from 12 percent at the end of 1981, to 14.5 percent in 1982 and to about 17 percent in 1983. This increase related only to fiduciary accounts, which are mainly denominated in U.S.dollars. In the more recent crisis in the Middle East shifts of asset from the Gulf to Switzerland have also been reported.[8]

A withholding tax of 35 percent is levied on deposits such as sight and time deposits of non-residents in Switzerland, but not on fiduciary accounts. As fiduciary deposits accounted for 65 percent of external non-bank deposits in 1989 the withholding tax actually applies to the smaller fraction of external deposits. The strong increase of the share of fiduciary accounts in the Seventies may be taken as an indicator for the attraction of tax-free investments in Switzerland. In section 4 we will investigate whether changes in the institutional factors discussed had a statistically significant impact on the Swiss market share.

A second group of determinants are regulatory measures which were implemented by the Swiss authorities to stop capital inflows throughout the Seventies.[9] Measures that were intended to limit the amount of deposits by non-residents in Switzerland included a ban on interest rate payments, a commission charge, the so-called negative interest rate, and minimum reserve requirements. In accordance with their purpose to prevent investments in Swiss francs a main feature of these capital control measures was, with the exception of minimum reserve requirements, that they only applied to deposits denominated in Swiss francs.

The ban on interest rate payments applied since the end of July 1971 on any increase

8 See Economist, September 15, 1990.

9 Apart from restrictions on deposits of non-residents these included restrictions on foreign exchange transactions (specifically ceilings on forward sales of Swiss francs to non-residents), and measures directed to prevent foreign investments in Swiss credit and capital markets. For a broader discussion of these measures see Cosandier (1987), Christensen (1986), and Lang (1981).

in Swiss franc denominated deposits by non-residents since that date. This restriction was lifted October 21, 1974 and reintroduced again November 21, 1974 applying now to increases in Swiss franc denominated deposits since October 21, 1974. Since January 1975 the interest rate ban applied to the overall stock of non-residents' deposits in Swiss francs. The interest rate ban was active for saving deposits with a maturity of at least six months till February 20, 1980, for demand deposits (including fiduciary accounts in Swiss francs) with maturities of at least three months till March 1980, and for all other deposits till the end of August 1980.

A commission charge of 2 percent per quarter was levied on all Swiss franc denominated deposits (including fiduciary accounts denominated in Swiss franc) of non-residents exceeding the balance at the end of July 1972.[10] After a suspension of this charge for about one year, from October 1973 to the end of October 1974, the charge was increased to 3 percent and applied to increases in Swiss franc denominated deposits that occurred since October 31, 1974. In January 1975 the charge was increased to 10 percent per quarter. The commission charge of 10 percent was applied till the end of October 1979 when it was reduced to 2.5 percent and to zero at the end of November 1979.

A third measure which was implemented at the end of July 1971 and which was effective till the end of February 1977 were minimum reserve requirements. Minimum reserve requirements applied to all deposits denominated in Swiss francs and foreign currencies including fiduciary accounts when they were invested in Switzerland. Since March 1973, reserve requirements varied across types of assets and had to be applied to increases in deposits as well as stocks.

Tentative conclusions with respect to the impact of the capital control measures on the Swiss market share can be made on the basis of the stylized facts summarized in the previous section. A first observation is that the capital control restrictions in the early Seventies appear to have induced a shift in the location of deposits and in their currency composition. The implementation of capital control restrictions in the years 1971 and 1972 and the tightening of these restrictions in January 1975 appear largely to be responsible for the strong drop in the Swiss market share in the period 1971-74. The impact of these policy measures is reflected in the negative growth rate of non-bank deposits in the years 1972 and 1974 when the stock of sight and demand deposits

---

10 Deposits of less than 100 000 Swiss franc were exempted from commission charges.

decreased by 12 percent and 35 percent, respectively (**Figure 2**). This decrease of non-bank deposits in absolute terms took place although the interest rate ban and the commission charge applied only to increases in stocks. Additional evidence for the impact of capital control measures provides the strong increase in the share of non-bank deposits held in foreign currencies in the period 1972-75 which can be explained by the discriminatory effect of the capital control measures against investments in Swiss francs by non-residents.

A second observation is that the lifting of the commission charges at the end of 1979 and of the ban on interest payments in the first half of 1980 appear to have had only a slight effect on the Swiss market share which increased from 16.5 percent at the end of 1979 to 17 percent at the end of 1980. In contrast to the overall Swiss market share, the share of deposits held in Swiss francs increased substantially during this period from 8.5 percent in 1979 to 21 percent in 1982. This increase, however, may not be fully attributed to the lifting of the policy control measures as Swiss interest rates increased during the same period from close to zero percent in 1978 to 9 percent in 1981.

The empirical analysis in section 4 cannot be used to test whether the implementation of the capital control measures at the beginning of the Seventies had a significant impact on market shares as higher frequency data (quarterly or monthly) is only available starting in 1975. The empirical analysis is therefore limited to testing whether the lifting of capital control measures had a significant effect on external liabilities of Swiss banks.

Economic factors are the third group of determinants which potentially have an impact on Swiss market shares. This group includes interest rate differentials, exchange rate expectation and the economic stability of the Swiss economy. These factors are in general considered to favor an investment in Swiss francs due to the combination of low inflations and high growth in Switzerland and the strong performance of the Swiss franc over most of the period under consideration. These economic factors, however, do not appear to have been the most important determinants of the decision of economic agents to deposit their wealth in Swiss banks when one considers the currency composition of external liabilities. The fact that since the mid-Seventies about 90 percent of external deposits of Swiss banks were held in foreign currencies suggests that non-residents did not deposit their money with Swiss banks to invest in Swiss francs for most of the period 1971 to 1989. It appears, instead, that investors appreciate characteristics of the Swiss banking system that are not directly related to the Swiss franc or the economic performance of the Swiss economy. These characteristics would include the institutional factors discussed above and the stability of the Swiss banking system in general. This, however, does not exclude the possibility that over some periods in the Seventies especially exchange rate expectations have been of importance for the Swiss market share as is suggested by the introduction of the strict capital control measures in the Seventies.

3. Theoretical Framework

Using the Almost Ideal Demand System (AIDS), which has been originally developed by Deaton, Muellbauer (1980) for consumer demand theory, asset share equations can be derived.[11] The solution of a constrained cost minimization problem yields share equations where asset shares are a function of AIDS prices and real wealth:

$$(1) \qquad s_{it} = \alpha_i + \sum_i \gamma_{ij} \ln rp_{jt} + \beta_i \ln(RW/rp)_t$$

where

$$s_{it} = a_{it}/W_t$$

$$rp_{it} = [(1+r_{it})(1-g_t)]^{-1}$$

$$rp_t = \sum_i s_i rp_{it}$$

$$RW_t = W_t/z_t$$

and r_{it} is the expected nominal return on asset i, g_t is the inflation rate, and z_t the price index. The main theoretical restrictions of the model are:

11 This section follows the approach by Barr, Cuthbertson (1989, 1990).

$$\textit{The adding up constraints,}\quad \sum_i \alpha_i = 1,\ \sum_i \gamma_{ij} = 0,\ \sum_i \beta_i = 0.$$

$$\textit{Homogeneity,}\qquad \sum_j \gamma_{ij} = 0.$$

$$\textit{Symmetry,}\qquad \gamma_{ij} = \gamma_{ji}.$$

A share equation for the short term is derived by allowing for sluggish adjustment:

$$\text{(2)}\qquad \Delta s_{it} = \sum_j c_{ij} \Delta lnrp_{jt} + k_i \Delta \ln(RW/rp)_t + l_i (s_i - s_i^*)_{t-1},$$

where s^*_i is the long-term share of asset holdings. Formally, equation 2 can be derived by minimizing a quadratic cost function. Although the use of a quadratic cost function for deriving asset demands is problematic as transaction costs in financial markets are unlikely to increase smoothly with the amount of assets exchanged the above specification is used here as a convenient way of introducing lagged adjustment. Substituting equation 1 for s^*_i into equation 2 yields

$$\text{(3)}\quad \Delta s_{it} = \alpha_i + \sum_j c_{ij} \Delta lnrp_{jt} + k_i \Delta \ln(RW/rp)_t + l_i s_{it-1} - l_i \big(\sum_j \gamma_{ij} lnrp_{jt-1} + \beta_i \ln(RW/rp)_{t-1}\big).$$

The expected sign of the own price effect is negative, of the cross-effect positive, and of the wealth effect positive. In vector notation a system of asset share equation can be written in the form

$$\text{(4)}\qquad \Delta S_t = A + C \Delta lnRP_t + K \Delta \ln(RW/rp)_t + LS_{t-1} - L(DlnRP_{t-1} + Bln(RW/rp)_{t-1}),$$

where S_t and S_{t-1} are vectors of asset shares, RP_t and RP_{t-1} are vectors of asset prices, A is a vector of constants, and C, K, L, D and B are matrices containing coefficients.

Investors in international financial markets face three basic decisions: The selection of the countries where they want to deposit their wealth, the choice of currencies, and the choice of the type of assets. The advantage of the above model is it that it permits to deal with each of these choices separately by specifying for each decision level a set of share equations. This is especially advantageous for the purpose of this paper as the main shifts of assets, which have been identified in section 2, can be analyzed separately. A second advantage is that factors which have been traditionally considered to be determinants of a country's market share can be more clearly distinguished according to whether they have an effect on the location of deposits, their currency composition or their diversification.

At the first or upper level decision wealth is assumed to be allocated across location of investments. At the second or middle level the decision is taken how to allocate the money which is invested in a country across currencies, and at the lower level the investor is assumed to decide about which types of assets to buy in each currency. At each of these levels only information that is appropriate at that stage is required and therefore each decision can be considered as a separate utility maximization problem.

A necessary and sufficient condition for multi-stage budgeting is that preferences are separable. If this condition holds assets can be partitioned into groups so that preferences within groups can be described independently of quantities in other groups.

Applying multi-stage budgeting, sets of asset share equations can be specified for each of the three levels. At the upper level the equation for the market share of Swiss banks in the international markets for non-bank deposits, s^u_{it}, is specified:

$$\text{(5)} \qquad \Delta s^u_{it} = \alpha_i + k_i \Delta \ln(RW/rp)_t + \sum_j \delta_{ij} x_{jt} + l_i s^u_{it-1} - l_i(\beta_i \ln(RW/rp)_{t-1}),$$

where the x_js stand for regulatory measures and institutional factors, and RW is the total value of external assets deflated by the price index for the industrial countries. The market share of all other countries could be computed by applying the budget constraint.

In contrast to equation 3, equation 5 does not include asset prices as explanatory variables. The exclusion of asset prices is based on the assumption that the interest rates paid on the large majority of nonresidents' deposits by Swiss banks is on average not different to that paid by banks abroad. Noting that about 90 percent of non-residents deposits in Switzerland are invested in foreign currencies this assumption appears to be justified. Differences between returns may still arise from differences between levels of commissions charged by banks in Switzerland and abroad. Mainly due to the lack of adequate data, the difference between commissions charged by banks in Switzerland and abroad is not further considered as an explanatory variable at this stage of the research.

To capture the impact of regulatory measures on the Swiss market share a dummy for the interest rate ban (IRB), and a dummy for the negative interest rate (NIR) were included in equation (5).[12] Both variables are included in the upper level share equation as the capital control restrictions can be considered to have lowered the general attractiveness of deposits in Switzerland although they only applied to deposits held in Swiss francs. As the capital control measures discriminated against investments in Swiss franc deposits, these variables will enter also the second level equation. Institutional factors which are considered to have determined the Swiss market share and of which proxies are included in equation (5) are the safe haven effect and bank secrecy (BS).[13] Changes in the price of gold were used as proxy to capture the safe haven effect. The use of the price of gold as proxy is based on the presumption that international political crisis and instabilities of the world economy were reflected in movements of the gold prices.

At the medium level the currencies shares of the external liabilities of Swiss banks are determined. The set of share equations is specified similarly to equation (4) with S^m_t being the vector of currency shares, RP_t the vector of asset prices based on the returns for each currency, and RW_t the total deposits by non-residents in Switzerland:

$$(6) \quad \Delta S_t^m = A + C\Delta lnRP_t + K\Delta \ln(RW/rp)_t + HX_t + LS_{t-1} - L(DlnRP_{t-1} + Bln(RW/rp)_{t-1}).$$

Expected asset prices were calculated by taking exchange rate movements into account. Returns on Swiss francs deposits were also adjusted for the interest rate ban and the negative interest rate. X_t is the vector which contains the dummies capturing the impact of the capital control measures. A dummy for the interest rate ban and one for the negative interest rate were considered.

---

12 IRB is set equal to one from the start of the sample period till August 1980 when the interest rate ban was lifted and zero otherwise. NIR is set equal to one till November 1979.

13 BS takes values of one starting in January 1983, when the Convention XVI entered into force, till the end of the sample period.

In the case of the lower level share equations for Swiss franc denominated deposits the vector S^l_t would include the share of the major types of deposits in the total non-residents deposits denominated in Swiss francs. The main categories of deposits would be fiduciary accounts, demand and sight deposits. Asset prices represented by RP_t would be computed on the basis of the interest rates paid on these deposits. The interest rate paid on sight and time deposits would have to be adjusted for the withholding tax.

4. Empirical Results

This section presents empirical results for the upper and medium-stage equations. The main objective is to test whether regulatory measures, institutional and economic factors are significant in explaining movements in the Swiss market share.

The upper and medium stage equations have been estimated over the period 1975:3 to 1990:6 and 1975:9 to 1990:12, respectively, using monthly data. The estimation period could only start in 1975 due to lack of data which makes it at this stage impossible to test empirically whether the implementation of the capital control measures in the early Seventies had a significant impact on the Swiss market share. The Swiss market share (equation 5) was computed using time series for external non-bank deposits of banks located in Switzerland and the aggregate for all countries, both from the IFS tape. Inspection of the data showed a 15 percent decrease of the world total in April 1978. Since this break in the data series is due to a change in the reporting system of the U.S. Treasury the percentage change in April was considered an outlier and therefore omitted in the regressions. Currency shares (equation 6) were computed using data from the Swiss National Bank. This monthly data has been compiled on the basis of the consolidated balance sheets, i.e. including branches abroad, of large banks in Switzerland whose number has been about seventy. A limitation of this data is that it does not follow the definition of the IMF which reports external liabilities of banks located in Switzerland. The monthly data is shown in **Figures 6** and **7**.

The upper level equation was estimated by OLS as specified in equation (5) but initially without variables for regulatory, institutional and economic factors (**Table 1**). The real value of the world total of non-bank deposits has the right sign but is insignificant at the 5 percent level. Only the lagged market share and the constant are significant. Overall, the explanatory power of this specification is with 3 percent very small.

FIGURE 5

SWISS MARKET SHARE IN NON-BANK DEPOSITS, IN %, MONTHLY DATA

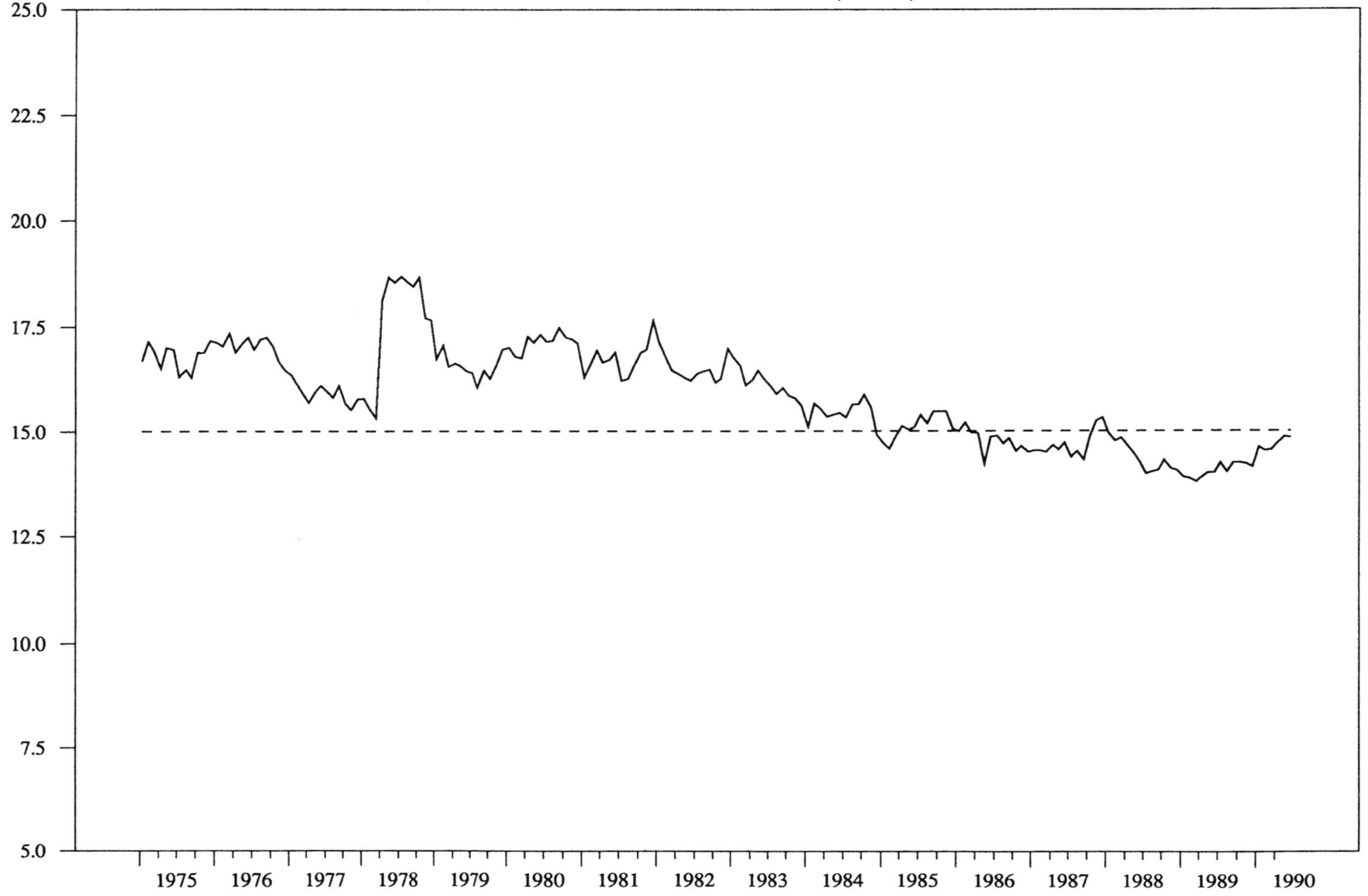

FIGURE 6

EXTERNAL LIABILITIES TO NON-BANKS BY CURRENCY, IN %, MONTHLY DATA

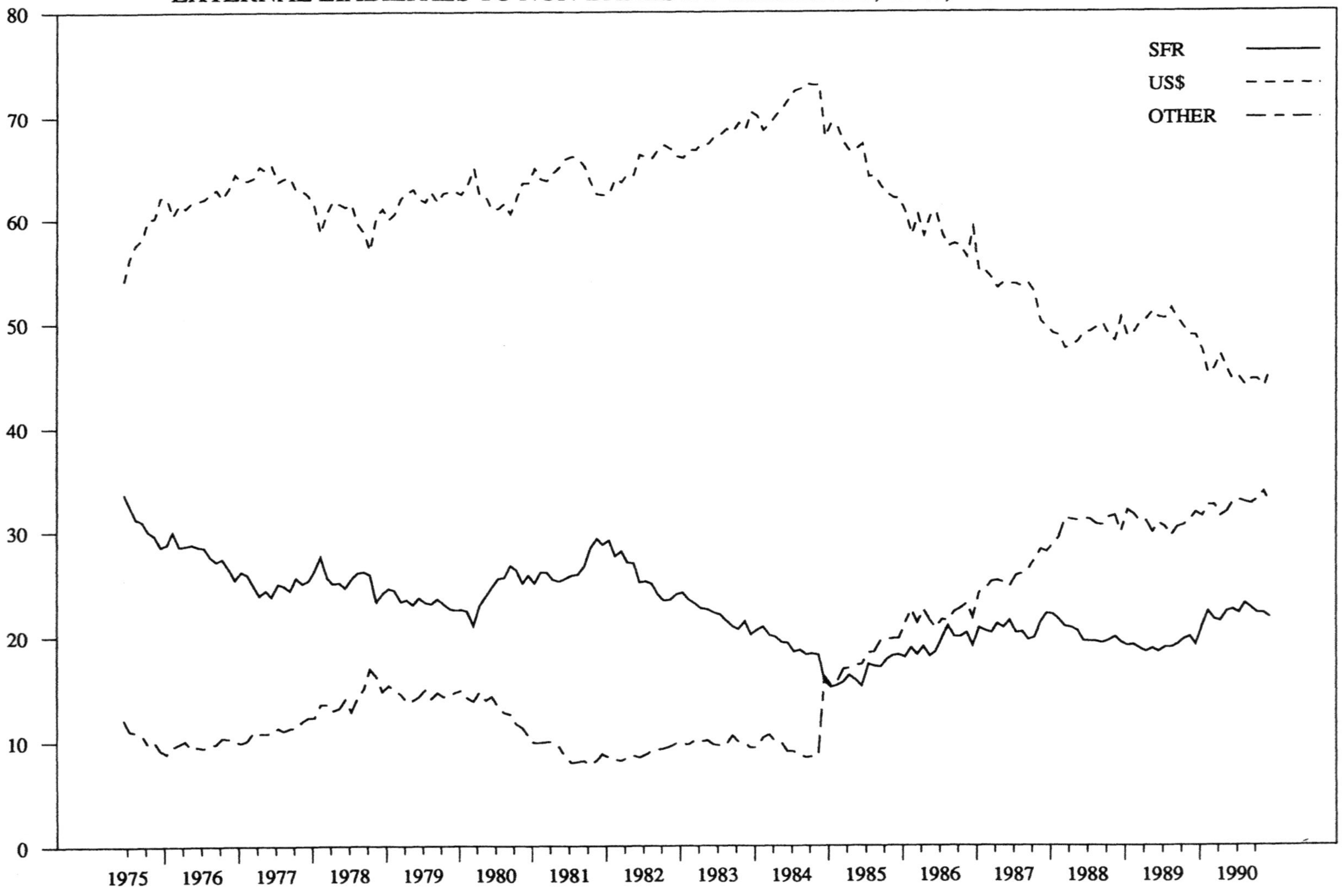

Table 1

Upper Level Share Equation

Dependent variable: Change in Swiss Market Share in Non-Bank Deposits

	1	2
Constant	0.11 (1.96)	0.18 (2.43)
Seasonals		not reported
BS		-0.01 (2.04)
NIR		-0.01 (1.55)
DSACHUS		-0.11 (2.73)
DPGOLD		0.07 (3.61)
DLRWRP	0.15 (1.79)	0.22 (2.22)
DUDLRWRP		-0.38 (2.31)
LNBCH(t-1)	-0.004 (2.55)	-0.007 (3.34)
LRWRP(t-1)	-0.006 (1.28)	-0.01 (1.62)
R^2	0.04	0.23
D-W	2.29	2.36

t-values are reported in parenthesis and R-square is R bar. BS is the dummy for banking secrecy; NIR is the dummy for the negative interest rate; CHA is a dummy for the "Chiasso affair"; DSACHUS is the percentage change in the Swiss franc- dollar rate; DPGOLD is the percentage change in the price of gold; DLRWRP percentage change in total non-bank deposits in real terms; DUDLRWRP as previous variable but multiplied by the NIR dummy; LNBCH is the log of the Swiss market share; LRWRP is the log of total non-bank deposits in real terms; and INFDIF is the difference between the inflation rate in Switzerland and in that in industrial countries.

In the second specification, regulatory, institutional, and economic factors were taken into account. Dummies for the relaxation of banking secrecy (BS) and for the negative interest (NIR) were included, apart from seasonal dummies and the variables included in the previous specification. Furthermore, changes in the Swiss franc-Dollar rate and in the price of gold were considered as explanatory variables. The former variable was included to take account of potential valuation effects and to test the hypothesis whether appreciations of the Swiss franc increase the Swiss market share. The latter variable was included as a proxy for instability in the world economy and the global political system.

This equation explains close to one quarter of monthly changes in the Swiss market share improving the explanatory power substantially compared to the first specification. Most variables including the real value of the world total of non-bank deposits are significant and have the right sign. The significance of the slope dummy for the period with the negative interest rate suggests that the slope parameter of the real value of world liabilities differed in the period with and without capital control measures. This result implies that the negative interest rate reduced the general attractiveness of Switzerland for non-residents to deposit money. The intercept, in contrast, does not seem to have changed in the period without capital control. A similarly result arises when a dummy for the interest rate ban (IRB) instead of the dummy for the negative interest rate.

Institutional factors appear also to have played a role in the determination of changes in the Swiss market share. The negative sign of the dummy for banking secrecy suggests that the share function shifted downward due to the loosening of banking secrecy. This result confirms the view that the lowering of the level of banking secrecy reduced the Swiss market share. Changes in the price of gold have the expected positive sign and are highly significant in explaining changes in the Swiss market share. To the extent that the price of gold is an indicator for instability in the global political system this result indicates the existence of a safe haven effect. The argument that a strong Swiss franc attracts foreign deposits is consistent with the highly significant negative coefficient of changes in the Swiss franc-Dollar rate. This result is somewhat surprising noting that only 10 percent of external liabilities of Swiss banks is held in Swiss francs. Seasonal movements appear to be present in the dependent variable as is suggested by the marginal significance level of the F-statistic (.06).

To test the hypothesis whether specific economic factors such as inflation differentials had a positive effect on the Swiss market share, the difference between the Swiss inflation rate and the average for all industrial countries was included as explanatory variables. The insignificance of the inflation differential confirms the view that the relative economic performance of the Swiss economy did not play an important role in explaining changes of the Swiss market share. A dummy, for testing whether the "Chiasso affair" in 1977 had a negative impact on the Swiss market share, proved also to be insignificant.

That only 25 percent of the changes in the Swiss market share is explained by the regression equation may be due to the exclusion of important external determinants from the equation. Such determinants could have been the loosening of capital controls in other countries than Switzerland.

The two medium level share equations, as specified in equation (6), were estimated by 3SLS using as instruments lags of currency shares, asset prices, and real wealth. A dummy variable is included in the two equations to take account of a break in external liabilities of Swiss banks in December 1984, which is due to a redefinition of this series. The asset price for Swiss franc deposits has been computed taking into account the interest rate ban and the commission charge. As proxy for exchange rate expectations the actual changes of exchange rates were used to compute expected asset prices.[14]

The relative real asset prices have the expected signs but are insignificant in both medium level equations (**Table 2a,b**). The coefficients of the real value of external liabilities of Swiss banks are significantly different from zero in both share equations. However, the real asset value has the wrong sign in the share equation for deposits in Swiss francs.

In an alternative specification nominal asset prices were employed instead of real asset prices. Relative nominal asset prices, in contrast to relative real asset prices, are highly significant in both share equations and they have the right sign.[15] In an estimation which is not reported in **Tables 2a** and **2b** the nominal asset price for deposits in Deutschmark was found to be insignificantly different from zero. In this case, the inclusion of a relative asset price imposes symmetry and homogeneity.

---

14 Using actual values as proxies for expectations leads under the rational expectation assumption to an errors-in-variables model. OLS estimates of regression parameters will be biased and inconsistent in such a case.

15 Using the Swiss franc instead of the US-dollar as base currency for calculating expected asset prices the signs of the coefficient of relative prices in both share equations switch.

Table 2a

Medium Level Share Equations

Dependent variable: Change in share of ext. liabilities held in sfr

	1	2	3
Constant	0.007 (0.04)	0.26 (1.07)	0.59 (1.52)
D1284	-0.15 (4.94)	-0.13 (4.37)	-0.14 (4.36)
NIR			-0.02 (1.74)
DLRNP		-0.71 (2.91)	-0.57 (2.20)
DLRRP	-0.24 (0.81)		
DLRWRP	-0.78 (3.01)	-1.02 (4.61)	-0.99 (2.08)
DUDLRWRP			0.48 (0.37)
LRNP(t-1)		-0.21 (1.55)	-0.17 (1.21)
LRRP(t-1)	-0.05 (0.26)		
LNBFCH(t-1)	-0.001 (1.39)	-0.007 (3.34)	-0.001 (1.05)
LRWRP(t-1)	-0.001 (0.07)	-0.01 (1.62)	-0.04 (1.41)
R^2	0.36	0.35	0.39
D-W	2.38	2.20	2.32

t-values are reported in parenthesis. NIR is the dummy for the negative interest rate; D1284 is a dummy for a break in external liabilities in December 1984; DLRNP, DLRRP are the relative asset prices for Swiss franc and US-dollar deposits in nominal and real terms, respectively; DLRWRP percentage change in total non-bank deposits in real terms; DUDLRWRP as the previous variable but multiplied by the NIR dummy; LRNP, LRRP are the log of the relative asset prices; LNBFCH is the log of the Swiss franc share; LRWRP is the log of total non-bank deposits in real terms.

Table 2b

Medium Level Share Equations

Dependent variable: Change in share of ext. liabilities held in US-$

	1	2	3
Constant	0.09 (0.75)	-0.06 (0.44)	-0.12 (0.49)
D1284	-0.07 (4.09)	-0.08 (4.82)	-0.08 (4.62)
NIR			-0.004 (0.56)
DLRNP		-0.32 (2.46)	0.30 (2.13)
DLRRP	0.14 (0.89)		
DLRWRP	-0.28 (1.94)	0.39 (3.22)	-0.39 (1.56)
DUDLRWRP			-0.08 (0.13)
LRNP(t-1)		0.15 (2.10)	0.15 (2.03)
LRRP(t-1)	-0.09 (0.93)		
LNBDCH(t-1)	-0.000 (0.36)	-0.000 (0.48)	-0.001 (0.53)
LRWRP(t-1)	-0.007 (0.77)	-0.002 (0.29)	0.003 (0.16)
R^2	0.35	0.42	0.39
D-W	2.47	2.40	2.32

t-values are reported in parenthesis. NIR is the dummy for the negative interest rate; D1284 is a dummy for a break in external liabilities in December 1984; DLRNP, DLRRP are the relative asset prices for Swiss franc and US-dollar deposits in nominal and real terms, respectively; DLRWRP percentage change in total non-bank deposits in real terms; DUDLRWRP as the previous variable but multiplied by the NIR dummy; LRNP, LRRP are the log of the relative asset prices; LNBDCH is the log of the US-dollar share; LRWRP is the log of total non-bank deposits in real terms.

To test whether the capital control measures affected the currency shares, dummies for the period with the negative interest rate (NIR) allowing for a change in the intercept and in the coefficient of real value of assets was included in each of the two share equations. In the share equation for Swiss franc deposits the intercept is suggested to be different across periods only at the 10 percent level and no change of the coefficient of the value of real assets is indicated by the insignificance of the slope dummy. These results are surprising as one would expect an effect of the capital control measures by Swiss authorities in the Seventies which discriminated against investments in Swiss francs on the currency composition of external liabilities of Swiss banks. A possible interpretation of this result would be that the lifting of the capital control measures did not lead to a permanent upward shift in the share of Swiss franc deposits and to a change in the coefficient of the real value of assets.

5. Concluding Remarks

This study attempted to analyze the role of institutional and regulatory determinants of the Swiss market share in the market for non-bank deposits within the framework of an explicit economic model. Whereas a significant effect of regulatory and institutional determinants on the Swiss share in the international market for non-bank deposits could be found, the lifting of regulatory factors does not appear to have had a lasting impact on currency shares for external liabilities of Swiss banks. Although the results are encouraging at least three issue have to be noted. Less than 25 percent of changes in the Swiss market share is explained by the upper level share equation. Variables to be included in future estimations are specifically foreign variables such as proxies for the loosening of capital controls in other countries than Switzerland. A second issue is the insignificance of dummies for capital control measures in the Swiss franc share equation and the negative coefficient of the real value of assets in this equation. A third issues is the treatment of exchange rate expectations.

Literature

Andrist, F., and Schlup, Th. (1990), Das Auslandsgeschäft der Banken 1975 - 1989, Volkswirtschaft, Mai 1990.

Barr, D.G., and Cuthbertson, K. (1990), The Demand of Financial Assets Held in the UK by the Overseas Sector: an Application of Two-Stage Budgeting, Bank of England, Discussion Papers, Technical Series No. 31, June.

Barr, D.G., and Cuthbertson, K. (1989), Modelling the Flow of Funds, Bank of England, Discussion Papers, Technical Series No. 21, February.

Blattner, N., Genberg, H., and Swoboda, A. (eds.) (1992), Competitiveness in Banking, Heidelberg: Physica-Verlag.

Camen, U. (1990), The Position of Swiss Banks in International Financial Markets: Their On-Balance-Sheet Activities and Fiduciary Transactions, Geneva, mimeo.

Christensen, B.V. (1986), Switzerland's Role as an International Financial Center, IMF, Occasional Paper 45, Washington, July.

Cosandier, P. (1987), Switzerland and the International Financial Integration. Recent History and New Theoretical Developments, Genève, Institut Universitaire de Hautes Etudes Internationales, Thèse no 422.

Deaton, A., and Muellbauer, J. (1980), Economics and Consumer Behaviour, Cambridge: Cambridge University Press.

Grilli, V. (1989), Financial Markets, Economic Policy, October.

Hirszowicz, Ch. (ed.) (1987), Internationale Wettbewerbsfähigkeit des Finanzplatzes Schweiz, Bern: Verlag Paul Haupt.

Lang, B. (1981), Exchange Rate Determination and Euromarkets with Special Reference to the Swiss Case Since 1973, Genève, Institut de Hautes Etudes Internationales, Thèse no. 351.

Sheldon, G. (1992), Explaining the Cross-Country Distribution of International Bank Deposits, in: Blattner et al. (1992).

Weale, M. (1986), The Structure of Personal Sector Short-Term Asset Holdings, The Manchester School, LIV(2), pp. 141-161.

Explaining the Cross-Country Distribution of International Bank Deposits

George Sheldon[1]

1. Introduction

International bank deposits consist of bank accounts where the depositor is not a resident of the country in which the account is held. The largest holders of cross-border accounts are other banks, their deposits contributing roughly 80% to the worldwide stock of international accounts (Grilli, 1989, p. 396). Interbank deposits constitute a far smaller percentage of cross-border accounts in Switzerland, however, making up only about a quarter of its non-resident accounts (Camen, 1990, p. 5). Consequently, Switzerland's share of the worldwide stock of interbank deposits is small. It amounts to less than 2% compared to 15% in the market for international non-bank deposits (Grilli, 1989, p. 398).

Cross-border deposits exhibit two distinguishing features: they are short-term and, as a rule, denominated in a foreign currency. Switzerland is no exception in this regard. Almost 80% of the non-resident accounts held in Switzerland consist of demand deposits or time deposits with less than 90-day maturities, and an equally large percentage are held in a foreign currency, principally in US dollars (50%) and D-Mark (12%) (SNB, 1990, p. 131). Judging by these characteristics one might tend to equate cross-border deposits with Eurocurrency accounts. However, the two types of deposits are not identical. Eurocurrency accounts, unlike cross-border deposits, can be held by residents, while cross-border accounts, unlike Eurocurrency deposits, can be denominated in domestic currencies. But as these cases represent more the exception than the rule, a great deal of overlap does in fact exist between both deposit forms.

The worldwide volume of non-resident deposits has expanded rapidly over the last two decades. Measured against the combined output of all OECD countries, the stock of

---

[1] The author thanks participants in the Conference on Competitiveness in Banking and my two discussants, Julian Alworth and Vittorio Grilli, for useful comments. Unfortunately, all errors are the author's.

cross-border bank deposits rose from 10% in 1972 to 35% in 1986 (Grilli, 1989, p. 396). Switzerland has not shared proportionately in this growth, however. Its share of cross-border bank deposits fell from 10 to 5% in the same time span (Grilli, 1989, p. 399). With Frankfurt, Paris and London vying for a greater share of the market, competition for international funds can be expected to increase in the future.

The loss of market share is no small matter for Switzerland. Some 40% of the deposits in Swiss banks come from abroad (SNB, 1990, p. 131). Only banks in Belgium and Luxembourg with shares of 64% and 84%, respectively, display a greater degree of foreign exposure (Grilli, 1989, p. 397). In addition, the banking sector is an important source of economic growth for Switzerland. Swiss banks contribute almost 9% to value-added, employ over 117,000 persons and add to Switzerland's current account surplus (Bossard et al., 1991).

Switzerland's market share loss comes somewhat as a surprise, as those factors that contributed to the strength of Switzerland as a financial center in the past still hold today. Its society continues to exhibit a high degree of political and social stability, trade has remained relatively unfettered, its courts continue to offer strong legal protection to market participants, its currency has maintained its value, and the quality and discretion of its banks are still renowned. However, Switzerland is no longer an exception in those regards. Competitor countries have been catching up. In the process, the weaknesses of the Swiss financial center have become more apparent. One major shortcoming according to an increasing number of Swiss authors (cf. AKW (1990), Braillard (1987), SBG (1990)) are taxes: for one, the comparatively high withholding tax on returns, but more importantly, the high stamp duty on security trading, which is held responsible for the fact that Switzerland has the only financial center without a developed money market. A recently published international cross-section study from Grilli (1989) appears to support the view that high taxes scare off depositors as it provides evidence that non-residents avoid depositing funds in countries with high withholding taxes. While the result seems plausible, the study nevertheless suffers from a number of weaknesses. For one, the underlying econometric model is quite restrictive and contains a number of counterintuitive implications. Secondly, some of the proxy variables used are rather rough.

The following paper represents an attempt to extend Grilli's work. It employs a less restrictive model structure, tries to improve on the quality of the data and utilizes additional variables in explaining a country's share of cross-border deposits.

The paper is set out as follows. The next section begins with a critical discussion of the econometric approach chosen by Grilli. His model is then contrasted with alternative specifications, which are estimated using data described in section 3. Our findings are presented in section 4. The final section summarizes the results and discusses their policy implications.

2. Econometric Modelling Schemes

2.1. Grilli's Model

Grilli bases his econometric analysis on the following regression model:

(1) $Y_{it} = \alpha_0 + \alpha' X_{it} + \varepsilon_{it}$ for $i = 1,\ldots,10$ and $t = 1972,\ldots,1987$, where

$$\varepsilon_{it} \sim N(0, \sigma^2),\ E(\varepsilon_{it}\varepsilon_{jt}) = 0 \text{ and } E(\varepsilon_{it}\varepsilon_{js}) = 0 \text{ for } t \neq s.$$

Y_{it} represents the stock of non-resident deposits in country i at time t expressed in US dollars. The vector X of explanatory variables encompasses statutory withholding tax rates on both non-resident bank deposits and dividends, a dummy for capital inflow restrictions, one for outflow restrictions, another one for the degree of bank secrecy, a time trend and GNP as a proxy for positive externalities associated with the size of the financial center. The data stem from the IMF and cover 10 countries: Belgium, Canada, France, Germany, Italy, Japan, the Netherlands, Switzerland, the US and the UK. Separate regressions are run on interbank and non-bank deposits.

The estimates suggest that high withholding taxes and capital flow restrictions discourage non-resident depositors while the degree of bank secrecy attracts them. Banks appear to react more to withholding taxes on dividends and GNP whereas non-banks are apparently more sensitive to withholding taxes on interest and the extent of bank secrecy.

The results do not seem surprising. Their reliability is questionable, however, as they rest on a number of restrictive and implausible assumptions.

- For one, the assumption of a common constant for all countries is problematical. It implies that if it were not for the cross-country variation in X, all countries would exhibit the same level of cross-border deposits on average. In other words, the model suggests that, with the exception of those characteristics incorporated in X or captured in ε, all countries are perfect substitutes in the eyes of non-resident depositors. Given the very rough characterization of a country that X provides, this assumption seems rather heroic. Unfortunately, should it prove wrong then not only is the estimated value of the intercept suspect, but the estimated slope parameters are questionable as well (cf. Hsiao, 1986, p. 6f).
- The regression model also stipulates that the level of cross-border deposits in a country depends solely on the characteristics of that same country. The efforts of other countries and/or their banks to attract deposits are necessarily of no avail according to (1). This assumption seems rather misplaced in a model intended to explain changing market shares. It either implies that banks situated in different countries are not competitors, which conflicts with the assumption inherent in a common constant. Or it suggests that they are indeed competitors but in an atomistic market where the market share loss of one country's banks has a negligible effect on the banks of any individual country. Yet in such a world, financial centers cannot exist by definition. In short, regression model (1) is self-contradictory.
- The issue of the assumed level of competition carries over to the stochastic term. In a competitive context one would expect that one country's stochastic gain could represent another's stochastic loss or, to put it more broadly, that common factors influence the stochastic disturbances of different countries. Model (1) precludes this possibility by excluding cross-country correlation. Incorrectly assuming this does not bias the results, however. The estimates are simply less efficient.
- A loss of efficiency is also the sole consequence of wrongly assuming a homoscedastic error term. The assumption implies, perhaps not unreasonably, that the relative variation of cross-border deposit levels decreases with their scale.

Grilli's findings also suffer from data problems.

- The deposit figures, taken from the IMF publication International Financial Statistics, do not specify the currency of deposit but rather combine deposits of different denomination into a US-dollar aggregate using spot exchange rates. Hence, deposit level variation in part reflects pure valuation effects. Furthermore, by not breaking down cross-border deposits by currency, the IMF data do not allow one to control for the fact that some of the capital flow restrictions and taxes contained in X only pertain to specific currencies. For example, the negative rate of interest on cross-border deposits imposed in Switzerland from July 1972 to February 1980 applied solely to accounts in Swiss francs. Further, the 15% withholding tax on bank deposit interest in Italy does not hold for non-resident accounts denominated in a foreign currency.

The data also do not indicate the specific country-of-residence of the depositors, although the returns from identical deposits can vary according to this factor. Tax reciprocity agreements are a case in point.

2.2. Theory-Based Approaches

Perhaps the most glaring shortcoming of regression model (1) is that it lacks an explicit theoretical foundation. The approach is essentially ad hoc. Grilli readily acknowledges this and lays blame on the fact that a well-developed theory of trade in international bank services does not yet exist. No doubt the missing model has something to do with the complexity of the problem. Bank services are notoriously heterogeneous. Hence, bank deposits unlike "classical" assets are not sufficiently characterized by the mean and variance of returns alone. For one, trust and discretion need to be dealt with (cf. Walter, 1985, p. 153ff). Still more factors come into play in an international setting: e.g. different currencies, socioeconomic systems, taxes and barriers to capital flows (cf. Cooper/Kaplanis, 1986). Furthermore, there is the variety of possible deposit motives to consider. A money launderer, a tax evader and a multinational firm cannot be cast in the mold of a representative depositor.

These problems need not stand in the way of a more theory-based approach, however. After all, theoretical consistency has taken a back seat to econometric necessity before. But to estimate one of the standard econometric portfolio selection models[2] requires at least data on returns. Three-month Euromarket interest rates are the natural choice given the short maturity of cross-border accounts. Yet country-specific time series do not generally exist, and when they do, they exhibit virtually no cross-country

2 Two main approaches exist in the literature (cf. Barr/Cuthbertson, 1989): the mean-variance model stemming from Markowitz (1952) and Tobin (1958) and the consumer-theoretic approach in the spirit of Friedman (1956). The latter modelling scheme has recently won support in Switzerland (cf. Müller, 1989; Sheldon, 1990; and Camen, 1991).

variation. Hence, they cannot be the cause of cross-country deposit share fluctuations. In short, the only progress that can be achieved at the moment is to eliminate the weaknesses in model (1) pointed out in the previous section. The following discussion serves that purpose.

2.3. SUR Models with Fixed Effects

Model (2) dispenses with the common-constant assumption by allowing for constants that vary by country and period, respectively, so-called fixed effects. Lowercase letters represent natural logarithms in (2), and D symbolizes a dummy variable. Logarithms are chosen in order to interpret the coefficients as elasticities.

(2) $$y_{it} = \alpha_{0i} + \alpha_{0t} + \alpha' x_{it} + \gamma' D_{it} + \varepsilon_{it}, \text{ where}$$

$$\varepsilon_{it} \sim N(0, \sigma_i^2), \; E(\varepsilon_{it}\varepsilon_{jt}) = \sigma_{ij} \text{ and } E(\varepsilon_{it}\varepsilon_{js}) = 0 \text{ for } t \neq s.$$

Country-specific constants (α_{0i}) capture relevant explanatory factors that are unique to a country yet remain constant through time (e.g. the socioeconomic framework), whereas period-specific constants (α_{0t}) absorb effects that are unique to a time period and uniform across countries (e.g. the world business cycle or seasonal effects). Period-specific constants can also represent a trend that, unlike in (1), varies through time. Fixed effects, too, can capture any constant country-specific or general period-specific measurement errors in the explanatory variables. Consequently, (2) is less sensitive to measurement error than (1), a convenient trait given the quality of some of the regressors.

The introduction of fixed effects leads to a marked increase in the number of parameters to estimate without contributing essentially to the explanatory power of the model, the constants serving solely to avoid the biases discussed in section 2.1. Measuring the variables in deviations from their respective period-specific means offers a simple solution to the problem. It reduces the number of constants while cancelling out all period effects and any period-specific measurement errors they may capture. Differencing in this manner yields (2a). Variables appearing in the equation without a country index represent means.

(2a) $$(y_{it} - y_t) = (\alpha_{0i} - \alpha_0) + \alpha'(x_{it} - x_t) + \gamma'(D_{it} - D_t) + (\varepsilon_{it} - \varepsilon_t)$$

Unlike (1) or (2), equation (2a) rests on the principle of comparative advantage; i.e., the level of cross-border deposits in a country no longer depends solely on factors within the same country. In fact, the value of determining factors can remain unchanged in a country and the volume of its deposits can still vary if developments in other countries move the mean against which a country's comparative advantage is measured. For the same reason, parallel movements of X in all countries have no effect on the dependent variable.

The slope parameters in (2) and (2a) measure both "own-country" and "cross-country" elasticities. This is seen by subtracting the regression equation (2a) of an arbitrary country j from that of another country i, yielding (2b).[3]

(2b) $$(y_{it} - y_{jt}) = (\alpha_{0i} - \alpha_{0j}) + \alpha'(x_{it} - x_{jt}) + \gamma'(D_{it} - D_{jt}) + (\varepsilon_{it} - \varepsilon_{jt})$$

As (2b) shows, negative values of the slope coefficients represent "cross-country" elasticities. However, according to (2b) these do not vary by country, implying in turn that no substitutional, i.e., competitive differential exists across countries. Allowing for country-specific coefficients does not change matters much either. It merely eliminates the equality between the absolute values of the "own-country" and "cross-country" elasticities. But the "cross-country" elasticities of country j to all other countries are still uniform. In order to allow for differing degrees of substitution among countries one has to break with model (2) altogether. Equation (3) offers an alternative that preserves many of the positive features of (2a).

(3) $$\ln(Y_{it}/Y_t) = \beta_{0i} + \beta_i'\ln(X_{it}/X_t) + \delta_i'(D_{it} - D_t) + \mu_{it}\text{, where}$$

$$\mu_{it} \sim N(0, \sigma_i^2),\ E(\mu_{it}\mu_{jt}) = \sigma_{ij} \text{ and } E(\mu_{it}\mu_{js}) = 0 \text{ for } t \neq s$$

---

3 Adding and subtracting the log of the sum of cross-border deposits to the left side of (2b) reveals that the left-hand variable is equivalent to the log of the market share ratio between two countries, or the so-called logit. This result might suggest basing (2a) on a random utility model of depositor behavior in the spirit of McFadden (1973). However, that would require assuming that a depositor does not spread his cross-border deposits across countries but, instead, views potential countries of deposit as mutually exclusive alternatives. Such an approach excludes the possibility of individual portfolio diversification.

The variables in (3) are measured in relative deviations from their means rather than, as in (2a), in absolute deviations from their mean log. Both specifications may seem identical at first glance, but they differ due to the non-linearity of the exponential function. As a consequence, the slope parameters no longer measure the effect of a change of comparative advantage between two countries on the ratio of their market shares, but rather the effect of such a change on the market share of just one of these countries, as (3a) demonstrates.[4]

$$\text{(3a)} \qquad \ln(Y_{it}/\Sigma_i Y_{it}) + \ln I = \beta_{0i} + \beta_i' \ln(X_{it}/X_t) + \delta_i'(D_{it} - D_t) + \mu_{it}$$

Despite this difference, (3) still exhibits most of the positive features of (2a). The period-specific constants as well as any corresponding measurements errors are again eliminated through the use of relative deviations from the mean. The country-specific constants still capture country-specific effects as long as these are proportional by a constant factor to a country's relative deviation to the mean. In this sense, (3) is more restrictive than (2a).

Despite the more flexible model structure compared to (1), models (2a) and (3) nevertheless contain restrictive assumptions. Separability and homotheticity assumptions underlie both specifications. Separability follows, for example, from excluding the possibility that developments outside the group of countries considered affect market shares within the group. In other words, our model assumes that the rise of offshore financial centers, say, in Singapore affected London and Vienna proportionately. Homotheticity, on the other hand, results from assuming that the scale of the deposit market does not influence market shares.

3. Data

3.1. Dependent Variable

Ideally the distribution of cross-border deposits across countries should be broken down by currency, maturity, the type of depositor and his or her country of residence, since

---

4 "I" represents the number of countries considered.

Figure 1: Cross-Border Deposits of Non-Banks in US Dollars

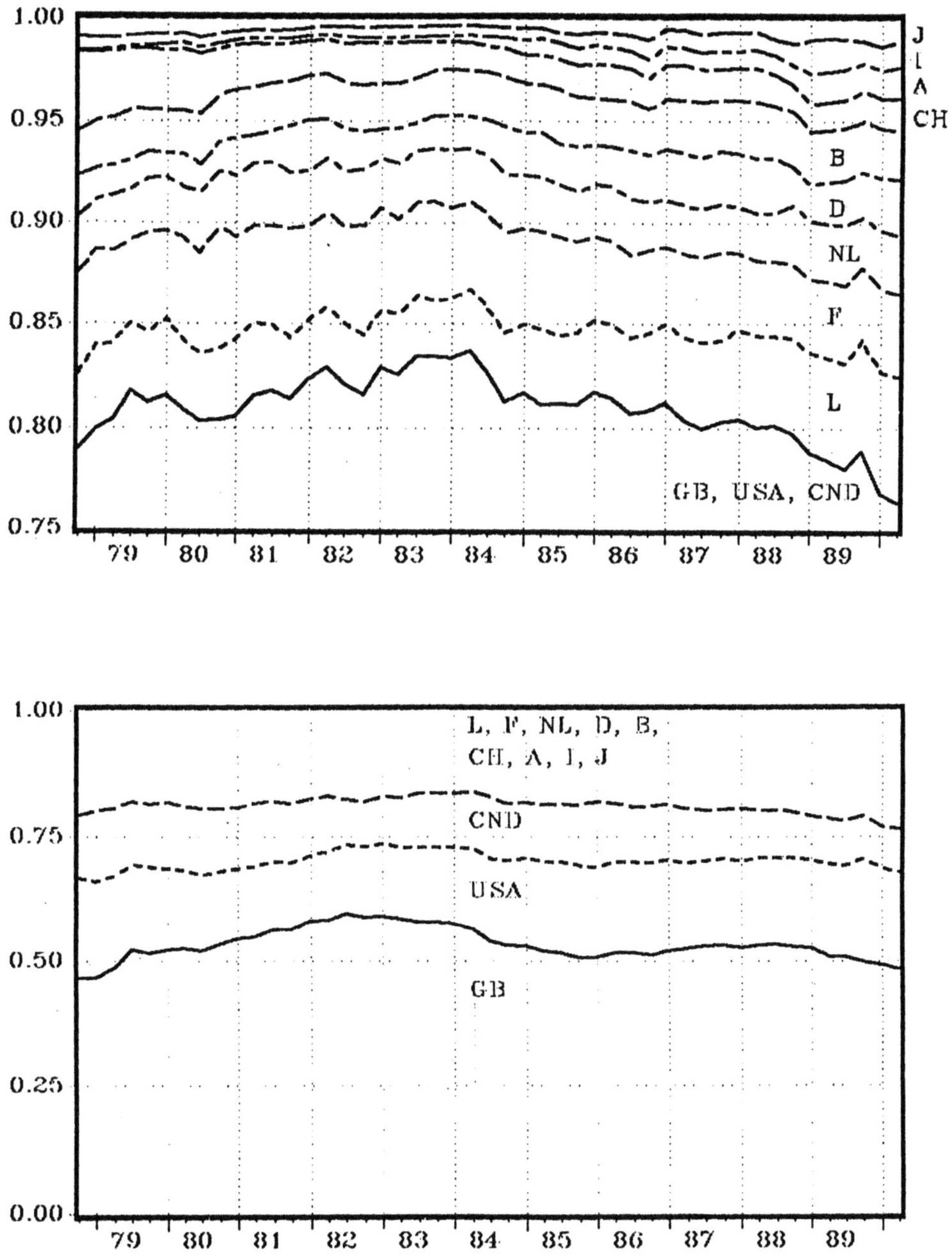

returns can be expected to vary with these factors. As pointed out earlier, the IMF data used in Grilli (1989) merely distinguish between non-bank and bank depositors. Our data, on the other hand, stem from the Bank for International Settlements (BIS)[5] and permit an additional breakdown by currency. We concentrate on deposits in US dollars, D-Mark and Swiss francs in this paper. The BIS databank does not carry information on the maturity of deposits but does record the depositors' country of residence. That information was not used in this study to keep our econometric model tractable. By so doing, one assumes that residents of different countries have common preferences and constraints with respect to their cross-border deposit choices. The importance of such factors as, say, geographical proximity is thus ruled out.

The BIS data employed here consist of quarterly figures and cover the period from the 4th quarter of 1977 (US dollar: 1978) to the 2nd quarter of 1990. In contrast, the IMF data analyzed by Grilli are annual and span the period from 1972 to 1987.[6] The countries compared in the following study include Luxembourg and Austria in addition to those countries considered by Grilli. Luxembourg and Austria were included due to their strict bank secrecy regulations, which apparently are on par with Switzerland's. Six deposit "markets" were analyzed in total. They result from combining the three currencies mentioned with the two types of depositors.

The BIS data indicate that the UK today has the largest share of cross-border deposits in five of the six markets considered. Only in the market for interbank deposits in US dollars is the UK second, having lost its position to Japan just in the last years. The UK has long led in the market for interbank deposits but first gained a leading position in the area of non-bank deposits (cf. **Figures 1-3**) in the second half of the 80s. The losers were principally Germany, whose share in the D-Mark sector fell from 55.3 to 22.5%, and Switzerland, whose share in Swiss franc deposits declined from 50.7 to 27.1%. Today more US dollars, D-Mark and Swiss francs are held in cross-border accounts in the UK and Japan than in the countries that issue these currencies.

The Swiss banks have lost ground in the other deposit markets as well. With the exception of interbank deposits in Swiss francs, Switzerland's banks have given up market

---

5 The author thanks the BIS, in particular Dr. Helmut Mayer and Dr. Karsten von Kleist, for providing him access to the BIS data. Their kind support made this study possible.

6 Our regression estimates also only cover the period up to 1987 due to data limitations with regard to the explanatory variables.

Figure 2: Cross-Border Deposits of Non-Banks in D-Mark

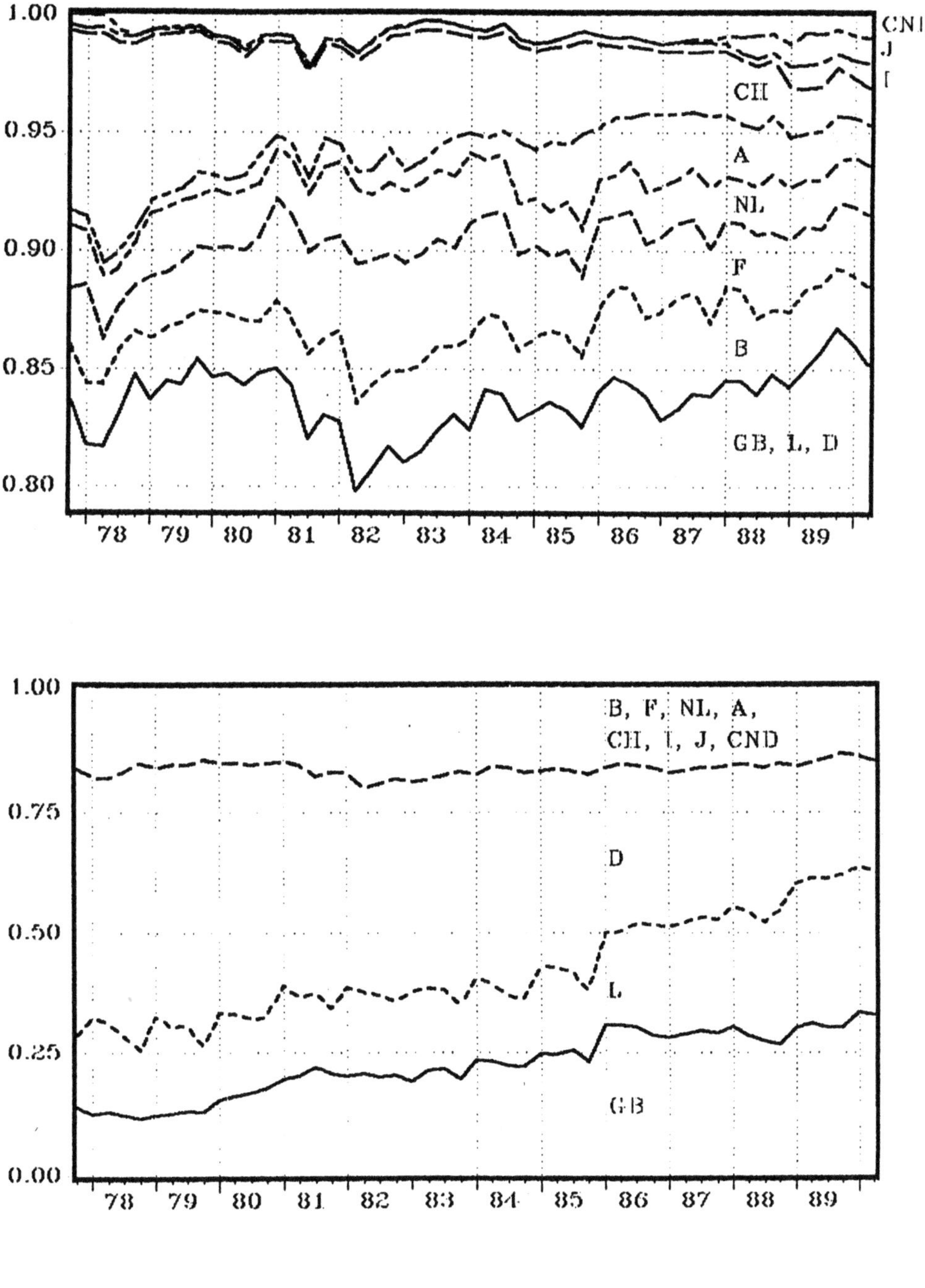

share in all the markets considered here. The losses in the market for non-bank deposits are particularly pronounced. Other general market shares losers include Germany, France and the Netherlands. Italy and Japan, on the other hand, count as overall market share winners. The banks in Austria, the UK and Luxembourg met with mixed success. The UK gave up ground in the market for interbank deposits in Swiss francs and, as already mentioned, in US dollars. On the other hand, its banks succeeded in making major inroads in all three non-bank depositor markets. The market share gains of Austria's and Luxembourg's banks were also achieved in the non-bank market, while they suffered losses in interbank deposits.

Overall, these developments have decreased share concentration in all markets save that for interbank deposits in US dollars. Otherwise, though, the reduction in concentration was greatest in the interbank market. In general, cross-country deposits today are more evenly distributed across the 12 countries studied than at the end of the 70s.

3.2. Explanatory Variables

We study the influence of the following variables on the non-resident deposit shares of a country: capital controls, bank secrecy, bank solidness, the size of the financial center, the level of money market fiduciary accounts, statutory withholding taxes on bank interest and dividends, and foreign trade volume.

Capital controls can encompass a myriad of measures. They may include the illegalization of certain capital transactions, case-by-case authorization requirements, surrender requirements, special reserve requirements, interest ceilings, etc. Finding a common scale of measurement for such diverse measures is a virtually impossible task. Hence, we follow Grilli (1989) and construct two dummy variables: one for capital inflow restrictions and one for capital outflow restrictions.

The outflow restriction dummies are drawn from the same source as in Grilli (1989): the annual IMF publication Exchange Arrangements and Exchange Restrictions.[7] The

---

[7] The "yes-no" information is taken directly from the row "restrictions on payments" in the Summary Table. The data refer primarily to exchange controls for residents. The yearly data were converted into quarterly observations on the basis of chronologies appearing in the IMF publication cited above as well as in OECD (1982, 1987a) and Bruni (1990).

Figure 3: Cross-Border Deposits of Non-Banks in Swiss Francs

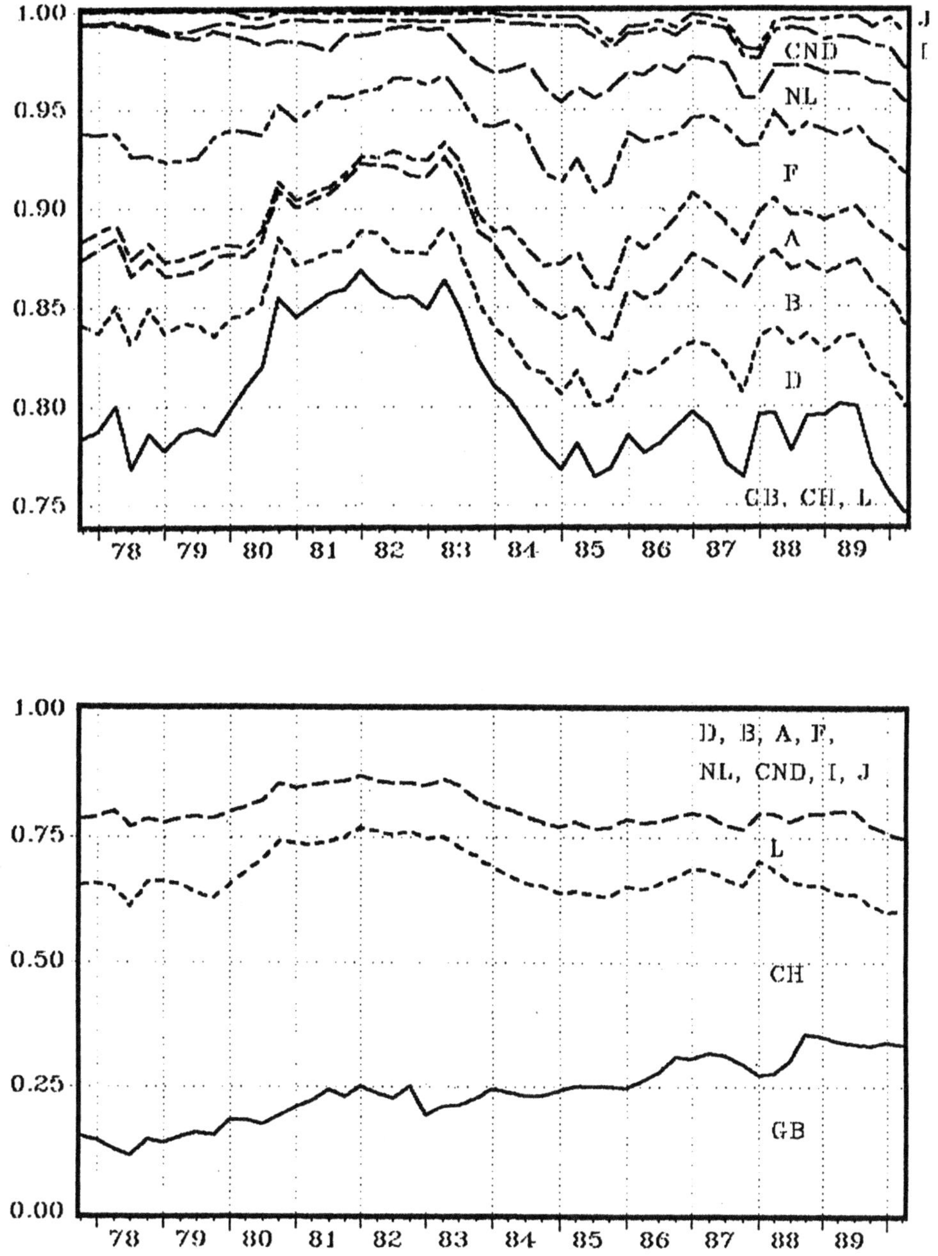

The IMF data indicate that Belgium, Canada, Germany, Luxembourg, the Netherlands, Switzerland and the USA never imposed capital inflow restrictions during the period of observation, while Austria and France never lifted theirs. The only regime changes occurred in the UK (which did away with exchange controls in the 4th quarter of 1979), in Italy (which strongly liberalized its exchange controls at the end of 1983 only to reimpose them for the 1st quarter in 1987) and in Japan (which ended restrictions with the implementation of the Foreign Exchange and Foreign Trade Control Law in December 1980).[8] The removal of exchange controls in the three countries mentioned reduced the capital outflow restriction differential across countries leading to a loss of comparative advantage for countries, like Switzerland, that never imposed such controls.

The values of the inflow restriction dummy are based on Grilli (1989) and the chronologies cited above. All sources agree that only Switzerland, Germany, Italy and Japan imposed restrictions during the period under study. These measures include special reserve requirements on foreign liabilities of banks (e.g. Germany, Italy, and Japan) and interest rate ceilings (e.g. Switzerland and Japan). Both measures have since been lifted,[9] leading to complete homogeneity across countries in this respect. Switzerland disposed itself of a comparative disadvantage by removing its restrictions.

Measuring the degree of bank secrecy in a country is no easy matter either, especially since the letter of the law and its application often differ. As a consequence, we rely on the opinion of experts, specifically on Braillard (1987), Chambost (1983) and Walter (1985). According to these authors Switzerland, Austria and Luxembourg treat bank secrecy in a similarly strict manner. The only noteworthy legal changes over the

---

8 Note that in accordance with (2a) and (3) only changes, such as these, that vary the relative attractiveness of countries can effect movements in their market shares. A constant cross-country differential is simply captured by the country-specific constants. Note, too, that it is impossible both to control for country-specific effects, as in (2a) and (3), and to identify, as in equation (1), those factors responsible for the average cross-country share differential the constants capture. Perfect multicollinearity would otherwise ensue.

9 The chronologies do not always agree with Grilli (1989) with respect to the period of change. Agreement exists as to when the elimination of the negative interest rate on cross-border deposits in Swiss francs took place, i.e. the end of 1979. But otherwise consensus does not exist. According to the IMF (1982, 33) no noteworthy capital inflow restrictions existed in Germany after the 1st quarter 1981, whereas Grilli, in breaking with his 0-1 coding, assigns Germany a value of 0.5 for the period 1979-81 and 0.2 for the period 1982-83. We adhere instead to the IMF judgment and, in addition, hold to the 0-1 coding throughout. The chronologies cited are not precise on when Japan and Italy removed their restrictions. So in these two cases we employ a method previously used by other authors (cf. Fukao/Hanazaki, 1987, 41, and the literature cited there) and view a domestic rate of interest on 3-month deposits higher than the Euromarket rate as a sign that inflow restrictions were still in force.

period under study also occurred in these countries. Switzerland passed a mutual assistance act (Bundesgesetz über die internationale Rechtshilfe in Strafsachen) in 1983 obliging it to divulge certain information in international criminal matters. This change is treated here as an easing of bank secrecy restrictions in Switzerland. Luxembourg enacted a law in April 1981 that, in an amendment to article 458 of the criminal code, places bank secrecy on par with medical confidentiality, with a similar threat of prosecution in case of violation. Austria introduced a new law in January 1979 comparable to article 47 of the Swiss Bank Act. The latter two enactments are viewed here as having tightened bank secrecy in those countries.[10] These changes in the law have led to a stronger polarization across countries with respect to bank secrecy and weakened Switzerland's position.

In light of the recent "savings-and-loan scandal" in the US, it would seem that the solidness of a country's banks, too, should effect its attractiveness for non-resident depositors. A natural choice as a measure of bank soundness is Moody's ratings. Unfortunately Moody's gives the short-term liability of large banks of all countries considered here the highest rating (P1) over the entire period of observation. Hence, we chose instead the ratio of equity to total liabilities of a country's large banks as calculated by the OECD (1985, 1987b, 1988).[11] According to the OECD figures, the large banks in Japan (2%), France (2.2%), Austria (2.4%) and Belgium (2.6%) were more highly leveraged over the time span considered than those in Switzerland (6%), the US (5%), Canada (4.5%) and the UK (4.5%). The cross-country differential decreased during the estimation period with Switzerland's position falling slightly.

Grilli (1989) maintains that firms enjoy positive external effects commensurate with the size and density of the market they serve: the larger the market, the greater is the cost advantage to firms. Accordingly, banks located in large financial centers should have a comparative cost advantage over banks serving smaller centers. Grilli uses a country's GNP as a rather rough gauge of these so-called thick market externalities. We

---

[10] Bank secrecy is without question hard to measure. Grilli uses a scale that - with the exception of Switzerland - ranges from -1 (France, Italy) to 1 (UK). Grilli assigns Switzerland a value of 5 up to 1978 and thereafter a value of 4. We could not identify the event that gave rise to the revaluation of Swiss bank secrecy. In order to ease comparison, we otherwise held to Grilli's scale but did not assign Switzerland a 4 until 1983 and gave Austria and Luxembourg a value of 3 before their new laws were enacted and a value of 4 thereafter.

[11] The yearly figures calculated by the OECD were converted into quarterly figures with the help of a cubic spline function.

view the volume of stock market trading as a more accurate indicator and apply it here instead. The data are drawn from the annual report of the International Federation of Stock Exchanges (FIBV) in Paris.[12] The data give evidence that the volume of transactions has converged somewhat across countries since 1977. Switzerland's position has weakened.

Fiduciary accounts are a unique feature of Swiss banking (cf. Braillard, 1987). The bank in its role as trustee merely acts as a go-between. It accepts funds from a depositor and invests them in its own name but at the risk of the depositor. The bank receives a fixed commission for its efforts. Fiduciary accounts are usually denominated in US dollars and constitute short-term agreements. They arose in the 50s and expanded dramatically in the wake of the second oil crisis when large sums of money flowed into the OPEC countries. Fiduciary accounts offer the advantages of Swiss bank accounts while stripping them of their drawbacks. The high Swiss withholding tax is avoided since fiduciary accounts are usually invested abroad, and the stamp duty does not apply because fiduciary accounts do not involve a security transaction. Furthermore, fiduciary account holders can remain anonymous more easily due to the so-called Form B, which - under certain conditions - exempts lawyers and private trustees from disclosing the identity of their clients, which the Diligence Agreement (Sorgfaltspflichtvereinbarung), introduced in 1977, otherwise requires. As a result of these features, non-resident depositors may increasingly substitute fiduciary accounts for cross-border deposits. If that is the case, the growth of fiduciary accounts should have slowed the expansion of cross-border deposits of non-banks in Switzerland and - to the extent that the entrusted funds were redeposited in other countries - have increased the volume of interbank deposits in the receiving countries.[13]

Tax avoidance may not only be the motivating factor behind the growth of fiduciary accounts but also the driving force behind the increase in cross-border deposits. High

---

[12] The annual data are denominated in domestic currencies. The data were first converted into US dollars using constant 1989 year-end exchange rates and then into quarterly figures with the help of a cubic spline function. The data suffer from the fact that the extent of coverage varies by country. For example, institutional investors are excluded in the figures for Canada, Germany and France. Note, though, that any country-specific measurement errors that remain constant through time are captured by the regression constants in (2a) and (3).

[13] The data on fiduciary accounts used here are taken from a time series kept by the Swiss National Bank that records the volume of fiduciary accounts stemming from funds received from abroad. The monthly figures cover only Swiss franc and US dollar accounts, both expressed in Swiss francs.

withholding taxes on bank account interest could provide the impetus. These tax rates also vary strongly by country. Of those countries considered, France tops the list with a withholding tax of 46%, followed by Switzerland with 35% and the US and the UK with roughly 30%. Germany, Luxembourg, the Netherlands and Italy (provided the cross-border deposit is in a foreign currency) do not withhold taxes on bank deposit interest. These rates were in force at the end of 1987. Between 1977 and then, tax rates increased in Austria (at first from 0 to 7.5% and latter just to 5%), Belgium (from 20 to 25%) and France (from 33 first to 40% and then to 46%). They declined in the UK (from 35 to 30%) and Italy (in the special case mentioned, from 15 to 0%). Through these changes the cross-country tax rate differential has increased slightly, with Switzerland's position improving.

Grilli (1989) points out that cross-border deposits may merely serve as way stations for money targeted for a securities market. In this case the withholding tax on stock dividends would appear to be the more appropriate tax indicator. These rates vary less across countries, however. With the exception of the UK, all 12 countries considered withhold taxes on dividends. Luxembourg deducts the least (15%), while Switzerland (35%), Italy (32%) and the US (30%) withhold the most. The cross-country differential has not changed much in the last years. Belgium raised its withholding tax rate in 1985 from 20 to 25%, and Italy in 1983 from 30 to 32.4%. Since Switzerland left its rate unchanged, its relative position improved.

The tax rates quoted are statutory rates.[14] As a result of reciprocity agreements these rates may seriously overstate the effective tax incidence and hence the true tax spread across countries. For example, in the case of withholding taxes on dividends, allowing for reciprocity agreements virtually eliminates any cross-country differential (cf. AKW, 1990, p. 20, fig. 13). We do not take reciprocity agreements into account here. To do so would necessitate differentiating depositors by country of residence and would make our econometric model unestimateable. Moreover, controlling for country of residence would not suffice. Tax-exempt institutional investors such as pension funds, charity foundations or churches lose the withholding taxes as they do not have profits from which to deduct them (cf. AKW, 1990, p. 21). Hence, statutory rates are more appropriate in these cases as well as in respect to secret money, i.e., non-declared wealth.

---

[14] The tax rates are drawn from listings of the Swiss Federal Tax Administration. Additional detailed information was provided by the International Office for Fiscal Documentation in Amsterdam.

Table 1: Development of the Cross-Country Attractiveness Differential

	all countries	Swiss position
outflow restrictions	decrease	loss
inflow restrictions	decrease	gain
bank secrecy	slight decrease	slight loss
equity ratio	increase	loss
stock exchange volume	decrease	loss
fiduciary accounts	increase	loss
interest tax	slight increase	slight gain
dividend tax	increase	slight gain
foreign trade	decrease	loss

FAI

Cross-border accounts are held not only for clandestine purposes, however. Multinational firms require foreign exchange balances, principally US dollars, simply to conduct international business (cf. Mishkin, 1989, p. 202). The transactions motive would lead one to expect higher levels of cross-border deposits in countries with large international trade flows. That follows from simple quantity theory or even renewal theory, for that matter.[15] We use the sum of exports and imports to capture this effect.[16] The data indicate that differences in international trade volume across the countries studied have narrowed. Switzerland has lost ground to the others.

Table 1 summarizes the changes over the estimation period of the relative attractiveness of the 12 countries considered with respect to the variables named.

---

[15] According to renewal theory, a stock (i.e. deposits) varies directly proportional to its flow (i.e. payments) in steady-state equilibrium.

[16] The data used stem from the International Financial Statistics of the IMF (series 70 and 71). The quarterly data appear in domestic currencies. They were converted into US dollars using 1989 year-end exchange rates.

4. Estimation Results

Models (2a) and (3) constitute equations systems. Each system represents a deposit market, with every system containing as many equations as countries analyzed. Model (2a) generates singular systems since the left-hand variable, by definition, sums to zero across equations. To avoid singularity and hence to make the parameters estimateable, one equation has to be dropped. Which one is eliminated does not affect the estimates of the remaining parameters as long as they are obtained by direct maximum likelihood estimation (MLE). That is the procedure we chose for model (2a). Model (3), on the other hand, is not singular. In this case we applied the less cumbersome feasible generalized least-squares (FGLS) method.

The assumption of a common intercept and common slopes (null hypothesis) implied by (1) were tested using equation (2a) and a likelihood ratio statistic based on the difference of the residual sums of squares and cross-products of the restricted and unrestricted model, respectively (cf. Greene, 1990, p. 519). Both null hypotheses were rejected at the 1% level of significance.[17] The regression constant and the "own-country" and "cross-country" elasticities thus appear to vary by country, implying that models (1) and (2a) are mis-specified in this respect. Hence, model (3) is more appropriate.

We also tested the SUR assumption $E(\mu_{it}\mu_{jt}) \neq 0$ underlying model (3). To do so we estimated each equation separately with OLS and then constructed a Lagrange multiplier statistic proposed by Breusch and Pagan (1980) from the estimated cross-equation correlations of the residuals within a system. The null hypothesis that no cross-equation correlation exists could be rejected in five of the six deposit markets analyzed, the exception being interbank deposits in US dollars. The chi-squared distributed test statistic exceeded the 1% critical value noticeably, except in the case of deposits of non-banks in Swiss francs (where the test statistic was significant at the 8% level of significance) and interbank deposits in US dollars (where the test statistic was significant at the 25% level). The equations system of the latter market was thus treated as if the SUR assumption did not hold and hence estimated with a single equation procedure.

---

17 The likelihood ratio statistic for the common-constant test ranged from 19.62 to 102.92. The 1% critical value from the chi-squared distribution with three degrees of freedom (only four country equations, i.e. 40 parameters can be estimated simultaneously with the MLE routine used) is 11.34. The likelihood ratio statistic for the test of common slopes varied from 140 to 236 compared to a 1% critical value of 46.96.

All equations in (3) were estimated with FGLS controlling for first-order within-country autocorrelation in situations where the Durbin-Watson statistic seemed low.[18] The Prais-Winsten FGLS estimator was used to preserve degrees of freedom. This is a two-step approach, followed by a third step to control for the SUR relationship (cf. Greene, 1990, p. 519). The multi-step procedure was not iterated to convergence as nothing is to be gained asymptotically. The FGLS estimator is efficient at every iteration, and iteration does not produce the MLE.

The estimation results for model (3) appear in **Table 2** (non-bank depositors) and **Table 3** (bank depositors). The variables were standardized prior to estimation in order to ease comparison of the relative strengths of the regressors within a given country.[19] Hence, the coefficients appearing in the tables are standardized elasticities, or so-called beta coefficients (cf. Maddala, 1977, p. 119). To conserve on space, the estimation results for Belgium, Canada and the Netherlands do not appear in the tables. Excluding the estimated parameters for these countries does not affect the overall picture, however.

From our discussion in section 3.2., one would expect that strict bank secrecy regulations, high equity ratios in the banking sector, large stock market turnover and sizeable foreign trade volume would increase a country's cross-border deposit share, while capital controls and high withholding taxes would decrease it. The results presented in the tables indicate that these effects hold only in certain instances. To start, roughly 55% of the signs are uncertain at a 5% level of significance.[20] In those cases nothing can be

---

[18] Unfortunately the inconclusive region of the Durbin-Watson statistic ranges roughly from 1 to 2 in our equations due to an inconvenient number of observations (41 or 37) and variables (8 or 9). Note that controlling for autocorrelation represents a generalization of the stochastic assumptions set out in section 2.3.

[19] Variables, such as fiduciary accounts or the withholding tax on dividends that varied in only one or two countries in the estimation period, exhibit relative little variation when measured against their respective cross-country mean because they pull the mean with them when their values change. The small variance leads to inordinately large elasticities, which give the false impression that the variable in question has a strong influence on deposit shares. The standardization eliminates this effect and at the same time increases the variation of those variables.

[20] This should not be misconstrued as indicating that the equations provide little explanatory power. The single-equation estimates (i.e., without the SUR assumption) yielded corrected R-squareds ranging from 0.42 to 0.96 and with a median value of 0.83.

Table 2: Regression Results for Non-Bank Deposits (SUR/FGLS)

		capital controls outflow	capital controls inflow	bank secrecy	equity ratio	stock volume	fidu- ciary	taxes on interest	taxes on dividend	foreign trade	Durbin-Watson
US$	AT	0.356*	0.205*	-0.037	0.101	0.232*	0.065	0.043	-0.473*	-0.077	1.625
		(0.185)	(0.099)	(0.048)	(0.167)	(0.096)	(0.196)	(0.130)	(0.200)	(0.063)	
	CH	-0.430*	-0.126*	-0.031	0.263*	0.011	-0.304*	0.150*	-0.080	0.295*	1.871
		(0.124)	(0.057)	(0.096)	(0.122)	(0.045)	(0.103)	(0.051)	(0.074)	(0.064)	
	DE	0.115	-0.144	0.263	1.042*	0.435	0.141	-0.340*	0.482	0.467*	2.004
		(0.341)	(0.241)	(0.198)	(0.238)	(0.274)	(0.268)	(0.120)	(0.293)	(0.121)	
	FR	1.336*	-0.409	-0.142	-0.246	-0.211	0.478	-0.639	1.005*	0.306	1.639
		(0.424)	(0.305)	(0.217)	(0.612)	(0.278)	(0.443)	(0.358)	(0.366)	(0.263)	
	GB	-0.012	0.471*	0.135	1.293*	0.239*	-1.703*	0.269*	0.441*	0.297*	1.871
		(0.090)	(0.133)	(0.097)	(0.211)	(0.092)	(0.188)	(0.125)	(0.133)	(0.128)	
	IT	-0.109	0.031	-0.093	0.702*	0.015	1.314*	-0.463*	-0.095	0.415*	1.927
		(0.086)	(0.067)	(0.094)	(0.195)	(0.073)	(0.111)	(0.126)	(0.167)	(0.148)	
	JP	-0.463*	0.142*	-0.078	-0.499*	0.159	1.590*	-0.235*	-1.130*	1.145*	2.165
		(0.123)	(0.055)	(0.067)	(0.135)	(0.100)	(0.159)	(0.082)	(0.181)	(0.186)	
	LU	-0.127	-0.334*	-0.281*	-0.614*	-0.137	-0.441	-0.378*	-0.215	0.226*	1.697
		(0.245)	(0.138)	(0.141)	(0.114)	(0.087)	(0.250)	(0.093)	(0.154)	(0.081)	
	US	-0.341	-0.006	0.152*	0.816*	-0.195*	1.035*	-0.097	-0.866*	-0.107	1.536
		(0.185)	(0.114)	(0.073)	(0.178)	(0.088)	(0.244)	(0.066)	(0.119)	(0.087)	
DM	AT	0.169	0.061	-0.033	-0.115	0.195*		-0.070	-0.611*	-0.059	2.144
		(0.207)	(0.134)	(0.077)	(0.091)	(0.074)		(0.108)	(0.160)	(0.082)	
	CH	-0.502*	0.231*	-0.519*	0.424*	0.261*		0.132*	0.171	0.210*	1.936
		(0.124)	(0.076)	(0.131)	(0.138)	(0.076)		(0.063)	(0.112)	(0.106)	
	DE	0.027	-0.039	0.003	-0.483*	-0.043		0.006	0.598*	-0.131	1.721
		(0.165)	(0.128)	(0.131)	(0.183)	(0.152)		(0.082)	(0.190)	(0.100)	
	FR	0.494*	-0.337	-0.551*	-0.422*	0.098		0.220	0.846*	0.312*	2.101
		(0.256)	(0.178)	(0.093)	(0.070)	(0.064)		(0.188)	(0.126)	(0.135)	
	GB	-0.072	0.098	-0.112	-0.227*	0.075		-0.194*	-0.489*	-0.107	1.851
		(0.075)	(0.101)	(0.077)	(0.084)	(0.071)		(0.089)	(0.099)	(0.080)	
	IT	0.176	-0.176	0.360*	-0.036	-0.155		-0.944*	-0.329*	0.612*	2.003
		(0.128)	(0.105)	(0.112)	(0.203)	(0.102)		(0.186)	(0.171)	(0.206)	
	JP	0.356*	-0.168	-0.142	0.940*	0.432*		0.341*	-0.702*	0.041	1.780
		(0.149)	(0.147)	(0.152)	(0.184)	(0.174)		(0.133)	(0.331)	(0.245)	
	LU	0.122	0.004	-0.213	-0.400*	-0.164		0.102	-0.409*	0.303*	2.081
		(0.244)	(0.172)	(0.170)	(0.089)	(0.097)		(0.112)	(0.179)	(0.109)	
SFr	AT	0.010	0.012	0.006	-0.204	0.060	0.323	0.436*	-0.499*	0.089	1.737
		(0.225)	(0.151)	(0.089)	(0.111)	(0.095)	(0.177)	(0.129)	(0.183)	(0.082)	
	CH	-0.474*	-0.101	-0.268	0.195	0.061	0.263*	0.217*	0.674*	0.090	1.633
		(0.147)	(0.087)	(0.143)	(0.148)	(0.083)	(0.115)	(0.069)	(0.124)	(0.108)	
	DE	0.159	0.098	0.280*	0.454*	0.006	1.270*	0.069	-0.366*	0.029	1.888
		(0.143)	(0.086)	(0.098)	(0.168)	(0.111)	(0.150)	(0.055)	(0.122)	(0.078)	
	FR	0.705	0.519	0.083	-0.129	0.026	1.615*	0.509	-0.208	-0.532*	1.666
		(0.485)	(0.345)	(0.236)	(0.154)	(0.154)	(0.381)	(0.376)	(0.277)	(0.230)	
	GB	0.289*	0.473*	-0.019	0.144*	0.349*	-0.278*	-0.275*	-0.264*	-0.097	1.929
		(0.074)	(0.101)	(0.064)	(0.069)	(0.059)	(0.089)	(0.077)	(0.076)	(0.074)	
	IT	-0.141	0.332*	-0.441*	0.151	0.112	1.277*	0.161	0.080	-0.256*	1.499
		(0.079)	(0.068)	(0.094)	(0.153)	(0.080)	(0.143)	(0.124)	(0.118)	(0.102)	
	JP	0.730*	0.136	0.080	0.028	0.168	-1.214*	0.130	-0.917*	0.207	2.009
		(0.165)	(0.100)	(0.102)	(0.122)	(0.116)	(0.188)	(0.084)	(0.234)	(0.171)	
	LU	0.285	0.233	0.341	0.160	0.329*	1.600*	-0.206*	-0.422*	-0.355*	1.650
		(0.273)	(0.177)	(0.192)	(0.111)	(0.116)	(0.230)	(0.106)	(0.179)	(0.100)	

*: significantly different from zero at a 5% level of significance (two-sided test)

Standard errors appear in parentheses.

said with generally accepted levels of statistical reliability about the direction of influence. Of the remaining coefficients approximately 55% carry the expected sign. Our a priori expectations are met most consistently (i.e., after weighing the number of significant "wrong" signs against the number of "correct" ones) with regard to deposits of non-banks in US dollars and D-Mark, whereas they are seldom confirmed in the case of interbank deposits in Swiss francs. This finding implies that the regressors are best suited to explaining the movement of cross-border deposits of non-banks denominated in a major reserve currency.

Foreign trade, capital outflow restrictions (principally exchange controls), stock market volume and withholding taxes on dividends exhibit the expected sign most consistently (again: net of wrong signs) whenever their coefficients are significant in a statistical sense. In these cases, the foreign trade variable carries the expected sign 80%, exchange controls 65%, and withholding taxes on dividends and stock market volume each 60% of the time. Trade appears to be an important factor in explaining the movement of cross-border deposits of non-banks in US dollars or D-Mark, which is what one would expect given their function as reserve currencies. Capital outflow restrictions, on the other hand, have their clearest effect in the interbank market, while stock market volume (or the size of the financial center) exhibits the expected sign most consistently in the non-bank depositor market. The level of withholding taxes on dividends seems to be more relevant in the case of cross-border deposits denominated in D-Mark and deposits of non-banks in Swiss francs. The latter finding is a direct result of controlling for autocorrelation. In a previous study (cf. Sheldon, 1991) in which autocorrelation was not considered, high withholding taxes just as often discouraged as attracted cross-border deposits. In fact, with respect to withholding taxes on deposit interest, which should bear a more direct effect on bank deposits, positive signs still dominate.

As differences across countries with regard to capital outflow restrictions, stock market volume and foreign trade narrowed during the estimation period (cf. **Table 1**), these factors may lie behind the overall decrease in cross-border deposit share concentration.

The sign to expect for non-resident fiduciary accounts in Switzerland is uncertain. Fiduciary accounts could serve as substitutes for cross-border deposits in Switzerland (negative sign), they could lead a life of their own (insignificant sign), or they could even act as complements (positive sign). In the case of cross-border deposits of non-banks in US dollars in Switzerland, fiduciary accounts appear to have had a dampening

Table 3: Regression Results for Interbank Deposits (SUR/FGLS)

		capital controls outflow	capital controls inflow	bank secrecy	equity ratio	stock volume	fiduciary	taxes on interest	taxes on dividend	foreign trade	Durbin-Watson
US$	AT	-0.176	0.283*	0.019	-0.434	0.151	0.149	0.448*	-0.170	0.143	1.998
		(0.226)	(0.147)	(0.066)	(0.297)	(0.171)	(0.313)	(0.196)	(0.274)	(0.074)	
	CH	-0.166	-0.045	0.203	-0.009	0.177	-0.213	0.203*	0.124	0.430*	1.963
		(0.229)	(0.113)	(0.198)	(0.243)	(0.093)	(0.202)	(0.101)	(0.153)	(0.128)	
	DE	0.033	0.216	0.019	0.045	-0.028	0.744*	0.053	0.045	0.133	1.929
		(0.198)	(0.147)	(0.117)	(0.143)	(0.168)	(0.161)	(0.074)	(0.179)	(0.074)	
	FR	0.158	0.050	0.583*	0.814	0.719*	-1.463*	-0.939*	1.392*	1.062*	1.767
		(0.456)	(0.329)	(0.234)	(0.674)	(0.312)	(0.464)	(0.401)	(0.394)	(0.299)	
	GB	-0.301*	-0.343	0.015	-0.606*	-0.458*	-0.638*	0.413*	0.090	0.353	2.086
		(0.136)	(0.179)	(0.129)	(0.303)	(0.134)	(0.247)	(0.178)	(0.180)	(0.191)	
	IT	0.091	-0.070	0.655*	0.192	-0.369*	-0.543*	0.856*	-0.938*	0.471	2.027
		(0.151)	(0.110)	(0.176)	(0.323)	(0.118)	(0.173)	(0.214)	(0.293)	(0.294)	
	JP	-0.016	-0.014	-0.070	-0.335	-0.110	0.031	-0.113	-0.269	-0.100	1.996
		(0.143)	(0.065)	(0.088)	(0.244)	(0.154)	(0.264)	(0.100)	(0.221)	(0.190)	
	LU	-0.312	0.076	-0.408*	0.391*	-0.044	-0.161	0.155*	0.332*	-0.046	2.019
		(0.189)	(0.115)	(0.144)	(0.113)	(0.096)	(0.205)	(0.079)	(0.135)	(0.077)	
	US	-0.337	0.215	0.022	-0.353	-0.221	-0.323	0.077	0.025	-0.025	2.012
		(0.235)	(0.169)	(0.122)	(0.444)	(0.217)	(0.435)	(0.129)	(0.289)	(0.147)	
DM	AT	0.316	0.402*	-0.117	0.307*	0.104		0.006	-0.590*	0.111	1.941
		(0.256)	(0.166)	(0.102)	(0.114)	(0.106)		(0.147)	(0.216)	(0.102)	
	CH	-0.569*	0.022	0.190	-0.273	-0.157*		0.051	-0.447*	0.527*	1.826
		(0.135)	(0.080)	(0.141)	(0.148)	(0.081)		(0.069)	(0.122)	(0.114)	
	DE	-0.081	0.211	-0.031	0.162	-0.362*		0.178*	0.345	0.040	1.701
		(0.174)	(0.132)	(0.133)	(0.179)	(0.163)		(0.092)	(0.198)	(0.103)	
	FR	-0.636	0.369	0.057	0.024	-0.141		0.329	0.498	-0.052	1.508
		(0.419)	(0.327)	(0.194)	(0.147)	(0.142)		(0.301)	(0.261)	(0.226)	
	GB	-0.012	-0.246	-0.029	-0.888*	-0.023		0.186	-0.368*	0.081	2.022
		(0.102)	(0.138)	(0.091)	(0.103)	(0.087)		(0.106)	(0.117)	(0.105)	
	IT	-0.278*	0.163	-0.123	0.404*	0.153		0.022	0.060	0.063	1.891
		(0.105)	(0.087)	(0.095)	(0.182)	(0.088)		(0.156)	(0.146)	(0.156)	
	JP	-0.332*	-0.210*	-0.044	-0.133	-0.076		-0.043	-0.305*	-0.113	1.707
		(0.068)	(0.063)	(0.072)	(0.083)	(0.080)		(0.060)	(0.145)	(0.103)	
	LU	-0.570*	-0.048	0.011	-0.343*	0.323*		-0.210*	0.383*	-0.066	1.886
		(0.148)	(0.109)	(0.102)	(0.061)	(0.068)		(0.069)	(0.111)	(0.065)	
SFr	AT	-0.039	-0.274	0.164	-0.136	0.136	-0.520*	0.415*	1.380*	0.030	1.189
		(0.288)	(0.205)	(0.116)	(0.154)	(0.126)	(0.244)	(0.163)	(0.249)	(0.103)	
	CH	-0.235	0.113	0.514*	0.182	-0.217*	0.208	0.234*	-0.191	0.286*	1.895
		(0.172)	(0.089)	(0.143)	(0.153)	(0.080)	(0.126)	(0.074)	(0.124)	(0.117)	
	DE	-0.265*	0.292*	-0.054	-0.080	-0.024*	0.428	-0.055	-0.002	-0.044	1.460
		(0.133)	(0.087)	(0.092)	(0.163)	(0.107)	(0.156)	(0.057)	(0.125)	(0.071)	
	FR	0.163	-0.076	-0.054	-0.111*	-0.050	0.409*	-0.338*	0.485*	-0.028	1.578
		(0.129)	(0.094)	(0.064)	(0.051)	(0.046)	(0.115)	(0.099)	(0.083)	(0.060)	
	GB	0.122	-0.520*	0.009	-1.088*	-0.458*	-0.394*	0.870*	-0.127	0.185	1.749
		(0.122)	(0.163)	(0.101)	(0.110)	(0.097)	(0.140)	(0.121)	(0.123)	(0.125)	
	IT	-0.155	0.002	-0.390*	-0.968*	0.308*	0.952*	-0.035	0.394	0.356	1.640
		(0.150)	(0.123)	(0.160)	(0.262)	(0.136)	(0.237)	(0.222)	(0.212)	(0.210)	
	JP	-0.020	-0.170*	0.251*	-0.192*	-0.083	-0.599*	-0.011	-0.177	-0.062	1.202
		(0.061)	(0.039)	(0.048)	(0.052)	(0.049)	(0.081)	(0.038)	(0.095)	(0.065)	
	LU	0.007	0.385*	-0.492*	0.244*	-0.218*	-0.963*	0.127	0.342*	-0.132	1.661
		(0.216)	(0.139)	(0.151)	(0.089)	(0.093)	(0.180)	(0.083)	(0.143)	(0.080)	

*: significantly different from zero at a 5% level of significance (two-sided test)
Standard errors appear in parentheses.

effect, i.e., served as substitutes. However, in the case of deposits in Swiss francs they seem to have acted as complements.

One has to take care in interpreting the sign of the fiduciary account variable for countries other than Switzerland. It is important to note that the value of this variable, i.e., its distance to the cross-country mean, constantly fell in these countries by definition. Hence, in countries in which the variable carries a positive sign the share of cross-border deposits there must have suffered from the growth of fiduciary accounts in Switzerland. That applies principally to Italy, the US, France and Germany. Since fiduciary funds are usually redeposited abroad in the name of the trustee bank, those countries with a negative fiduciary-account coefficient in the interbank markets appear to have been the principal recipients of these re-invested funds. Japan, the UK and Luxembourg seem to have been among the main beneficiaries. These results accord well with cursory observation (cf. Braillard, 1987, p. 155).

It is interesting to investigate whether those countries which liberalized their capital controls, amended their bank secrecy regulations or changed their withholding tax rates benefited or suffered from these measures. In general, the results do not point to a uniform effect. The removal of exchange controls in the UK in 1980 proved beneficial to interbank deposits in US dollars but detrimental to deposits of non-banks in Swiss francs. The latter finding also holds for the lifting of exchange controls in Japan in the same year. Japan's share of deposits of non-banks in Swiss francs did not profit from this measure. Yet its share of non-bank deposits in US dollars and interbank deposits in D-Mark did increase. Italy's share in the latter market also rose in the wake of exchange control removal after 1984.

The lifting of capital inflow restrictions in Switzerland and Germany did not produce a uniform effect. Surprisingly, the removal of the negative interest rate on cross-border deposits in Switzerland saw its non-bank deposit share in US dollars increase although the measure applied only to Swiss franc accounts.

Tightening of bank secrecy regulations in Austria and Luxembourg proved to be counterproductive, if effective at all. On the basis of the statistically significant coefficients Luxembourg loss market share in US dollar deposits as a result of this measure. Surprisingly, Switzerland suffered losses in the market for interbank deposits following the enactment of the mutual assistance agreement in 1983, although the law probably applied more to non-bank depositors. However, in those markets the agreement seems to have had a positive effect.

The estimation results provide little support for the benefits of international tax competition. Italy and the UK lowered their withholding taxes on deposit interest and achieved a mixed return. Gains in the non-bank market were generally paired with losses in the interbank market. French banks also suffered losses in the interbank market but as a result of raising their withholding taxes on deposit interest. Austrian banks, on the other hand, posted a deposit gain despite an increase in the withholding tax. Increasing the withholding tax on dividends in Italy proved to be clearly detrimental to the cross-border deposit shares of its banks in those markets in which the corresponding coefficient is statistically significant.

Concentrating now on the results for Switzerland, we find that foreign trade and exchange controls had the expected effect on the Swiss share of cross-border bank deposits most often. The coefficient for the foreign trade variable is statistically significant and carries the expected sign in five out of six markets, and the coefficient of the exchange control variable in four of the six. The relative strength of the capital outflow variable on deposit share movement, however, surpasses that of the foreign trade variable in those markets where both are statistically significant. The equity ratio variable always displays the expected positive sign when it is significant. The sign of the withholding tax rate on interest, on the other hand, is consistently significant and "wrong" inasmuch as it implies relative higher withholding taxes would increase rather decrease Switzerland's share of cross-border deposits. The effects of the other variables are not uniform. Stock market volume is seen to have a positive influence on Switzerland's share of non-bank deposits in D-Marks, but a negative effect on interbank deposits in D-Mark and Swiss francs. The bank secrecy variable, strangely enough, only carries a significant expected sign in an interbank market.

5. Conclusions

This study has attempted to extend previous work on the determinants of the cross-country distribution of international bank deposits by developing an econometric model that is less restrictive and at the same time less sensitive to measurement error than the pooled regression approach employed in Grilli (1989). The more flexible modelling scheme controls for cross-country effects and allows for country-specific regression constants and slopes. Tests performed in the study reject the pooled approach and support the broader modelling procedure.

The results provided by the more robust modelling approach present a decidedly different picture than those offered by a pooled regression. In contrast to Grilli (1989) we find scant evidence that the regressors have uniform effects. The influence of a variable generally depends on the country, the currency and/or type of depositor concerned. This result should come as no surprise, however. Few are the markets in which one would expect to find uniform own and cross elasticities. The market for cross-border deposits is no exception. To assume otherwise, according to our findings, leads to biased results.

Foreign trade and exchange controls exhibit the most consistent effect. That suggests that these factors are the prime force behind cross-border deposit share movements, not secret money operations. This interpretation is further supported by the finding that withholding tax rates perform rather poorly, as one would expect if income is usually reported and hence subject to the lower tax rates stemming from reciprocity agreements. The importance of foreign trade leads one to believe, too, that real factors are at the heart of deposit level movements. This stands in contrast to, say, exchange markets where real causes play a backseat role to financial motives. It may be the case, however, that our static modelling scheme is biased against finding financial causes important since it fails to control for announcement effects.

Our overall findings carry over to Switzerland, too, where, in addition, fiduciary accounts seem to be important. According to our results, non-resident depositors feel increasingly encouraged to place US dollars in fiduciary accounts instead of depositing them in a normal bank account. This may be a result of the high withholding taxes in Switzerland, although these rates apparently do not discourage depositors directly. Moreover, fiduciary accounts do not appear to compete with deposit accounts in the Swiss franc deposit market. Hence, in general one should not expect lowering withholding taxes to have a marked influence on Switzerland's share of cross-border deposits.

Our results provide little reason to expect Switzerland's cross-border deposit share to grow in the future. The on-going integration process in the EC should increase trade among the EC member nations and decrease capital controls, which according to our findings will make it increasingly difficult for Swiss banks to attract non-resident deposits. The expected continued growth of fiduciary accounts should also have a dampening effect. Of course funds deposited in other countries are not lost forever. They can be repatriated, albeit at Euromarket interest rates. Hence, consistently below-average interest rates could increasingly become a thing of the past in Switzerland. Swiss banks need not suffer from these developments, however. As multinational firms they earn profits worldwide. But the income-generating strength of the Finanzplatz Schweiz may be in jeopardy.

Literature

Arbeitskreis Kapital und Wirtschaft (AKW) (1990), Standort Schweiz im internationalen Wettbewerb - Produktionsfaktor Kapital, Zürich, October.

Barr, D., and Cuthbertson, K. (1989), "Modelling the Flow of Funds", Bank of England, Discussion Papers, Technical Series, No. 21, February.

Bossard, A., Wirth, M., and Blattner, N. (1992), "The Swiss Banking Sector: Development and Outlook," in this volume.

Braillard, Ph. (1987), Der Finanzplatz Schweiz. Regierungspolitik und internationale Konkurrenzfähigkeit, Geneva.

Breusch, T., and Pagan, A. (1980), "The Lagrange Multiplier Test and its Application to Model Specification in Econometrics," in: Review of Economic Studies, Vol. 47, pp. 1287-94.

Bruni, F. (1990), "Banking and Financial Reregulation towards 1992: The Italian Case," in: J. Dermine (ed.), European Banking in the 1990s, Oxford, pp. 231-257.

Camen, U. (1990), "The Position of Swiss Banks in International Financial Markets: Their On-Balance-Sheet Activities and Fiduciary Transactions," paper presented at the 2nd workshop of the NFP28 project team FAI/ICMB in Geneva, September.

Camen, U. (1992), "The Swiss Position in the International Market for Non-Bank Deposits," in this volume.

Chambost, E. (1982), Die Bankgeheimnisse in den Ländern der Welt, München/Zürich.

Cooper, I., Kaplanis, E. (1986), "Costs to Crossborder Investment and International Equity Market Equilibrium," in: C. Mayer, St. Shafer (ed.), Recent Developments in Corporate Finance, Cambridge, pp. 209-240.

La Federation Internationale des Bourses de Valeur (FIBV) (various years), Activités et Statistiques, Paris.

Friedman, M. (1956), "The Quantity Theory of Money: A Restatement," in: M. Friedman (ed.), Studies in the Quantity Theory of Money, Chicago.

Fukao, M., Hanazaki, M. (1987), "Internationalisation of Financial Markets and the Allocation of Capital," in OECD Economic Studies, No. 8, Spring, pp. 35-92.

Greene, W. (1990), Econometric Analysis, New York.

Grilli, V. (1989), "Europe 1992: Issues and Prospects for the Financial Markets," in: Economic Policy, October, pp. 388-421.

Hsiao, C. (1986), Analysis of Panel Data, Cambridge.

International Monetary Fund (IMF) (various years), Exchange Arrangements and Exchange Restrictions, Annual Report, Washington.

McFadden, D. (1973), "Conditional Logit Analysis of Qualitative Choice Behavior," in: P. Zarembka (ed.), Frontiers in Econometrics, New York, pp. 105-42.

Maddala, G. (1977), Econometrics, New York.

Markowitz, H. (1952), "Portfolio Selection," in: Journal of Finance, Vol. 7, pp. 77-91.

Mishkin, F. (1989), The Economics of Money, Banking, and Financial Markets, Glenview.

Müller, U. (1989), "Die Passivseite der Bankbilanz. Ein Portfolioansatz," in: Schweizerische Zeitschrift für Volkswirtschaft und Statistik, Vol. 125, pp. 55-66.

OECD (1982), Controls on International Capital Movements, Paris.

OECD (1985), Cost and Margins in Banking, Paris.

OECD (1987a), Italy, OECD Economic Surveys, Paris.

OECD (1987b), Bank Profitability, Paris.

OECD (1988), Bank Profitability, Paris.

Schweizerische Bankgesellschaft (SBG) (1991), "Swiss Banks Face the 1990s," in: UBS International Finance, Winter, pp.1-8.

Schweizerische Nationalbank (SNB) (1990), Das schweizerische Bankwesen, Zürich.

Sheldon, G. (1990), "Explaining the Swiss Position in the Market for International Bank Deposits," paper presented at the 2nd workshop of the NFP28 project team FAI/ICMB in Geneva, September.

Sheldon, G. (1991), "Die Stellung der Schweiz im Wettbewerb um internationale Bankeinlagen: Eine internationale Querschnittsanalyse," in: Schweizerische Zeitschrift für Volkswirtschaft und Statistik, Vol. 127, pp. 55-79.

Tobin, J. (1958), "Liquidity Preference as Behavior towards Risk," in: Review of Economic Studies, Vol. 25, pp. 65-86.

Walter, I. (1985), Secret Money, London.

Comment on

Ulrich Camen: "The Swiss Position in the International Market for Non-Bank Deposits"

Jean-Pierre Danthine

This paper focuses on the Swiss share of cross-border non-bank deposits. The key stylized fact is illustrated in **Figure 1** which reveals a dramatic evolution with the Swiss market share being cut in half between 1971 and 1989. The objective is to explain this evolution and thus be in a position to assess future prospects. The paper also contains information on the composition of international non-bank deposits in Switzerland. In the light of this information it appears that the author's choice to include fiduciary accounts in his analysis was judicious since they may have substituted in large part for other deposits. See Sheldon (this volume) for a different perspective.

It is important to distinguish two subperiods in the considered time interval with 1975 being the cut-off point. This is true not only because the evolution of the Swiss market share of international bank-deposits appears quite different before and after that date, but also because the nature of the available data and, as a consequence, the method of analysis differs. Thus the econometric analysis is restricted, for the better or for the worse, to the second subperiod.

Now it appears that, in terms of the loss in market share, most, if not all, of the action is concentrated in the first of the two subperiods, in fact between 1971 and 1974. This is interpreted by the author as "the result of the implementation of capital control restrictions in the years 1971 and 1972 and the tightening of these restrictions in January 1975" (p. 174). While this interpretation is plausible, and indeed must be kept in mind when assessing later the importance of regulatory factors for explaining the evolution of market shares, it is not fully satisfactory in the sense that it does not say why the capital control restrictions of the early Seventies had a once and for all effect that was not offset when the restrictions were lifted. Indeed, the quantitative estimate of the impact of lifting the NIR regulation in 1979 and the significance of the IRB dummy do not appear consistent with the evolution of the early Seventies unless one can justify an asymmetric impact of such measures or one assumes the presence of switching costs. However, none of these considerations find a place in the later modeling.

The post 1975 evolution in the Swiss market share is not so dramatic and in fact does not reveal any obvious trend. This makes the econometric analysis all the more necessary for identifying key determinants and assessing future prospects.

The chosen model is one where the representative consumer selects sequentially and independently the country of investment, then the currency(ies) in which he will invest and finally the type of asset (sight, time deposit or fiduciary accounts). At the first level (the choice of country) it is assumed that one may omit to take expected returns into account, them being essentially the same for the same currency in all countries. While this is reasonable as far as **gross** returns are concerned it may not be so for **returns net of commissions and transaction costs**. Indeed the omission of the latter is regrettable and may go some way towards explaining the relatively low R^2 in the final equation.

Institutional and regulatory factors are thus assumed to dominate and three of them are indeed shown to play a role: banking secrecy, represented by a dummy taking the value of one in January 1983, the "safe haven" property proxied by the price of gold and the negative interest rate justifying a dummy taking the value one until November 1979, zero thereafter.

The main shortcoming of Camen's modeling is the fact that only Swiss institutional variables are given attention. This is inappropriate, even when focusing on the Swiss market share, because what is relevant is Switzerland's position relative to its competitors, not its absolute position. This statement accords with the underlying model since the other first stage equation deals with the market share of the "Rest of the world", for which it is difficult to argue that only Swiss variables matter. More importantly it is often argued that the bulk of the recent changes in financial markets relevant for Switzerland have occurred abroad and that it is by standing still that the Swiss position has deteriorated. The incriminated omission is thus likely to be of substance. It is also damaging statistically because there is very little action on the right hand side of the estimated equation (**Table 1**): besides lagged level variables, the explanatory power is concentrated in the two dummies, the price of gold and the SFR/$ exchange rate whose presence is not fully in the spirit of the model.

This being said, interpreting the results of this equation at face value leads to an appreciation that is considerably less pessimistic than the impression obtained from the initial look at **Figure 1**. Yes the loosening of banking secrecy matters, but, by and large, its effect is to offset the removal of the negative interest rate regulation. The "safe haven" role of deposits in SFR appears to continue being significant. And all in all the long run implications of the equation, while not fully clear, are not obviously unfavourable[1].

Table 2 records the results of the second stage estimation, representing the choice of currency. The necessity of proper estimation of price variables, i.e. risk adjusted expected rates of returns, is unescapable at this stage and the results, implying a role for nominal but not real rates, generate some skepticism about whether this notoriously difficult task has been handled satisfactorily. While this observation undermines our confidence in the results of the estimated second stage equation, it also serves to underline the usefulness of the independence hypothesis enabling to do without this requirement at the level of the country choice.

The author observes with surprise that at this stage of budgeting the lifting of the negative interest rate regulation does not appear to play a role. This is indeed paradoxical since it is at the level of the choice of currency that one would have expected this regulation to bite. One possible interpretation serves to remind us of the usual identification problems. It is clear that the capital control regulations were instituted in the early Seventies in the face of changes in the demand for deposits in Swiss francs. They were then removed when the demand pressures subsided. The absence of any discernable impact of the equilibrium quantities simply could mean that the regulatory change was well adapted to the demand shift. By the same token, this observation highlights the fact that the measures taken in the early seventies were certainly excessive and, as we have seen, the cost of this excess may well be permanent[2].

---

1 As an illustration, one may observe that equation 1 (**Table 1**) implies a positive steady state value for the dependent variable. Indeed with the sample means of LNBCH and LRWRP equal to, respectively, 15.87 and 6.53 (these figures are courtesy of the author), the negative terms in the equation add up to a steady state value of .103 which is smaller than the constant term, while it is clear from Figure 1 that the sample mean of LRWRP is positive.

2 Unless the effect was precisely the one wanted which is difficult to believe. Pre-1971 data would be very helpful here. They would tell us in particular whether the 30% market share of 1971 was exceptional in which case the drop of the next three years could appear as a return to normalcy contrary to what is implicitely assumed in the text.

To conclude, one may want to ask whether it was a good idea to adopt a purely time series approach? My feeling is that, at least when restricting the scope to Swiss variables only, there has not been enough changes in institutional and regulatory variables to explain convincingly the evolution of the Swiss market share in international non-bank deposits. As a result, at this stage of the analysis, we cannot claim enough confidence in our understanding of the decisive factors to venture a reasonably safe appreciation of future prospects.

Comment on

George Sheldon: "Explaining the Cross-Country Distribution of International Bank Deposits"

Vittorio Grilli

The rapid and extensive changes occured in international financial markets during the 1980's are arguably one of the most impressive economic phenomena in recent years. The process of integration of the European markets triggered by the 1992 project and the possibility of a future European monetary union suggest that more changes will be occurring. It is surprising, therefore, that so little academic research has been devoted to the analysis of international financial markets and of international commercial banking.

In several OECD countries, deposits held by non-residents represent a significant part of banks' balance sheets, but their importance differs across countries (ranging from 20% to 80% of total liabilities). Moreover, countries' shares of the world market for non-resident deposits have experienced large changes in the past few years. In order to forecast future trends in this market, it is crucial to understand and explain these cross-country differences and time series variations. Sheldon's paper is a welcomed contribution in this, still young, area of research.

When I initially approached the problem (Grilli, 1989) I was surprised by the absence of research in the field. This implied a lack of any established theoretical modelling or econometric practice on this topic. Having to start from scratch, my analysis was, in several respect, somewhat primitive. Sheldon's paper addresses some of the issues for which my analysis was the least satisfactory, and introduces several important improvements.

There are several directions in which substantial contributions in the area could be made: in the theoretical modelling, in the data collection and in the econometric methodology. This paper does not address any theoretical issue but, instead, concentrates on the empirical aspects of the problem.[1] In the following, I shall discuss

---

1 Other papers in this volume try to model theoretically the problem of international trade in banking services.

the major innovations of this paper, contrasting them with my previous analysis, and try to identify the parts that I consider important and valuable and the ones on which I disagree.

The first issue I want is address to the paper's last, i.e. its conclusions. Sheldon summarizes its findings in three main conclusions. First, and contrary to my results, tax treatment and secrecy laws are not important considerations for international depositors. Second, exchange rate controls are the most important institutional determinant of non-resident deposits. Third, Switzerland will find it difficult to reverse the negative trend that its world share of international deposits have displayed in recent years. While I agree in principle with the last two points, I strongly disagree with the first. My skepticism is motivated by two distinct considerations. First, the author's results do not support this strong conclusion. Second, and perhaps more importantly, the econometric methodology employed in the paper cannot capture the importance of institutional aspects. Let me start with the first point. One major problem in interpreting the author's results is the large number of estimated coefficients (about 500) that must be analyzed. Reaching a conclusion inevitably involves some judgement. One way of summarizing the results is by asking how many times a variable is significant and, at the same time, has the expected sign. This is done in **Table 1**. From the table it is clear that bank secrecy and withholding taxes do not perform any worse than the other variables. In fact, they are amongst the most significant. Another way to look at the findings is to ask whether the results for each country are consistent across different currency markets. In other words, if we find that withholding taxes are important for dollar deposits in France, they should be important for DMark deposits in France, since regulations are identical across currencies within the same country. **Table 2** summarizes for each country, which variables are significant and with the correct sign, in at least two out of the three currency markets. From this table as well it is difficult to reach the conclusion that secrecy and, especially, tax treatment, are of no importance.

While taxes and secrecy do not seem to perform worse than the other variables under investigation, it is true that the global explanatory power of the regressions is quite low. Only 20% of the coefficients with the expected sign are also significant. Why this poor performance? This leads us to the second point of the discussion: the econometric methodology. The paper introduces several potential improvements over my previous analysis. First of all, Sheldon correctly points out that there might be additional country specific characteristics that are not captured by the institutional dummy variables. He argues, therefore, in favour of introducing of fixed effects in the analysis. Given the author has access to quarterly data, and not just annual data as in my study, degrees of freedom are not a problem and the introduction of fixed effects would have been an interesting exercise. This, however, was not done in the paper. Second, Sheldon argues that the assumption that a country's share of foreign deposits is only affected by that country's own variables is too restrictive. If foreign variables are also important, their omission could bias the estimates. While this is a good point in principle, I doubt that in this specific instance biases in the estimates are likely to occur. For this to be the case, in fact, the omitted variables must be correlated with the explanatory variables. It is unlikely that institutional characteristics, like capital controls and tax treatment, are correlated across countries. This does not mean that including these variables would be of no use, since the explanatory power of the regression is likely to increase.

In order to capture these cross-country effects, Sheldon does not pool the data of all countries together by using a panel estimation strategy, as in my previous work. Instead, he estimated a system of single-country equations. The influence of foreign variables is introduced by constructing explanatory variables in terms of deviations from the cross-country means. While this approach is theoretically sound, the nature of the variables under investigation makes it unadvisable and, I believe, this is the reason of the low level of explanatory power of the analysis. The problem is that the crucial explanatory variables - exchange rate controls, tax treatment, secrecy laws - show almost no variations overtime. All the information contained in this data set is the cross-country variation. It is crucial, therefore, to use a cross-section approach and not just a time series approach. Understanding why the ability of a country in attracting foreign deposits has changed over time and determining the different roles played by institutional factors in different countries are important issues and a time series analysis of the type employed by Sheldon is, in principle, the appropriate way to proceed. However, with the data at hand, this approach is unfeasible.

While I disagree on the choice of econometric strategy, the quality of the data used in this study is certainly superior to that of those used in my previous work. Instead of IMF annual series on total non-resident deposits, Sheldon uses quarterly BIS data which have the advantage of being disaggregated both by currency of denomination and by residency of the depositors. The quality of the data is, indeed, an important improvement of this paper. The use of deposit data disaggregated by currency of denomination eliminates valuation problems that contaminate the IMF data. Given that currency disaggregation is available, Sheldon should have controlled not only for the characteristics of the country in which a deposit is held, but also for the characteristics of the currency in which it is denominated. In particular, it would have been important to include, as explanatory variables, some measure of expected change and volatility of the relevant exchange rates. It is also disappointing that the author did not make use of the information on the country of residence of the depositors. This, among other things, could have allowed for a more appropriate identification of the relevant withholding taxes. It is also awkward that the author decided to estimate jointly the equations referring to deposits denominated in the same currency but held in different countries while, at the same time, he assumed that the markets for foreign deposits denominated in different currencies within the same country are independent. Finally, I find the inclusion of fiduciary accounts as an explanatory variable troublesome. While it is clear that foreign deposit and fiduciary account decisions are related to one another, this relationship goes both ways and, thus, fiduciary accounts are not a proper independent variable.

In conclusion, this paper is a serious and careful study of the markets for foreign deposits, However, like all empirical work, there is still scope for improvements and extensions.

Literature

Grilli, V. (1989), "Europe 1992: Issues and Prospects for the Financial Markets", in: Economic Policy, October.

Table 1 Number of Significant Coefficients with Correct Sign*

Non Banks							
KO	KI	SEC	EQR	STK	TXI	TXD	FT
4	2	3	9	7	8	14	9
Banks							
KO	KI	SEC	EQR	STK	TXI	TXD	FT
6	3	4	4	3	3	5	4

* Fiduciary accounts have been excluded since they have a theoretically ambiguous sign.

KO = controls on capital outflow
KI = controls on capital inflow
SEC = bank secrecy
EQR = equity ratio
STK = stock volume
TXI = withholding tax on interest income
TXD = withholding tax on dividend income
FT = foreign trade volume

Table 2 Consistency Across Currency Markets* (2 out of 3 Markets)

Country	Non Banks	Banks
AT	STK, TXD	-
CH	KO, EQR, FT	FT
GER	EQR	-
FRA	-	TXI
UK	TXI, TXD	-
ITA	TXI	-
JAP	TXD	KI
LUX	TXI, TXD	SEC

* Fiduciary accounts have been excluded since they have a theoretically ambiguous sign.

KO = controls on capital outflow
KI = controls on capital inflow
SEC = bank secrecy
EQR = equity ratio
STK = stock volume
TXI = withholding tax on interest income
TXD = withholding tax on dividend income
FT = foreign trade volume

Comment on

Ulrich Camen: "The Swiss Position in the International Market for Non-Bank Deposits"

George Sheldon: "Explaining the Cross-Country Distribution of International Bank Deposits"

Julian S. Alworth*

The papers by Camen and Sheldon represent important contributions to the better understanding of the determinants of banks' funding behaviour in the international market. I shall comment on each of the papers separately, although some of my remarks apply to both studies.

While the major trend identified in the paper by Camen - the decline in the share of non-bank deposits held with banks in Switzerland - is probably broadly correct, it is difficult to draw precise inferences from international banking data such as those of the IMF over such a long period. The coverage and quality of the banking data - both for banks in Switzerland and for banks in other countries - have varied significantly over time. For example, a quick perusal of International Financial Statistics (IFS) published by the IMF reveals that the Cayman Islands and the Bahamas started reporting figures on deposits by non-banks only at end-1979 and end-1983 respectively. Taken together, at end-1983 the two centres had roughly the same volume of non-bank deposits as reported in IFS for banks in Switzerland (including trustee accounts). Such breaks in series undoubtedly account for significant changes in the recorded market share of banks in Switzerland. They may also bias the econometric results. For example, in the econometric section the coefficient on the dummy variable for Convention XVI is interpreted as indicating that the relaxation of banking secrecy rules in 1983 influenced the market share of Switzerland. Another interpretation might be that the data changed in 1983.

* These comments reflect the author's own views and not necessarily those of the BIS.

Furthermore, I am surprised that, in comparing the typology of deposits, fiduciary ("trustee") accounts are compared with deposits of Swiss banks worldwide. A comparison between fiduciary accounts held with banks in Switzerland and foreign deposits by non-banks in Switzerland would have been more relevant and certainly more dramatic. At end-1990 fiduciary accounts with banks in Switzerland amounted to well over $200 billion, whereas straight non-bank deposits represented only $16 billion in all currencies.

I should also like to add that these data-related problems are magnified when utilising monthly data. To my knowledge only a very small number of countries supply such data to the IMF, and information on banks located in offshore centres, particularly in the Caribbean, is notoriously unreliable.

As regards the estimations, I have only one comment. As far as detailed coefficient values are concerned, I am not surprised at the marked responsiveness of the share of non-bank deposits in Switzerland to exchange rate movements. If the non-dollar component of non-bank deposits is higher in Switzerland than it is on average in other centres - as indeed happens to be the case - an appreciation of the Swiss franc relative to the dollar (which for most periods corresponds by and large to an appreciation of all currencies relative to the dollar) raises, for accounting reasons, the share of non-bank deposits in Switzerland relative to those elsewhere. Although Camen is conscious of such valuation effects, he interprets the coefficients as indicating an improvement in Swiss banks' competitiveness.

Sheldon's paper represents a serious attempt to explain some of the determinants of international banking activity. It is also one of the first to exploit the data on international banking activity collected by the Bank for International Settlements (BIS), which hitherto has not been sufficiently utilised for analytical empirical studies of the financial markets. I am in broad agreement with the somewhat "ad hoc" modelling strategy employed, and with Sheldon's comments on the previous paper by Grilli, particularly in respect of the cross-centre effects. At the same time, I would add that Grilli was unable to utilise the same sort of information available for this study.

My comments, therefore, will be of three types. Firstly, I shall highlight some of the pitfalls in using the BIS data which may have affected the econometric study. Secondly, I shall present a brief assessment of the estimations, particularly of the variables employed. Finally, I shall comment on some of the problems involved in extrapolating these results in order to assess the influence of locational factors.

The BIS quarterly data present the most complete and detailed picture of international banking activity currently available. Figures are reported on a quarterly basis by fourteen industrial countries on banks' external business broken down by currency, location and type of counterparty (bank/non-bank). For example, the statistics reported to the BIS include data on Deutsche Mark deposits by German non-bank residents in Luxembourg. The published data, however, are presented in a more aggregated form. The data from end-1977 to end-1990 with the exception of minor breaks in series are reasonably reliable for the purposes of this type of study. Information has also been available since end-1983 on banks' international business in the most important offshore centres, although some of the breakdowns are not reported.

There are two important developments which are not mentioned in Sheldon's paper but which have affected the character of business carried out in several financial centres. One, apparently not considered in Sheldon's paper, was the opening of International Banking Facilities in New York and the Japan Offshore Market in Tokyo in December 1981 and December 1986 respectively. While the specific regulatory details governing these two offshore accounts differ, they are similar in two important respects: (a) deposits on these accounts are not subject to reserve requirements, and (b) they are exempt from withholding tax. These changes had important implications for the funding behaviour of banks in these two centres. In the case of the IBF, a considerable volume of assets was rebooked from the offshore centres in the Caribbean to the offshore accounts in these two centres following their opening, which subsequently, generated a considerable volume of new business, especially in the case of Japan. In essence, the opening of these offshore centres means that there are two financial centres for foreign depositors in each of these countries.

The second development of some importance is the growth of securities issued by banks, for which it is not possible to obtain a bank/non-bank breakdown owing to the negotiable and bearer nature of the instruments involved. In particular, for most CDs issued by banks in London a bank/non-bank breakdown is not available.

I shall now turn to the equations. Let me begin with what I believe to be two mis-specifications of the tax effects. The first concerns the treatment of fiduciary accounts as an independent variable rather than as a separate set of accounts. The basic difference between a fiduciary account and an account with a Swiss bank is that the former is exempt from withholding tax. Since most of the funds are channelled to related offices of banks in Switzerland, from the standpoint of an individual bank there is no real difference between a fiduciary account and a deposit. The relative stagnation of non-bank deposits in Switzerland and the rapid growth of trustee accounts is an indication of a strong tax effect unless the opposite can be shown to be the case. Hence, in my view, it would be more appropriate to model trustee accounts as a separate financial centre. The second mis-specification of tax effects arises from the omission of interest rate variables. Although posted interbank deposit rates are uniform worldwide the actual interest payments received by individuals depend on the level of withholding taxes in various centres. The higher the level of nominal interest rates, the larger the absolute interest differential resulting from withholding taxes. In other words, location matters more with high levels of nominal interest rates than with low levels. Using Euro-rates and statutory withholding taxes to compute a tax wedge would also have the advantage of creating variability in the tax parameter over time.

Another important variable not considered by Sheldon is reserve requirements. To be sure, special reserve requirements on capital inflows such as those imposed in Germany in the early 1970s are captured by the inflow restriction dummy. But general reserve requirements also matter for individual banks' funding decisions of their international business. Dollar deposits in New York and dollar deposits in London are not the same thing. In this case, too, the level of interest rates is important: the interest rate differential between Euro and domestic deposits widens as interest rates increase.

As for the variables employed in this paper, I find the explanation of the significance of withholding taxes on dividends somewhat perplexing: namely that deposits are temporarily parked in a country before they are invested in shares. The volume of cross-border investments in shares is minuscule in comparison with that of deposits, and transaction-motivated deposits in the international markets cannot really be considered to be of prime importance. Dividend taxes are probably just a proxy for "environmental" factors which are not captured by other variables. However, they may matter in another, more subtle way. Banks earn a greater margin on business with non-banks than on that with other banks. They may wish to earn profits and distribute dividends from countries with low profit and dividend taxes. Accordingly, banks with worldwide operations will try to attract non-bank funds where they want profits to be realised, i.e. countries with low dividend taxes.

I am somewhat bemused by the use of the catch-phrase "thick-market externalities" to describe financial market centres in terms of their international deposits (though this expression was originally used by Grilli). The Bahamas and the Cayman Islands, two locations not considered in Sheldon's paper, are "large" banking centres in terms of the size of their deposits. There is no great cost advantage in terms of physical facilities or financial infrastructure in these centres. In fact, the books are run from New York and no physical presence is needed. GNP or stock market trading (if there is such a thing) would not be a rough indicator of thick-market externalities in this case and certainly not a useful explanatory variable of cross-border deposits.

I am also perplexed by the equating of banking nationality with location implicit in using the ratio of equity capital to total liabilities (the soundness proxy). Let us take, for example, the, admittedly extreme, case of London: deposits with British banks account for only 21% of total cross-border deposits. Do changes in the equity capital of British banks indicate a change in the desirability of placing deposits with a Swiss or German bank in London?

Finally, I would note the omission of seasonal variables. There are very pronounced seasonal movements in the case of certain groups of institutions, most notably banks in Japan. Moreover, seasonal patterns of banks' behaviour had changed over. In the early 1980s, European banks' end-of-year business was the most important source of seasonal savings. As the Japanese have grown in relative importance, the building up of positions at end-March and end-September has become of greater significance.

Let me now turn to what I consider to be the three most important drawbacks of using such studies to assess whether or not a particular centre is attractive - drawbacks for which, I should add, the authors cannot be blamed given the nature of the data at their disposal. One specific major drawback, as I see it, is the lack of information on the country breakdown of depositors. This is important for two reasons. Firstly, BIS data reveal that cross-border deposits in a particular currency are dominated by depositors from the country of issue of that currency: German depositors in Deutsche Mark, US depositors in dollars, etc. It is the preferences of these depositors for different financial centres which tend to determine where banks are located. For example, why are 38% of German residents' Deutsche Mark deposits in the Euro-market held in Luxembourg but only 1% of US residents' dollar deposits placed in that country? Secondly, although there have been some important changes in recent years, there tends to be a "home country bank bias" when non-banks place funds abroad. German residents place deposits in Luxembourg with German banks, US money market mutual funds tend to place funds in London with US banks, etc. Clearly there are important interactions between where banks of particular nationalities wish to locate and where depositors from specific countries will place their deposits.

Another drawback of these studies is that they tend to focus on only one set of locational factors: viz. those affecting cross-border deposits by banks or non-banks. Banks carry out other activities: lending, foreign exchange market transactions, securities dealing, etc. Each of these types of activity has its own characteristics which find the environment to which they are best suited in different financial centres. For example, before the implementation of banking supervision on a consolidated basis in the early 1980s one of the reasons for shifting activity abroad was to escape domestic regulations governing large exposures and capital constraints on leverage. Moreover, foreign banks may also be active in domestic business in each of the financial centres in which they operate. In the United States, for example, the agencies, branches and subsidiaries of foreign banks accounted for about 25% of industrial and commercial bank loans in 1985-89.

Finally, much international banking activity is of a purely domestic character. For example, in Japan restrictions on domestic money markets have encouraged banks to channel funds through offshore banking units (JOM) to other offshore centres and return these funds by way of their domestic accounts. It is doubtful whether the growth of the international books of banks in Japan as a result of such round-tripping can be interpreted as an increase in the competitiveness of Japan as a financial centre.

In summary, I consider that Sheldon's careful study of the determinants of non-bank deposits in various centres represents a very useful contribution to our understanding of the determinants of international banking activity. Its results will provide a useful benchmark for assessing future work in this area.

Part V: International Financial Centres

On the Attractiveness of International Financial Centres

Matthias Jeger, Urs Haegler, Roland Theiss

1. Introduction

In spite of its growing importance the problem of measuring and explaining the extent to which a financial centre succeeds in attracting competitors from other centres has not yet received a lot of attention in research. A paper by Choi et al. (1986) is among the more creative exceptions to this rule. The authors address the issue of attractiveness (which is one aspect of competitiveness) by investigating the following questions:

In which financial centres are foreign banks represented? How are the financial centres connected with each other? Has the pattern of interconnectedness changed over time? Why do banks prefer some of the centres more than others?

To answer these questions Choi et al. study the distribution of the outlets of the world's Top 300 banks across important financial centres in 1970 and 1980, respectively. In this paper, we continue their study by updating their data to 1989 and by analysing the observed distributional changes that have taken place since their work (sections 3 to 5). In addition we attempt to give some theoretical arguments (section 6) and then pursue the insights they provide using extended empirical specifications (sections 7 to 9).

2. Identification of Financial Centres

Choi et al. (1986) first identify which financial centres are important by drawing on Reed (1981), who reports on the opinions of experts. Consensus opinion deems the following centres as being significant: London (LO), New York (NY), Paris (PA), Frankfurt and Hamburg (FH), Tokyo (TK), Singapore (SI), Hong Kong (HK), Los Angeles and San Francisco (LS), Zurich and Geneva (ZG), Amsterdam (AM), Brussels (BR), Panama (PN), Milan and Rome (MR), Toronto and Montreal (TM).

Financial centres of a country were condensed into one if geographically not too distant. In order to ensure comparability with Choi et al. (1986) we did not alter their selection of the centres.

3. The Matrices of Interconnectedness

Tables 1 and 2 are matrices describing the headquarters and offices ("offices" stands for simple representative offices, branches and subsidiaries or, in some cases, majority joint ventures) of the Top 300 banks in the world across the financial centres chosen above. The diagonal elements give the number of banks headquartered in the centres. The off-diagonal elements show the number of their offices located in other centres. The Top 300 banks were chosen from the annual publication "The Banker" on the basis of either equity or assets and according to whether they are headquartered in one of the financial centres selected.

These criteria were met by 104 banks in 1989, i.e. the sample is comparable in size (but not necessarily in composition) to the one in Choi et al. (105 banks for 1980). Offices are counted only once, even if a bank has several offices in a centre. Office locations were determined by relying on "The Banker's Almanac and Yearbook". **Table 1** gives the office distribution for 1970 and 1980; **Table 2** contains the corresponding values for 1989. The column totals in the tables indicate the total number of banks in the sample that are present in a given centre. Instead of the number of banks in a centre it would be interesting to know how many persons a bank employs in a centre. But in most cases this information cannot be drawn from "The Banker's Almanac".

The tables confirm the dominance of London, New York and Tokyo as financial centres. London has recovered from the setback in the 1970s and regained the first position. London, New York, Tokyo and, slightly less pronounced, Hong Kong are today's most important financial centres. In the 1980s Hong Kong overtook Frankfurt/Hamburg and has almost caught up with Tokyo. Hong Kong is followed by Frankfurt/Hamburg, Singapore and Zurich/Geneva, i.e. Zurich/ Geneva gained significantly on the others during the last decade and advanced from rank 12 to rank 7.

Table 1: Head Offices of Major Banks and Their Representation in Other Centers, 1970 and 1980*

FROM \ TO	LO	NY	PA	FH	TO	SI	HK	LS	ZG	AM	BR	PN	MR	TM	Σ
LO	14	9	8	4	4	1	1	2	1	7	2	0	2	0	55
	8	*8*	*6*	*5*	*8*	*4*	*7*	*4*	*3*	*3*	*4*	*1*	*2*	*4*	*67*
NY	10	13	8	7	8	3	6	0	3	5	4	2	5	1	75
	9	*10*	*8*	*8*	*8*	*9*	*8*	*7*	*5*	*3*	*4*	*4*	*7*	*4*	*94*
PA	5	3	7	3	3	1	1	1	1	4	3	1	4	0	37
	11	*13*	*14*	*8*	*9*	*6*	*9*	*4*	*2*	*5*	*3*	*3*	*8*	*2*	*97*
FH	3	2	1	12	1	1	0	0	0	0	0	0	0	0	20
	4	*6*	*2*	*12*	*4*	*3*	*5*	*1*	*0*	*0*	*1*	*1*	*1*	*2*	*42*
TO	8	8	2	2	17	2	2	6	1	1	1	0	1	1	52
	14	*15*	*7*	*10*	*23*	*11*	*8*	*11*	*4*	*2*	*3*	*2*	*1*	*6*	*117*
SI	0	0	0	0	0	1	1	0	0	0	0	0	0	0	2
	1	*1*	*0*	*0*	*1*	*1*	*1*	*0*	*0*	*0*	*0*	*0*	*0*	*0*	*5*
HK	1	1	1	1	1	1	1	1	0	0	0	0	0	0	8
	1	*1*	*1*	*1*	*1*	*1*	*1*	*1*	*1*	*1*	*0*	*0*	*0*	*1*	*11*
LS	5	4	1	2	5	1	5	8	1	1	2	1	1	0	37
	4	*4*	*3*	*4*	*4*	*4*	*4*	*4*	*1*	*1*	*1*	*1*	*2*	*2*	*39*
ZG	1	1	1	0	1	1	1	1	3	1	0	0	0	1	12
	3	*3*	*2*	*0*	*3*	*2*	*3*	*3*	*5*	*1*	*0*	*0*	*0*	*2*	*27*
AM	2	2	0	0	1	0	2	1	0	3	0	0	0	0	11
	2	*3*	*0*	*0*	*2*	*2*	*2*	*2*	*0*	*4*	*1*	*1*	*1*	*0*	*20*
BR	0	1	0	1	0	0	0	0	0	0	3	0	0	0	5
	3	*3*	*1*	*1*	*3*	*3*	*2*	*0*	*2*	*0*	*7*	*0*	*2*	*0*	*27*
PN	0	0	0	0	0	0	0	0	0	0	0	1	0	0	1
	0	*1*	*0*	*0*	*0*	*0*	*0*	*0*	*0*	*0*	*0*	*1*	*0*	*0*	*2*
MR	4	5	4	5	0	1	0	1	2	0	3	0	12	1	38
	7	*7*	*4*	*6*	*5*	*4*	*3*	*4*	*0*	*0*	*4*	*0*	*10*	*3*	*57*
TM	5	5	2	2	4	0	4	4	1	1	2	0	1	7	38
	5	*5*	*4*	*4*	*5*	*4*	*5*	*5*	*1*	*1*	*1*	*2*	*2*	*5*	*49*
Σ	58	54	35	39	45	13	24	25	13	23	20	5	26	11	391
	72	*80*	*52*	*59*	*76*	*54*	*58*	*46*	*24*	*21*	*29*	*16*	*36*	*31*	*654*
Rank	1	2	5	4	3	11	8	7	11	9	10	14	6	13	
	3	*1*	*7*	*4*	*2*	*6*	*5*	*8*	*12*	*13*	*11*	*14*	*9*	*10*	

[a] The figures for 1980 are shown in italics below the figures for 1970. - Sum of main diagonal: 102 in 1970 and 105 in 1980.

Source: The Banker [1971; 1981]; The Bankers' Almanac and Yearbook [1970-1971; 1980-1981].

Choi et al. (1987), p. 50. **FAI**

Table 2 Table of Interconnectedness 1989

From \ To	AM	BR	FH	HK	LO	LS	MR	NY	PA	PN	SI	TK	TM	ZG	sum		max
AM	3	3	3	3	3	2	2	3	3		3	3	1	3	35		3
BR	1	7		3	4	1	2	4	2		2	3		3	32		7
FH	2	2	13	7	8	5	2	7	3		5	5	3	5	67		13
HK			1	1	1			1		1	1	1			7		1
LO	3	3	1	6	8	2	4	6	5		4	7	4	4	57		8
LS	1	1	2	3	4	4	1	4	1	1	4	4	1	2	33		4
MR	2	4	9	7	9	5	12	8	7		2	5	2	4	76		12
NY	3	4	9	10	10	5	9	10	9	1	10	8	6	8	102		10
PA	5	5	9	9	10	6	9	10	10	3	9	8	6	7	106		10
PN										1					1		1
SI				2	3	3		3			3	3			17		3
TK	3	5	12	16	20	13	4	21	9	7	14	22	9	13	168		22
TM	1	1	4	6	5	4	3	6	3	1	5	6	6	1	52		6
ZG			2	3	3	2		3	1	2	2	3	2	4	27		4
sum	24	35	65	76	88	52	48	86	53	17	64	78	40	54	780		104
Rank	13	12	5	4	1	9	10	2	8	14	6	3	11	7			

Sources: The Banker's Almanac and Yearbook (1990), The Banker (1990) FAI

Even more impressive is Singapore's thrust. Having been level with Zurich/Geneva in 1970, it has since outdistanced the Swiss financial centre.

4. The Significance of the Differentiation between Representative Offices, Branches and Subsidiaries

Generally, offices are staffed by only a few employees and in most cases economically less important than branches or subsidiaries. Especially in Frankfurt/Hamburg and Los Angeles/San Francisco the share of representative offices lies above average. The type of representation chosen is expected to depend on factors like taxation as well as regulatory and other entry conditions.

Unlike branches and subsidiaries, simple representative offices are in most cases easier to establish. Canada, for instance, does not permit the establishment of foreign banks. In Japan a strict reciprocity requirement holds, and the procedures are involved. For instance, at least until 1987 not a single foreign bank acquired a Japanese bank, "above all because of the many legal problems" (Braillard, 1987, p. 59).

Given the fact that in Japan licenses are given only case by case, it is quite amazing that so many banks are represented in Tokyo. This is another hint at the significance of Japan. Perhaps, the financial strength of this country is even greater than expressed by our figures. These observations are to be taken into consideration when we analyse the determinants of establishing either representative offices, branches or subsidiaries in a foreign country.

5. The Degree of Interconnectedness

Choi et al. use four measures to quantify the degree of interconnectedness:

a) The first measure gives the ratio of actual to potential links. The numerator is the number of nonzero cells and the denominator is the total number of off-diagonal cells. In a matrix of $n=14$ financial centres, at most $(n^2-n)=182$ direct links between two centres exist.

b) The second measure presents the percentage of pairs of centres (i,j) which display a direct link in at least one direction. The numerator consists of the number of cells in which either Y_{ij} or Y_{ji} is different from zero, and the denominator is equal to one half of the number of off-diagonal cells (=91).

c) In analogy to b) we can also ascertain the percentage of pairs of centres which display direct links in both directions. The numerator then consists of the number of cells in which both Y_{ij} and Y_{ji} are different from zero, and the denominator is again equal to 91.

d) As a fourth measure Choi et al. use Cohen's $\varkappa$:

$$\varkappa = 1 - \frac{\Sigma_i P_{ij} - \Sigma_i P_{i.} \cdot P_{.j}}{1 - \Sigma_i P_{i.} \cdot P_{.j}} \tag{5.1}$$

where $P_{ij} = Y_{ij} / \Sigma_i \Sigma_j Y_{ij}$.

$\varkappa$ can take any value between one and zero. A value of one indicates complete dispersion, i.e. every bank from each centre has a representative office, branch or subsidiary in every other centre. A zero signals extreme concentration on the main diagonal or no interpenetration. The measure takes into account the actual cell frequencies, not just the presence or absence of a direct link.

Table 3 presents the results for all four measures. The findings for 1970 and 1980 are those of Choi et al., while those for 1989 are new. From 1970 to 1989 all four measures rose. We interpret this as an increase in the interconnectedness between the financial centres. But at least two caveats are in order. Firstly, we are only looking at the offices of the banks in our sample. Secondly, banks vary to a degree from sample to sample.

A comparison of the measures across time indicates how the links have changed. The following points stick out.

Increases in the four measures of interconnectedness are most visible between 1970 and 1980, while the measures for 1980 and 1989 are practically identical. But this finding does not preclude changes between 1980 and 1989. The difference between the measures only capture net changes. It is possible that in some cases increases in interconnectedness have been offset by corresponding declines. A comparison of the cells of 1980 and 1989 shows that, indeed, some major gross changes have taken place.

Let us first have a look at the changes in the one-way links. Unlike in 1989, no link existed in 1980 between FH and AM, FH and ZG, MR and ZG, ZG and PN as well as between HK and PN. The offices from AM, FH or LO in PN disappeared completely.

Table 3 The Degree of Interconnectedness

Number of links				
	a) total	b) one-way	c) two-way	
1970	109	71	54	
1980	140	83	58	
1989	141	85	59	
	Percentages of links			
	a) total	b) one-way	c) two-way	d) Cohen's κ
1970	60	78	59	0.82
1980	77	91	64	0.92
1989	79	93	65	0.94

FAI

New links in both directions arose between AM and the centres of the EC countries. Banks from MR, BR and FH have opened offices in AM since 1980. In return, banks from AM established themselves in PA and TM. Hong Kong banks have closed all their offices in LS, TM, AM, ZG and PA. Likewise, the mutual link between PN and NY has vanished. On the other hand a two-sided link between FH and ZG has arisen.

If one considers only the branches or only the subsidiaries, one recognizes that the degree of interconnectedness with respect to born branches and subsidiaries was lower in 1989 than in 1970.

6. Some Theoretical Reflections on Foreign Direct Investment by Banks

Before proceeding to an empirical analysis we present some theoretical reflections that form the basis of the specifications which we estimate afterwards.

Basic to the ideas presented is the presumption that in going to other financial centres, banks either follow the non-bank multinational enterprises originating from their own centre or move with their country's exports in order to meet the growing demand for banking services in connection with international trade, i.e., to support these transactions by geographical closeness to importers. There are some descriptive statistics in the literature on foreign direct investment (FDI) that seem to confirm this point of view. For example, one can find data for the U.S. that demonstrate a more or less parallel development of total FDI flows and finance FDI flows.[1] Grubel (1977, p.354) points to another important role that multinational banks can play. They can offer intermediation between smaller local banks from different centres.[2] By fulfilling this task in wholesale banking, they provide an information network that without them would not have come into existence or only at much higher cost.

Why do banks not carry out these functions from their home centre but instead accept the eventual disadvantages connected with establishing an office in another financial centre? A plausible explanation for this is related to the special characteristics of banking services. Unlike non-service goods, financial services can in general not be stored. Consequently, in most cases a permanent relationship exists between the supplier (the bank) and the consumer (the customer). Since very often considerable uncertainty and information problems are involved in banking services, the contact between the two ought to be sufficiently close.[3]

---

1 See Graham and Krugman (1989), p. 18.

2 By "local" we mean "not active internationally".

3 See Kindleberger (1974), p. 8.

We are not merely talking about providing tourists and businessmen with familiar banking services abroad, although the scope for this kind of activity must not be underestimated. Presumably more important is a certain degree of information on firms or customers from which potential competitive advantages may accrue to banks settled in more than one centre. The financial strengths and weaknesses and the behaviour of a given firm might be better known to a bank located in the same country. In many cases there might exist a long-term business relationship. By following its home client to other centres a bank might benefit from this advantage in information. On the other hand, if the bank stays out it risks losing its customer.[4] Other potential reasons to expand a bank's business through an office in another centre are to provide local customers with information on potential foreign trading partners and on the special characteristics of the payment systems in the different countries involved as well as to carry out international transactions in the securities markets.[5]

Since the information argument is valid for all banking services, it is only of minor significance whether we concentrate on commercial or investment banking, although a more detailed inquiry might deliver further interesting findings. The decisive aspect here is that a bank, independent of its field of activity, tries to benefit from the kind of advantages in information described above. Undisputedly, financial firms, in full analogy to other multinational enterprises deciding on their FDI, might also try to avoid unfavourable taxation or other government regulations, i.e., to behave partly like other multinational firms. But focusing on these general factors exclusively would not be adequate in the case of banks. Bank specific phenomena like "house bank relationships" and market segmentation have to be accounted for, too.

Suppose that some banks from different centres intend to open an office in a given financial centre where they have not been represented before. The question they have to answer is whether the prices they expect to set in an equilibrium offer positive profits to them. Otherwise, it would of course not pay to move. Thus, we have to focus on the effects of changes in exogenous quantities on (potential) profits.

---

4 See Grubel (1977), p. 352, and Vastrup (1983), p. 120.

5 Grubel (1977, p. 352) points explicitly to the defensive character that bankers obviously attach to these measures. If a bank fails to make use of the informational advantages it enjoys with certain firms that are active in a foreign centre, it will possibly not only lose these customers. It also runs the risk that local banks themselves will begin to build up information by expanding commercial relationships with the firms and thereby eventually enter the bank's own home market.

To start, we can identify what makes the financial centre attractive to both banks, independent of their origin. One can expect that an increase in the total number of potential customers has a positive influence on the profits of both banks. The sheer size of a market stimulates profits of all banks that will be present in this financial centre. This stems from the fact that the potential to cover the fixed costs grows with an increase in aggregate demand.[6]

Another category of determinants has a strong impact only on the profits of banks from a specific source centre while their influence on the other banks' profits is weak and eventually ambiguous. These are the bilateral factors (i.e., the opportunities of banks from a given centre offered by our potential target centre). An increase in these quantities causes the profits of one bank to rise while it tends to lower the profits of the other bank. The reason for this is the information structure which is favourable only to a subset of the foreign banks.

As a third group of exogenous variables, we take government action into consideration. If equally valid for all banks present in a financial centre, regulatory change (e.g., changes in reserve requirements or taxes of various kinds) can be introduced in the model as a surcharge on all prices. This would affect the banks' profits in the same way as a decrease in aggregate demand for banking services since it makes them more expensive. A comparable effect would be caused by entry barriers.

Finally, it is almost trivial to add that fixed and variable costs parameters have a negative impact on profits.

We can conclude that the decision of a bank to establish an office in another financial centre depends not only on the general regulatory environment in a specific potential target centre but also on variables that have an (almost) exclusive effect on banks from a specific source centre. These bilateral factors in the sense of the previously mentioned export flows and foreign direct investment are responsible for the following observation: being an attractive financial centre for banks from one country is neither a necessary nor a sufficient condition for general attractiveness.

---

6 Besides, market size could be responsible for an additional positive effect, namely "thick market externalities", mentioned by Grilli (1989), p. 391.

7. Statistical Methods

We now turn to the question of econometric modelling. Whether a bank decides to go to another financial centre depends on the expected profits. A bank will go there if the expected profits are positive; otherwise it will not. We assume that the probability of reaching the break-even point largely depends on the kind of exogenous variables discussed in the previous section.

In our empirical estimations the dependent variable Y_{ij} (i.e., the off-diagonals of **Tables 1** and **2**) is taken to show us for how many banks the prospect of positive profits held true. We assume that each bank at the beginning of each period has to decide whether to go elsewhere or to stay where it has been before. Therefore, we treat every bank in a given centre as if they all were alike. This assumption causes some problems, however. The situation of an incumbent will generally be different from that of a new entrant, even if they are of the same origin. But since our data are related to the centres rather than to the banks, we are obliged to treat the banks as if they were homogeneous.

The variable to be explained consists of count data. In principle, we could analyze them using multiple linear regression, as we actually do in section 8. But the preponderance of zeros and small values and the clearly discrete nature of Y_{ij} suggest that we could improve on least squares with a model that accounts for these characteristics. The Poisson regression model has been widely used to study such data (cf. for example Mc Cullagh and Nelder, 1983).

The Poisson model stipulates that each Y_{ij} is drawn from a Poisson distribution with the probability density

$$\Pr\{y_{ij}=Y_{ij}\} = \frac{\exp(-\lambda_{ij}) \bullet (\lambda_{ij})^{Y_{ij}}}{Y_{ij}!} \qquad Y_{ij} = 0,1,2,.. \tag{7.1}$$

where Y_{ij} is the realized value of the random variable. This is a one-parameter distribution with mean and variance of y_{ij} equal to λ_{ij}. To incorporate exogenous variables x_{ij} including a constant, the parameter λ_{ij} is specified to be

$$E(y_{ij}) = \lambda_{ij} = \exp(\beta' x_{ij})$$

where

$$\ln \lambda_{ij} = \beta' x_{ij} \tag{7.3}$$

The Poisson model was estimated with the maximum likelihood method.

The Negative Binomial model is an extension of the Poisson model which allows the variance of the distribution to differ from the mean. The model follows from the Poisson model by specifying

$$\ln \lambda_{ij} = \beta' x_{ij} + \varepsilon \tag{7.4}$$

where ε has a Gamma distribution (cf. Cameron and Trivedi, 1986). This model has an additional parameter, θ, where

$$Var(y_{ij}) = E(y_{ij})[1 + \theta\, E(y_{ij})] \tag{7.5}$$

The model is estimated using maximum likelihood. Starting values are obtained from the Poisson parameters and an estimate of the variance of Y_{ij}. In the next chapter we report on the estimations of the Negative Binomial model only in the cases where the parameter estimates of θ are significantly different from zero. Theta can only take on positive values. So the model allows to test for overdispersion (i.e. the variance exceeds the mean). If underdispersion is the problem then the truncated Poisson model could be appropriate (see below).

A further potential problem is that the dependent variable is bounded from above and below in our sample. While fitted values of Y_{ij} below zero are not possible because of our specifications, values greater than the maximum of the realized observations are. With a truncated Poisson model it is possible to set an upper limit. Therefore we estimate the equations with truncated Poisson and Negative Binomial models based on

maximum likelihood. In addition, with the exception of the dummy variables we only use the natural logarithm of the explanatory variables.

It may be interesting to begin by comparing our results with those of Choi et al. They deal with the problem of count data by applying Non-Linear Weighted Least Squares (NLWLS). They also use Ordinary Least Squares. To have a better base for comparison we also estimate the equations with OLS. The OLS models we fit have the form

$$Y_{ij} = \beta' x_{ij} + \varepsilon \tag{7.6}$$

where Y_{ij} is as before the vector of the dependent and x_{ij} the vector of the independent variables. β is the parameter vector and ε a spherical error term. The dependent variable again consists of the elements Y_{ij} from **Table 1** and 2.

Since we are interested in elasticities we take the natural logarithm of the variables. We use the Box-Cox transform (cf. Box and Cox, 1964) of Y_{ij} with parameters $\lambda_1=0$ and $\lambda_2=0.5$. In other words, we add 0.5 to all elements of Y_{ij} rather than omit zero cells from the estimations. A test with values for λ_2 of 0.1 and 1 indicates, as it did in Choi et al., that the results are not sensitive to the location shift. So the dependent variable in the OLS estimations have the form $\ln(Y_{ij} + 0.5)$.

Later, we introduce a couple of new variables not used by Choi et al. Some of these measures are closely in line with the reflections of section 6. Since the Poisson model is more appropriate for analyzing count data only the results obtained by this technique are presented in the case of the extended specifications.

8. Updating of Choi et al. (1986) and Comparison of Results

In this section we test some specifications chosen by Choi et al. (1986) with data for 1989 and compare results. Besides some revenue and cost proxies a few variables representing interconnectedness, regulation and behaviour are incorporated in the estimations. All models deal with the issue of explaining the entries in the off-diagonal cells.

The estimations contained in **Table 5** consist of 182 observations. As already mentioned, the variable $\ln(Y_{ij} + 0.5)$ is applied when using OLS. In the Models I and IA the first explanatory variable, $TO_j = Y_{.j} - Y_{ij}$, is derived directly from the interconnectedness matrix. It equals the sum of all banks (offices) in a centre j except the ones from i. TO_j can be viewed as a proxy for the total number of customers present in j (see section 6). The bigger it is the more banks are able to coexist. This variable also should capture "thick market externalities" existing in j. Because of effects of additional competition both elements are expected to be characterized by diminishing marginal returns. Thus, the expected sign of the coefficient for TOj is positive, its absolute value, however, should be less than 1.

In the Models II and IIA CGNP is introduced, alternatively to TO_j, as a measure of a centre's economic importance. CGNP corresponds to a financial centre's contribution to gross national product. It was calculated by multiplying the population of each centre with real per capita income in 1988 of the country under consideration. The resulting values were converted into 1980 US-Dollars. The Fischer Weltalmanach provided us with population numbers.

$FROM_i$ reflects the number of headquarters in the source centre. This control variable is necessary, since a financial centre cannot "send" more offices to another centre than it has headquarters. In the OLS estimations we expect a coefficient for $FROM_i$ which is positive and increasing over time.[7]

The variable $DIST_{ij}$ describes the flight distance between i and j. The data were gathered from the SWISSAIR guide. Since in our study some centres consist of two cities, we have calculated the average distances in these cases.

$DIST_{ij}$ is intended to capture a cost element. However, the expected sign of the coefficient is unclear. FDI and international trade literature says that the costs of mastering cultural and geographical distance reduce bilateral exchange. Considering this in isolation implies a negative sign. But the establishment of an office can also be cost saving. If transactions are carried out from the headquarter, variable costs increase with growing distance. The more distant two centres are the more probable it becomes that the foreign centre is served by a local office. So, we might also expect a positive sign.

---

7 Choi et al. confirm this by pointing out that the interconnectedness increased from 1970 to 1980, a tendency that was again confirmed for 1989.

The impact of regulatory action is examined in the case of JPN. This is a dummy variable which takes on the value of 1 if the source centre is Tokyo. In the course of the last two decades, the Japanese government has relaxed step by step the legal restrictions concerning the establishment of bank offices by Japanese banks in foreign countries. Nevertheless, according to Choi et al. only a few Japanese banks were actually allowed to open branches abroad.

Choi et al. introduced variables that focus on the effects of interconnectedness between certain centres. Whether a bank settles in another centre depends also on the other banks' expected reactions. Y_{ji} , i.e. the opposite flow of Y_{ij} , is a variable that captures reciprocity. Choi et al. point to a literature that emphasises rivalry and threat elements in connection with FDI. This would imply that some firms from i invest in j if competitors from j have invested in i before so that the latter do not succeed in gaining an advantage. The specifications IA and IIA leave out Y_{ji} as an explanatory variable, however.

The purpose of the next variables is to shed light on the effects of cooperative behaviour. Steuber (1977) emphasizes the massive restrictions and non-competitiveness stemming from cooperation among large European banks. These phenomena are captured by the dummy variable EURO, which equals 1 for the links between PA, BR, AM, FH and MR and 0 otherwise.

SWISS is another dummy that is set equal to 1 if i=ZG and j is one of the five previously mentioned European centres. According to Paltzer (1977), large Swiss banks are likely to refrain from opening offices in other European countries. The Swiss banks are said to have been content to let their customers come to them rather than to follow them in other centres. Finally, we introduce the dummy variable FHZG that is intended to capture a possible "non-aggression pact" between FH and ZG, a claim that has been made frequently in the past (see, e.g., World Business Weekly (1980)).

The variables presented in this section are summarized in **Table 4**. The results by Choi et al. for 1970 and 1980 as well as our corresponding OLS estimations for 1989 are listed in **Table 5**, where we have omitted the models IA and IIA, while the findings of our Poisson estimations for 1989 are shown in **Table 6**.

Both tables show that TO_j as a proxy for the attractiveness of a financial centre is highly significant. For the dummies we expect a negative sign throughout. Since the

Table 4 List of Variables in the Specification by Choi et al. (1986)

Dependent Variable	
Y_{ij}	off-diagonal cell entries (cf. tables 1 and 2)
Independent Variables	
TO_j	$Y_{.j} - Y_{ij}$
CGNP	GNP of a centre
$FROM_i$	Y_{ii}
$DIST_{ij}$	distance between two centres
Y_{ji}	reverse flow to Y_{ij}
JPN	(0,1)-variable with the value of 1 if i=TK and 0 otherwise
EURO	(0,1)-variable with the value of 1 if Y_{ij} represents a flow between any two of the five centres PA, BR, AM, FH and MR
SWISS	(0,1)-variable with the value of 1 if i=ZG and j=PA,BR,AM,FH,MR
FHZG	(0,1)-variable with the value of 1 if i,j=FH,ZG

FAI

foreign activities of Japanese banks are no longer restricted as rigorously, we cannot be sure of obtaining a negative sign for JPN, particularly in 1989. The same holds true for FHZG. Choi et al. point out that signs exist that hint at the breakdown of the "Swiss-German alliance". Indeed this appears to be confirmed by our results. In contrast to 1980 the coefficients of FHZG are no longer significantly different from zero in 1989, independent of the regression method chosen. Hence, there are no more signs for the existence of a stand-still agreement between Frankfurt and Zurich. As far as JPN is concerned, the claim that Tokyo maintains significantly less presence in foreign centres is, if it was ever valid at all, not confirmed anymore, which is demonstrated by the fact,

Table 5 Results 1970, 1980, 1989: Models I, II (OLS) (t-statistics in brackets)

	Results by Choi et al. 1970	1970	1980	1980	1989	1989
	I	II	I	II	I	II
Const.	-1.42 (-1.10)	-.11 (-.19)	-3.20 (-3.94)*	-1.30 (-2.54)*	-2.98 (-4.99)*	-1.65 (-2.68)*
Ln TOj (1)	.38 (.93)		.62 (3.36)*		.77 (7.50)*	
Ln CGNP		-.12 (-1.02)		.12 (2.28)*		.19 (4.12)*
Ln FROMi	.50 (5.84)*	.40 (5.43)*	.78 (13.29)*	.76 (12.85)*	.84 (14.40)*	.82 (12.82)*
Ln DISTij	-.04 (-1.64)	-.01 (-.15)	.06 (1.09)	.06 (.96)	-.06 (-1.20)	-.07 (-1.30)
Ln Yji (1)	-.29 (-1.07)	.74 (3.12)*	.18 (2.34)*	.22 (2.59)*	.06 (1.18)	.01 (.08)
JPN	-.15 (-.65)	-.22 (-.95)	-.31 (-1.44)	-.38 (-1.74)*	.32 (1.58)	.21 (.97)
EURO	-.35 (-1.46)	-.23 (-.92)	-.46 (-2.34)*	-.51 (-2.60)*	-.10 (-.53)	-.25 (-1.20)
SWISS	-.27 (-.72)	-.36 (-.96)	-.65 (-2.00)*	-.72 (-2.18)*	-1.04 (-3.44)*	-1.18 (-3.51)*
FHZG	-.83 (-1.27)	-.24 (-.39)	-1.17 (-2.35)*	-1.11 (-2.19)*	.27 (.60)	.53 (1.08)
R2	.44	.44	.61	.60	.69	.63
Adj. R2					.68	.62
F-stat.	16.70	16.74	34.16	32.31	49.50	37.36
Obs.	182.00	182.00	182.00	182.00	182.00	182.00

1) in Choi et al: estimated values (see text)
* significant (95%, one-tailed test)

Source: Choi et al. (1986), own computations FAI

Table 6 Results 1989: Models I , II (Poisson and Negbin) (t-statistics in brackets)

	POISSON				NEGBIN
	I	IA	II	IIA	II
Const.	-4.22 (-6.97)*	-4.34 (-7.26)*	-1.86 (-3.52)*	-2.01 (-4.21)*	-1.93 (-2.43)*
Ln TOj	.90 (7.95)*	.94 (8.76)*			
Ln CGNP			.14 (3.52)*	.15 (5.75)*	.14 (2.59)*
Ln FROMi	1.03 (12.68)*	1.03 (12.75)*	.99 (12.22)*	.99 (12.27)*	1.02 (9.71)*
Ln DISTij	-.01 (-.37)	-.02 (-.38)	-.04 (-.86)	-.03 (-.91)	-.03 (-.46)
Ln Yji	.06 (1.37)		.04 (.78)		-.04 (.56)
JPN	.16 (1.16)	.19 (1.40)	.03 (.20)	.04 (.28)	-.05 (-.31)
EURO	-.01 (-.07)	.02 (.10)	-.27 (-1.70)*	-.25 (-1.63)	-.24 (-1.08)
SWISS	-1.10 (-1.85)*	-1.06 (-1.78)*	-1.31 (-2.21)*	-1.29 (-2.18)*	-1.30 (-1.69)*
FHZG	-.06 (-.16)	-.07 (-.17)	-.03 (-.06)	-.02 (-.04)	.08 (.11)
Theta					.09 (1.85)*
Chi-squar.	169.00	170.00	225.00	226.00	
Log-likl.	-325.00	-326.00	-354.80	-355.00	-347.10
Obs.	182.00	182.00	182.00	182.00	182.00

* significant (95%, one-tailed test)

FAI

that only the corresponding coefficient of model II for 1980 is significant.

The signs for the coefficients of SWISS and EURO are in line with expectations but as far as the latter is concerned they are not significant. The view according to which there are agreements among large European banks is not confirmed by this model. Possibly, there has been a change here, because the absolute values for the EURO coefficient were clearly higher in 1980.

On the other hand, one can still find some evidence for the conservative behaviour of Swiss banks. However, the most recent developments point to a change in attitude. While in 1988, e.g., not a single large Swiss bank was represented in Italy, since then every one of them has established some kind of office there.

There is no 1989 estimation showing a significantly positive influence of Y_{ji} (reverse flow). Here, we also have a deviation from the results of 1970 and 1980. A plausible reason for this has not yet been found.

The coefficient of $FROM_i$ is highly significant while the distance variable does not seem to be of much importance for the locational decision. Perhaps, the opposing forces described before neutralize each other.

In Model IA (see **Table 6**) Y_{ji} has been omitted. Since its influence in Model I was very small, the outcomes as compared to I are hardly different. Comparing **Tables 5** and **6** one can also see that the change of estimation methods does not greatly affect results. In Models II we substitute CGNP for TO_j.[8] The parameter of CGNP is significantly positive. The values for R^2 and for log likelihood are also smaller than in Model I. All the other differences between the two models are small. The coefficient of EURO is significantly negative in the Poisson regression of Model II. The fact that in 1980 JPN was significant and in 1989 it was not, suggests that the liberalization in Japan now allows Japanese banks, ceteris paribus, to open even more offices in foreign centers than their competitors from other countries. No major differences between Models II and IIA appear in **Table 6**.

---

8 Considering the log-likelihood ratio tests as well as the Wald tests the Negative Binomial model is to be preferred over the Poisson model. The estimated t-value for θ suggests that the variance of the dependent varialbles is significantly greater than their average.

9. Estimation of New Specifications

9.1. The Models and Specifications

We turn now to the estimation of the extended specifications. Here, we apply the Poisson regression model exclusively. In section 6 we emphasized the importance of an advantage in information. Unfortunately, it was not possible to find a proxy for the extent of the informational differences that made sense. One could perhaps have used a variable that differentiates, say, between more bank-oriented and more market-oriented countries, under the assumption that the banks originating from the latter group are better informed than the other ones. But we chose not to. However, for measuring the extent of the potential set of customers we can make use of the bilateral data that are to be found in international trade statistics (1989 exports from the country with centre i to the country with centre j; EX_{ij})[9] as well as in statistics on foreign direct investment (number of foreign affiliates of multinationals from country i in the country j; FDI_{ij}).[10]

In addition, we introduce variables which are supposed to give information about the general legal environment. STAMP provides indications on the 1989 stamp duties on stock market transactions. An AKW documentation as well as a survey on international taxation (Coopers and Lybrand, 1990) served as data sources. All other things equal, an office is preferably opened where tax legislation is most favourable; that is why we expect a negative sign.

The same holds for the variables that are thought to capture capital controls in the widest sense. CONRES is a dummy variable that takes on the value of 1, if residents are subject to capital controls and of 0 otherwise. CONFOR is an analogous variable for non-residents. Both variables stand for the degree of regulation of financial markets in general. Bertero and Mayer (1990) served as a source; unfortunately, we do not benefit from a complete data series. For this reason, the effects of these variables, which are expected to be negative, are only examined in equations with a reduced number of dependent variables.

---

9 Sources: OECD, Monthly Statistics of Foreign Trage, January 1991, Paris; IMF, International Trade Statistics, various issues, Washington, D.C.

10 As a consequence of the lack of complete bilateral data on the extent of FDI stocks we had to use the number of foreign affiliates as listed in the tables of the UNCTC (1985). These data that refer to 1980, unfortunately, are the most actual indications to be found in the completeness required by our matrix. The information for Panama as an origin and the two links between Singapore and Hong Kong, however, are still missing.

As a further conceivable reason for establishing an office in a certain centre we have taken banking secrecy (SEC) into account. Financial transactions might benefit from a high level of discretion. If a bank wants to participate in this business, it has to be present physically. Thus, we expect the sign of the parameter to be positive. Grilli (1989) developed a scale for secrecy which we adopt in our estimations. Grilli chose the highest value for Switzerland. This view is supported by Braillard (1987, p. 99) who suggests that "with the exception of Luxembourg, Austria and Liechtenstein the Swiss banking secrecy is still a great advantage compared to the extent of the protection of privacy in other industrial countries".

Grilli (1989) provides no information on Singapore and Hong Kong. We have adopted the Swiss values for these centres, although, according to Braillard (1987, p. 99), these countries exhibit secrecy laws that are even stricter than those of Switzerland: "The Swiss banking secrecy is far from being the most rigid one, if one compares it with the ones on Cayman Island, the Bahamas, Panama or even Singapore and Hong Kong".

Since the scaling appears somewhat arbitrary we formed a second dummy variable for secrecy (SEC01) that equals 1 for Panama, Zurich, Singapore and Hong Kong and zero otherwise (see Appendix). We assume in accordance with Braillard (1987, p. 99) that a high degree of discretion is guaranteed in these centres.[11]

In all the new specifications we omitted FHZG. As shown by the results of the previous section, the evidence of a Swiss-German alliance vanished.

In a first group of specifications (Models III) we want to test the effects of the variables for which we have an (almost) complete data set. Since for EX_{ij} we lack only two observations, namely the streams within the U.S. (from NY to LS and from LS to NY), we still have 180 data points. The distance variable $Dist_{ij}$ in Model IIIA is substituted in Models IIIB and IIIC by the time zone variable TZ, which takes the value of 1 for destinations situated in another time zone and zero otherwise. We distinguished four different time zones.

---

11 Eventually, this is no longer valid for Panama because of political instability there. That is why we have also estimated samples excluding Panama.

Table 7 List of New Variables

EX_{ij}	exports from country with centre i to country with centre j
FDI_{ij}	number of foreign affiliates of multinational enterprises from country with centre i to country with centre j
STAMP	stamp duties on transactions at a centre's stock market
CONRES	(0,1)-variable with the value of 1 if residents are subject to capital controls and 0 otherwise
CONFOR	(0,1)-variable with the value of 1 if nonresidents are subject to capital controls and 0 otherwise
SEC	secrecy variable
SEC01	(0,1)-variable for secrecy with the value of 1 if j =PN,ZG,HK,SI
TZ	(0,1)-variable with the value of 1 if the two centres are in different time zones
TURN	turnover of a centre's stock market

FAI

In a second group of specifications (Models IV) the sample size is reduced to 167 and 165 observations, respectively. The two samples, however, are not identical with respect to everything else. In IVA and IVB we take the FDI_{ij} as an explanatory variable. For these models the values for PN as a source centre and the ones for the link between SI and HK were not available. The specifications IVA and IVB, on the other hand, include the variable TURN for which no data could be found, whenever Panama was the destination. The turnover in the share markets (TURN) in each centre can be viewed as another demand variable. The data for TURN measure total stock market turnover in 1989 and are taken from the yearbook of the Fédération Internationale de Bourses de Valeurs (FIBV). The higher the turnover is in j, the more attractive this centre becomes for other banks. As an explanatory variable TURN as well as STAMP have the disadvantage that our sample contains not only universal banks but also pure commercial banks. However, it is possible that commercial banks establish themselves in a foreign centre just because they are allowed to engage in investment banking there. Of course, the expected sign is positive.

In Model IVA we estimate an equation where FDI_{ij} appears in addition to EX_{ij} whereas the latter has been left out in Model IVB.

Table 7 lists all the dependent variables that are newly introduced in this section.

9.2. The Results

In section 8 we had a multicollinearity problem with the two attractiveness variables TOj and CGNP. Since we introduce some new attractiveness variables this problem may become worse. Therefore we first computed the correlations of the different variables (see **Table 8**).

Table 8 Correlation Coefficients

	ln TO_j	ln CGNP	ln TURN[1]
ln TO_j	1	0.66	0.51
ln CGNP		1	0.34
ln TURN			1

[1] number of observations = 169 FAI

Unfortunately, there are missing data in our series. For the turnover in shares variable we do not have the data where the destination is Panama. In the case of FDI_{ij} we have missing data where the origin is Panama. A check of the correlations shows that there are two groups of variables related to each other. TO_j, CGNP and TURN belong to the first group (see **Table 8**). But there exists also a strong correlation between the two trade variables EX_{ij} and FDI_{ij} of 0.68 (165 observations). The correlations are helpful for the model specifications.

Tables 9 and **10** present the results for the models III and IV. Again the coefficient of $FROM_i$ is positive and statistically significant. The same can be said about TO_j. The coefficient of this variable has the right (positive) sign and is significant as well. In addition, the value of the coefficient is less than 1 (as in section 8).

We refer to the model with TO_j as model III B and to the one with CGNP as model III C. The coefficient of CGNP is highly significant. But the t-value of the parameter of CGNP is smaller than that of TO_j . Also, as can be seen from the log likelihoods, the model with TO_j performs better than that with CGNP. A reason for this may be that TO_j not only reflects the aggregate demand for bank services but also "thick market externalities" mentioned above.

In the models III the new variable EX_{ij} shows the expected positive influence on the establishment of new offices and the coefficient is also significant. Among the regulatory variables the secrecy variable seems to play an important role in explaining the opening of offices. The coefficient of SEC is positive and significant in all specifications.

This result does not change if we introduce the second secrecy dummy SEC01 instead of SEC in estimations not reported here. In all equations SEC fitted better than SEC01. This result is not surprising since it was already suggested that banks follow their customers abroad. Banking secrecy can be of major importance to non-residents.

In comparison to the models I and II, the coefficient of the distance variable changes its sign and becomes positive in model IIIA. But the coefficient is still not significant. The introduction of the time zone variable in place of the distance variables does not necessarily lead to more clarity. The parameter remains insignificant. However, the sign of the coefficient always has the correct (positive) sign. This result may be due to the crudity of our approach relative to the complexity of the issue. Each European centre is homogeneous in terms of the time zone, however, this does not mean that banks outside Europe will establish an office in each European centre. Also, the postulated agreements among European banks not to establish offices in each other's countries seem to have broken down (if they ever existed at all). The coefficient of

Table 9 **Results 1989: Models III (Poisson) (t-statistics in brackets)**

	POISSON		
	III A	III B	III C
Const.	-4.98 (-8.18)*	-4.49 (-9.52)*	-3.89 (-8.10)*
Ln TOj	.63 (5.27)*	.62 (5.21)*	
Ln CGNP			.16 (3.33)*
Ln FROMi	.88 (10.47)*	.87 (10.37)*	.82 (9.99)*
Ln DISTij	.06 (1.45)		
TZ		.13 (1.35)	.11 (1.11)
Ln Yji	.13 (1.98)*	.13 (1.93)*	.17 (2.49)*
JPN	.09 (.65)	.11 (.85)	.04 (.29)
EURO	.14 (.79)		
SWISS	-.81 (-1.37)	-.89 (-1.52)	-.85 (-1.44)
Ln EXij	.17 (4.54)*	.18 (4.70)*	.18 (4.93)*
SEC	.13 (3.80)*	.12 (3.86)*	.22 (6.93)*
Ln STAMP	-.07 (-1.21)	-.06 (-1.14)	-.08 (-1.33)
Chi-squar.	145.00	145.00	164.00
Log-likl.	-306.00	-306.00	-314.00
Obs.	180.00	180.00.	180.00

* significant (95%, one-tailed test) FAI

Table 10 Results 1989: Models IV (Poisson) (t-statistics in brackets)

	POISSON			
	IVA	IVB	IVC	IVD
Const.	-4.45 (-9.10)*	-4.46 (-9.00)*	-4.60 (-4.87)*	-3.21 (-7.41)*
Ln TOj	.70 (5.49)*	.82 (6.93)*	.55 (2.66)*	
Ln FROMi	.81 (8.80)*	.86 (9.58)*	.89 (10.23)*	.86 (9.95)*
TZ	.09 (.93)	.01 (.08)	.14 (1.29)	.16 (1.59)
Ln Yji	.10 (1.36)	.09 (1.33)	.10 (1.40)	.12 (1.64)
JPN	.26 (1.84)*	.34 (2.43)*	.07 (.50)	.06 (.03)
SWISS	-1.05 (-1.79)*	-1.18 (-2.01)*	-.88 (-1.50)	-.86 (-1.45)
Ln EXij	.11 (2.10)*		.17 (3.82)*	.18 (4.36)*
Ln FDIij	.05 (1.48)	.11 (3.96)*		
SEC	.10 (2.97)*	.07 (2.31)*	.10 (2.07)*	.15 (4.71)*
Ln STAMP	-.05 (-.90)	-.05 (-.88)	-.10 (-1.12)	-.18 (-3.26)*
CONFOR			.70 (.48)	
CONRES			.03 (.19)	
Ln TURN			.03 (.93)	.08 (3.22)*
Chi-squar.	134.00	138.00	128.00	138.00
Log-likl.	-297.00	-299.00	-286.00	-291.00
Obs.	165.00	165.00	167.00	167.00

* significant (95%, one-tailed test) FAI

EURO still has a negative sign but it is no longer significant, so we dropped this variable in most of our estimations.

Y_{ji} , the reverse flow to Y_{ij} , is significant in the equations of model III but loses its significance in model IV. However, the coefficient remains positive, as expected, in all estimations. In the extended specifications, the SWISS and JPN dummies also lose their significance in almost all equations. On the other hand, the JPN dummy is confirmed to have a positive coefficient now instead of the negative coefficient found for the years 1970 and 1980.

In model IVA the variables EX_{ij} and FDI_{ij} are jointly estimated. In contrast to Model IVB, where EX_{ij} is dropped, the coefficient of FDI_{ij} is not significant.

This result is a strong indication of some collinearity between FDI_{ij} and EX_{ij} which is confirmed by the strong correlation coefficient of 0.65 between these two variables.

In the models IVC and IVD the newly introduced regulatory variables do not seem to be important. The coefficients of CONFOR and CONRES are small, carry the wrong sign and are never significant. On the other hand, the turnover in shares seems to influence the settlement of banks in a positive, but not significant direction. Here, the collinearity problem already mentioned arises again. We therefore estimated a specification with TURN but without TO_j (see model IVD).

As expected, TURN has a positive and significant sign. Not surprisingly and in accordance with the theoretical background we can see from the log likelihoods that the models with TO_j and CGNP have a better fit than those with TURN. In contrast to the former specifications STAMP gets a significantly negative sign in model IVD, too. However, we have to be careful in interpreting this result. STAMP also strongly correlates with an entry barrier dummy, ENT, not included in our estimations (p=0.71). Therefore, with STAMP we might just measure the height of the general entry barriers surrounding centre j. With nine different categories of regulatory obstacles we constructed an index of ENT shown in the appendix. But it is hardly possible to quantify these different effects and it is even more difficult to compare them.

Anyway, we made an attempt to measure them with the help of publications by OECD, Walter (1985,1988) and The Department of Treasury (1990). Of course, our list of different forms of entry barriers is far from complete and the weighting of the individual obstacles causes some problems. In addition, we did not find complete data sets for all the measures. Because of these shortcomings we do not report the results of the estimations including the ENT variable here, although its coefficient had the expected (but not significant) negative sign.

Furthermore, one can see that in models IV C and D there are only minor changes with respect to the other variables already appearing in former specifications.

Representative offices are often small and usually not as important as branches or subsidiaries. Therefore, our results so far might be distorted in some way. As a consequence, we excluded the representative offices from the dependent variable (Y_{ij}) in a couple of estimations not reported here. From the results thus obtained the same conclusions as before can be drawn. Only the coefficient of the JPN-dummy gets an opposite (negative) sign, indicating that in comparison to banks from other countries, Japanese banks prefer to send out representative offices.

10. Summary of Results and Conclusions

The results emerging from the empirical estimates reported in sections 8 and 9 can be summarized as follows:

1. The attractiveness of a centre as a potential site for establishing an office is clearly related to the size of the local economy and to the number of banks that are already there. Also the stock market turnover is a good measure of a centre's attractiveness. In all models the coefficients of the corresponding demand variables have the expected and highly significant positive sign. The same is true for the bilateral trade flow and foreign direct investment variables. The overall economic relations with another country seem to play an important role in explaining the establishment of an office in other financial centres.

2. In section 8, the OLS as well as the Poisson regressions show quite similar results. With a few exceptions, most results obtained by Choi et al. (1986) are confirmed by our estimations for 1989. However, in 1989 the suppression of competition among continental European banks as well as the cooperative behaviour between German and

Swiss banks seem to have broken down. This result especially emerges from the expanded models in section 9. The dummy variable indicating the penetration of Swiss banks into other European centres is still consistently negative but, especially in the expanded models, mostly loses its significance. Nowadays, Japanese banks, ceteris paribus, have a stronger tendency to establish themselves abroad than their counterparts from other countries. As a result, the corresponding dummy has changed its sign since 1970.

3. The distance as well as the time zone variables have only little if any explanatory power. Foreign bank presence in a bank's home centre encourages the establishment of an office in the foreign banks' home centre, indicating some international rivalry behaviour. But only in the specifications of model III is the coefficient capturing this effect significant.

4. Among the newly introduced regulatory variables, banking secrecy is confirmed by our results as an attraction for foreign banks. The coefficients of the corresponding variables are always positive and significant. The other regulatory variables measuring the extent of capital controls, stamp duties and general "entry barriers" seem to play a minor role with respect to our analysis.

Obviously, the attractiveness of a financial centre is not only dependent on the general environment of banking regulation but also on the activity of the "real" economy surrounding it. Particularly important are the extent of international trade as well as the amount of foreign direct investment in the countries involved. If one wishes to increase the number of foreign banks in one's own country - perhaps to stimulate competition or simply to increase the share of highly productive economic activities - it is recommended to continue to reduce trade barriers and to liberalize (direct) investment in general.

This points to an important implication for Switzerland in particular. Today, the most effective international integration movement takes place within the EC. Switzerland is not a member of the EC. Currently, the prospects of a successful treaty on an European Economic Space, binding together the EC- and EFTA-countries are rather bleak. Alternatives to full membership are difficult to imagine. Therefore, if Switzerland continues to stay out of the EC, this could be detrimental to the attractivity of the Swiss financial centre to foreign banks (as well as to the attractiveness of the foreign financial centres to Swiss banks). On the other hand, the results with respect to banking secrecy also point into the opposite direction. Should Switzerland's banking secrecy suffer from closer links to the EC, integration might imply attractivity losses for Switzerland.

Another conclusion that one could draw from the results is that there exists something like comparative advantages also between financial centres. While one centre attracts predominantly banks from one range of countries another one offers particularly favourable conditions for banks from other places. Thus, in spite of the possible existence of thick market externalities one hardly has to expect concentration leading to the survival of only just a few financial centres, or worse, just one financial centre in Europe or the whole world. This observation provides some comfort with respect to the future of smaller financial centers than London, New York and Tokyo. The nature of the comparative advantages as well as limits of the thick market externalities responsible for this finding have, however, to be investigated further in order to be better understood and eventually exploited in practice.

APPENDIX

Table 1 The Secrecy and Capital Control Variables

	AM	BR	FH	HK	NY/LS	LO	MR	PN	SI	TM	ZG	PA	TK
SEC (1)	0	1	0.5	4	0	1	-1	4	4	0	4	-1	0.5
SEC01(2)	0	0	0	1	0	0	0	1	1	0	1	0	0
CONRES (3)	0	1	0	0	0	0	1	NA	0	1	0	1	0
CONFOR (3)	0	0	0	0	0	0	0	NA	1	0	1	1	0

(1) Sources: Grilli (1989), Braillard (1987)
(2) Source: Braillard (1987)
(3) Source: Bertero and Mayer (1990)

Table 2 The Entry Barriers Variable (ENT)

	AM	BR	FH	HK	NY/LS	LO	MR	PN	SI	TM	ZG	PA	TK
ENT	3	3	3	NA	3	2	6	NA	2 ?	3	3	4	6

The index was constructed according to the 9 following subjects:

* Limitation on foreign banks solicitation of certain kinds of deposits
* Restrictions on repatriation profits or funds
* Reciprocity tests
* Prohibition by law of foreign banks entering via branches
* Supervisory control on the opening of new domestic branches by authorised institutions
* Stock exchange membership restrictions
* Limited foreign participation in primary an secondary markets
* Interest rate deregulation
* Limitations in raising funds

Sources: OECD (1984), OECD (1987a), OECD (1987b), OECD (1989)
Braillard (1987)
The Department of Treasury (1990)
Walter (1985), Walter (1988)

REFERENCES

Arbeitskreis Kapital und Wirtschaft [AKW] (1990). Standort Schweiz im internationalen Wettbewerb - Produktionsfaktor Kapital. Zürich.

The Banker, June 1990.

The Banker's Almanac and Yearbook, 1990.

Bertero, E. and Mayer, C. (1990). "Structure and Performance: Global Interdependence of Stock Markets around the Crash of October 1987". European Economic Review, 34, pp 1155-1180.

Braillard, P. (1987). Der Finanzplatz Schweiz. Genf.

Box, G.E. and Cox, D.R. (1964). An Analysis of Transformations". Journal of the Royal Statistical Society, pp. 211-252.

Choi, S.-R.; Tschoegl, A.E. and Yu, C.-M. (1986). "Banks and the World's Major Financial Centers, 1970-1980. Weltwirtschaftliches Archiv, 122, pp. 48-64.

Coopers & Lybrand (1990). 1990 International Tax Summaries. John Wiley & Sons, New York.

Department of Treasury (1990). 1990 Report on Foreign Treatment of U.S. Financial Institutions.

Fédération internationale des bourses de valeurs [FIBV] (1990). Activities and Statistics, 1989 Report. Paris.

Graham, E.M. and Krugman, P.R. (1989). Foreign Direct Investment in the United States. Institute for International Economics, Washington, DC.

Grilli, V. (1989). "Financial Markets". Economic Policy, vol. 4, pp. 387-421.

Grubel, H.G. (1977). "A Theory of Multinational Banking". Banca Nazionale del Lavoro Quarterly Review, 123, pp. 349-364.

IMF, International Trade Statistics, various issues, Washington, D.C.

Kindleberger, Ch. P. (1974). The Formation of Financial Centers: A Study in Comparative Economic History. Princeton Studies in International Finance, No. 36, Princeton, NJ.

Mc Cullagh, P. and Nelder, J. (1983). Generalised Linear Models. London.

OECD (1984). International Trade in Services: Banking. Indication and Analysis of Obstacles. Paris.

OECD (1987a). International Trade in Services: Securities. Paris.

OECD (1987b). Prudential Supervision in Banking. Paris.

OECD (1989). Competition in Banking (by G. Broeker). Paris.

OECD (1991). Monthly Statistics of Foreign Trade, January 1991, Paris.

Paltzer, E.F. (1977). "Internationalization of Banking by Foreign Bases and Addresses", in: Wadsworth, Wilson and Fournier: The Development of Financial Institutions in Europe, 1956-1976, pp. 167-174.

Reed, H. (1981). The Preeminence of Financial Centres. New York.

Steuber, U. (1977). "International Co-Operation an Competition among Banks in Europe", in: Wasdsworth, Wilson and Fournier: The Development of Financial Institutions in Europe, 1956-1976, pp. 175-189.

Trivedi, P.K. and Cameron, A.C. (1986). "Econometric Models Based on Count Data: Comparisons and Applications of Some Extimators and Tests", Journal of Applied Econometrics, vol. 1, pp. 29-53.

UNCTC (1985) Transnational Corporations in World Development, Third Survey. London.

Vastrup, C. (1983). "Economic Motives for Foreign Banking: The Danish Case". Kredit und Kapital, 16, pp. 117-125.

Walter, I. (1985). Barriers to Trade Banking and Financial Services. London.

Walter, I. (1988). Global Competition in Financial Services: Market Structure, Protection, and Trade Liberalization. Cambridge, Mass.

World Business Weekly (1980).

Comment on
Matthias Jeger, Urs Haegler, Roland Theiss: "On the Attractiveness of International Financial Centers"

Peter Buomberger*

Reading the Jeger, Haegler and Theiss paper reminded me of an incident a couple of years ago. The economic research department at UBS had been asked to survey the reasons why Swiss firms chose to invest in Texas. After reviewing the literature and talking with half a dozen of firms that had recently made such investments - and getting few sensible answers - we began to question instead why UBS itself had established a presence in this "financial center" back in 1980.

First and most important: We wanted to better serve major corporate customers in the southern "sun belt", then the fastest growing region in the United States with a big potential for private banking. Many of the Top 500 are located there.

Second: We wanted a place with a good infrastructure such as international air connections and telecommunications facilities, and a competitive labor market.

Finally, the clincher for Houston was that our major Swiss competitors were already operating in Atlanta and Miami, the only other two U.S. cities that met the other criteria.

I relate this anecdote not to suggest that the UBS Houston location decision was typical, but rather to illustrate the problem the authors face when trying to find a few variables that explain what is inherently a very complex process.

The first reason, a growing economy, would get picked up by the authors in their economic size variable, at least in the inter-temporal comparison when the larger Texas economy should have been attracting more banks between 1970 and 1980, but

---

* The author would like to thank Dr. William Gasser for substantial input in this paper.

probably fewer by 1989. This assumes that recent growth is the best estimate of future growth, the decision parameter banks would use. Market growth should be a better variable. Past growth is not the best estimate of the future, but it still no doubt misguides many actual decisions.

The infrastructure needs of banks are no doubt getting picked up by the TO variable, the presence of other foreign banks. But this variable likely captures a lot of other things as well. I'm not surprised that it is highly collinear with other variables in the empirical model, but I am surprised that it matches their GNP in the market center so closely.

The final reason, locating where other major Swiss banks are not already present, will not get picked up in the model, except maybe by the dummy variable SWISS that suggests Swiss banks are conservative in locating abroad. Is this dummy variable actually capturing a specific aspect of market size, the limited market for Swiss commercial and private banking services abroad?

I would also like to point out that these three factors were not the only ones considered before we established a presence in Houston. They were simply the ones that seemed most important as the decision was finalized. In other cases other things might be critical. To see the broad scope of factors that can influence these decisions, consider the following factors taken from the index of a recent feasibility study for a new operation in Europe. These are not ordered by their importance. Any one of them could be the factor that tips the scale for or against a particular location.

Factors in Locating International Banking Operations

- Political Situation
- Social and Cultural Aspects
- Economic Situation
    - Country
    - Financial Center
    - Interdependence with other markets and centers
- Market Structure and Opportunities
    - Size
    - Potential Customer Segments
    - Products and Services Offered

- Competition
  - In General
  - Domestic Banks
  - Foreign Banks Locally Present
  - Swiss Banks Locally Present
- Labor Market
- Legal Aspects
- Tax Aspects
  - Local Transactions
  - International Transactions
- Business Objectives
- Strategy
  - Legal Form of Presence
  - Customer Segments
  - Services and Products
  - Marketing Priorities
  - Marketing Coordination

Actually, Houston is not one of the financial markets considered by the authors. I don't have a problem with this, except to note that the decision of which centers to include and which to exclude seems more important than the paper admits. One way out of this problem would be to define a market to include Houston, Atlanta and Miami. For corporate lending and private banking the region is relatively homogeneous. But investment banking and funds management can best be done in New York, and these other centers cannot be separated for such banking activities. The problem is not unique to Houston. Why are Zurich and Geneva really combined? Why are Los Angeles-San Fransisco and New York separated? What happened to Chicago? For that matter, where are Luxembourg and Sydney?

A critical question related to the EC single financial market is whether centers like Paris, Frankfurt, London, Luxembourg and even Zurich can coexist once some of the artificial regulatory barriers are removed. It might even help to put a few less successful cities like Vienna, Copenhagen or Stockholm into the equations to improve the robustness of the explanations. Differences in market focus, like the evolution of commodities markets in Chicago, may make some centers attractive for unique reasons. More careful definitions of banking markets may help explain the success of some centers like Luxembourg or Geneva in highly specialized activities and put more light on the problem of inter-regional coexistence.

In the same sense, it would also be useful to consider what attracts banks from non-financial centers. Why are Asian, Middle Eastern or Latin American banks attracted to these centers? The more limited matrix approach of Choi et al. (1987) is interesting and provides some insight into changing location patterns among major international banks, but it is not well suited to empirical testing of some of the more important relationships that must underlie location decisions for all banks.

I don't blame the authors at this stage for the poor state of the literature identifying financial markets. These markets are changing rapidly as technology changes the way financial intermediation is efficiently conducted. In any case, the authors already give us a "three-in-one" paper and I would not add a fourth part at this time.

The first "paper" brings the statistical results of Choi et al. for 1970 and 1980 up to date as of 1989. The results are interesting and correspond with our own evaluations, but are not very useful in determining the attractiveness of financial centers.

The second "paper" discusses some theoretical issues related to attractiveness. This is also interesting, but in my view does not help much either in interpreting the Choi results or in identifying better variables for the empirical work. Indeed it still leaves the expected directions of many possibly important relationships ambiguous.

Finally, in the third "paper", the authors put some economics into the explanation of the changing patterns in the Choi et al. model and some initiative into creating data to undertake new tests. While I have reservations about the statistical technique employed, about the logic of the empirical model, and about the data itself, I find this the most useful of the three papers. Anything we can say about what makes a financial center attractive would be immensely valuable, both to the banks that must make these decisions regularly and to public policy makers who make rules that will attract or repel investment and employment in banking.

I can only applaud the care which the authors have taken to identify their empirical variables. This points out some of the problems with the study, but also suggests directions for further research.

Let me first turn to the dependent variable(s). The number of banks in a location presents problems. Branches and subsidiaries are not the same as representative offices, as the authors note. But not all branches and subsidiaries are equal either. I would prefer to see the dependent variable specified as the number of persons employed. This would help differentiate between "tax addresses" and a market center in which real financial intermediation is being done. It could also produce much more useful results. For instance, how many Swiss jobs does the stamp tax cost?

I am most disturbed by the two variables for market scale on the independent variable side of the empirical work. My reservation is about using other "outside" banks operating in the market. It may give a good overall fit, but it says nothing about why these other banks are there or why the market is attractive. There are no doubt market economies in international banking - other banks with which to do business, depth trading in various instruments, a strong labor pool, good legal and technical support, and a regulatory environment that should be attentive to the needs of outside bankers. But I think most of these factors can and should be modelled separately.

The alternative market scale variable presented, the economic size of the market, is commendable in principle, especially when used in connection with variables that measure market potential specific to foreign banks, like bilateral trade and investment links with the foreign banks' home countries. But the proxy used, GNP per capita multiplied by the population of the "center", strikes me as pretty weak. Most centers enjoy a level of income well above their national average. Canton Zurich is 27% above the national average; Geneva 29% higher. Most other centers are likely even more skewed. On the other hand, the economic region being served is likely larger than the financial center itself. Zurich-Geneva or Paris, like New York, serve all of their nation for many kinds of banking services. Most operations in Singapore serve much of Southeast Asia.

I see no simple answer to this problem, but suggest that the national income contribution of the financial sector in a country would usually be a better proxy for the relative size of its financial market. This, combined with variables measuring bilateral trade and direct investment activity, should give a better measure of market potential than local income alone. I suspect that the variable for turnover (TURN) in the local securities market is already picking up some of this potential depth of financial business.

There are inherent problems with some of the variables like banking secrecy, capital controls, and barriers to entry, and I see no good alternative to the dummy variable and rank order approach used. Capital controls and entry barriers are very complex. The presence of a law often matters less than the vigour with which laws are applied and the various laws themselves have different effects. The OECD and U.S. Treasury studies do about as well as can be expected. The resident/non-resident breakdown of capital controls also appears about as detailed as one can effectively get.

I would, however, augment the banking secrecy variable, partly because of its special importance to Switzerland. It seems that many countries offer the same kind of banking secrecy on paper as does Switzerland, but an important distinction can be made in the likely durability of this secrecy. Panama and Hong Kong are cases in point. Does Panama offer the same protection today as it did five years ago? Will Hong Kong be as secret after 1996? For lack of a better measure, I would suggest using years since the banking secrecy laws have been in place to weigh the dummy variables. The judgmentally weighted variable SEC seems to fit better than the simple dummy SEC01 in the results presented and further refinement appears in order.

The distance variable raises more basic problems. The failure to determine an a priori sign for distance suggests their nature. If one considers distance a proxy for cultural or business ties, one expects a negative sign. But we already have two variables, trade and direct investment flows, to capture these business relationships directly. Distance is also a poor proxy for the cost of supporting a foreign operation. Local living expenses, wages, office space and telecommunications differ by much more than distance from headquarters. Even transportation and travel expenses are more likely to depend on competition in the transportation markets than distance. With all of this, I would expect a positive sign on distance, if one could control for the other factors. Banking is information intensive and most of the qualitative information needed to make credit and investment decisions can be most efficiently collected and monitored close to its source.

The time zone variable also appears needlessly limited. It should matter more (negatively) whether a bank already has an office in the same time zone than the difference between the time zone of a particular center and the home country. I suggest this change because the data would already appear to be on hand, but the time zone problem is likely as complex as distance. I am not surprised to find no significance.

Finally, I should say that dummy variables like the non-aggression pact between German and Swiss banks make little sense to me. But I suppose there is nothing wrong with testing and eliminating some of the more curious hypotheses around. The declining significance of the cross-European banking dummy variable is interesting.

In conclusion let me say that despite my reservations on some of the particulars, I am happy to see this paper. Bankers and politicians make far too many decisions without testing the empirical relevance of their arguments. The public policy decisions now faced by Switzerland, such as the stamp duty, overall tax compatibility, the withholding tax and possibly even banking secrecy, are too important to be taken without better empirical support.

Regarding the conclusions the paper gives for Switzerland, I do not think that the Swiss financial center will necessarily be disadvantaged if Switzerland stays out of the European Community. But Switzerland will have to work hard to remain internationally competitive whether it is in a single financial European market or not.

The opportunity to compete on equal terms in the Community makes entry attractive to most large Swiss banks. Moreover, the Swiss economy may suffer in general if it is not well integrated in an emerging single European market and this would be bad for domestic banking. I also see advantages in remaining outside of the Community. If Switzerland can get inflation under control, a strong franc and low interest rates might again offer an attractive alternative to future EC markets that may have to rely on an Ecu as their home currency. On the other hand, London has done well as a financial center without being part of the hard currency bloc in Europe. Similarly, banking secrecy itself may no longer be a solid base for comparative advantage. Too many centers now offer secrecy for legal transactions and neither Swiss nor world opinion will tolerate secrecy as an excuse for hiding gains from illegal activities. Still, a combination of secrecy, safety, and political neutrality may well define a "niche" that a center can effectively exploit. Call it "private banking". This might be more successfully pursued outside the political confines of the European Community, but we need more evidence on the magnitudes involved.

Another result of international competition is that domestic Swiss business will also be lost to foreign centers unless our market becomes more competitive. Swiss institutional investors, a growing segment in our financial markets, are now more performance oriented and less concerned with privacy. Reducing the stamp duty only for foreign transactions and retaining high withholding on domestic resident earnings, for example, leaves banks located in Switzerland disadvantaged in dealing with domestic residents. The growing volume of trading in Swiss securities in London and the growth in Luxembourg funds, for instance, suggests that financial operations in Switzerland are significantly disadvantaged by these taxes. We may be getting into details here that are too refined to be captured efficiently within the global approach to financial centers modelled by the authors, but it is important to consider such features more carefully in order to seriously analyze the attractiveness of the Swiss financial center.

Part VI: Monopoly Power

Monopoly Power in Swiss Financial Markets

Hans Genberg, Thomas Helbling, Salih Neftci

I. Introduction

This paper investigates the degree of integration between local Swiss credit markets and corresponding external markets. The motivation for the paper is the frequently asserted proposition that Switzerland in a low-interest-rate country and an interest-rate island (Aeberhardt, Zumstein (1990)) on which interest rates move relatively independently of interest rates abroad.

Some of the specific issues that we wish to address are illustrated by the following questions:

- Is it true that Swiss and external financial markets are poorly integrated? If so, what is the reason, and it is likely to continue in the indefinite future?

- Does the existence of interest differentials between Swiss and external financial markets imply that the Swiss National Bank has an additional degree of monetary independence beyond what is offered by a flexible exchange rate?

- Is the degree of capital mobility (appropriate defined) small in the case of Switzerland?

Previous empirical studies of these issues can be grouped into three broad categories, those that test the covered and uncovered interest parity condition in the Euro Swiss Franc market, those that investigate the linkages between interest rates in the Euro market and interest rates on large deposits in Zurich, and those that investigate the linkages between foreign-currency interest rates and Swiss Franc interest rates.[1] In the first category of studies we find, for example, the papers by Cumby, Obstfeld (1984) and by Gaab et al. (1986). Cumby, Obstfeld (1984) tested and rejected the uncovered interest parity hypothesis for the Swiss franc US-Dollar exchange rate (among others) with weekly data for the period of January 1976 to June 1981. Gaab et al. (1986) came to the same conclusion in their paper in which they tested three hypothesis about the uncovered interest parity for the Swiss Franc exchange rate with respect to the $, DM,

---

1 For a recent comprehensive review of empirical studies see Hauser (1991).

FF and the £ with monthly data for the period January 1975 to August 1984. They had to reject their strong form in which the risk premium is constant and close to zero. However, they could not reject the weak form in which the average exchange rate change over the entire sample equals the average interest rate differential, but the variance of the residuals was very large in this case.

Examples of the second category of studies, i.e. those that investigate the linkages between interest rates on Euro deposits and those on large-denomination deposits in Zurich, are Cosandier (1987) and Frankel, MacArthur (1988). Basing themselves on average interest differentials and on correlation coefficients, both sets of authors argue that there is a high degree of integration between these two markets, especially since the second part of the 1970s.

Finally, a third line of research, exemplified by papers such as Genberg et al. (1982), Kirchgässner, Wolters (1985), and Genberg, Salemi (1987) focuses on the relationship between Swiss interest rates and interest rates in foreign countries with the view to investigate transmission mechanisms and possible causality patterns. A general conclusion of these studies is that foreign interest rate shocks are important determinants of movements in Swiss Franc interest rates. Rich (1990) argues that this dependence of Swiss interest rates on foreign credit conditions is much weaker in more recent data than in those used in these studies.

The structure of the remainder of the paper is as follows. In Section II we present some stylized facts concerning the relationship between selected Swiss interest rates and corresponding external interest rates. We conduct two types of comparisons: between rates denominated in Swiss Francs and other currencies on the one hand, and between Euro Swiss Franc (off-shore) rates and domestic (on-shore) rates on the other. Our comparisons confirm the results of other studies which conclude that interest rates are tightly linked on the Euro-markets, and that interest rates on large domestic deposits follow Euro Swiss Franc rates quite closely. Our comparisons also suggest, however, that the off-shore/on-shore association between interest rates at the retail level has been less than perfect.

In Section III we present a model of segmentation and monopoly power in the domestic market for retail term deposits intended to explain the imperfect correlation between off-shore and on-shore interest rates. The theoretical model is an adaptation of Barro's 1972 model of monopolistic price adjustment. Some of its implications are tested and found to be consistent with observed domestic interest rate movements. The results also suggest that the degree of market segmentation and monopoly power has diminished over time to the point where during the latter part of the 1980ies off-shore and on-shore interest rate differentials are largely eliminated.

Section IV investigates the extent to which monetary policy has influenced the observed differential between external and internal interest rates. The purpose is to examine whether the National Bank has the ability to influence domestic interest rates through channels other than those operating via the actual and expected exchange rate.

In the last and concluding section we summarize briefly the main empirical results of the paper and propose directions for future research that naturally follow from our analysis.

II. Domestic and External Interest Rates: Some Stylized Facts.

Studies of interest-rate linkages between countries often start by establishing that the covered interest parity condition holds on the Euro-market. Hypotheses relating to integration of financial markets or, loosely speaking, the degree of capital mobility can then be investigated by comparing interest rates in the country in question (on-shore rates) with corresponding Euro (off-shore) rates. We follow this procedure here.

Figure 1 shows that the differential between the 12-month Euro Swiss Franc deposit rate in London and the 12-month Euro DM rate is closely matched by a discount (or premium) on the forward market. Differences are likely to be due in part to transactions costs and in part to observation errors stemming from less that perfectly matched timing of the observations rather than arbitrage opportunities. In fact, quotes by banks for forward exchange rates and euro deposit rates are often said to be made using the interest parity condition.

Although movements in the forward premium do provide a potential for independent movements in the two interest rates, it is interesting to note that the medium- and long-term movements in Swiss Franc and DM interest rates are quite similar. This presumable reflects the similarity of the monetary policy objectives of the Swiss National Bank and the German Bundesbank. It is also interesting to note that many short-term fluctuations are similar. To investigate whether this is due to an active coordination of interest rate policies of the two central banks or whether it is due to the market forces would be an interesting area of research.

FIGURE 1

12 MONTH EURO SFR AND 12 MONTH EURO DM RATE

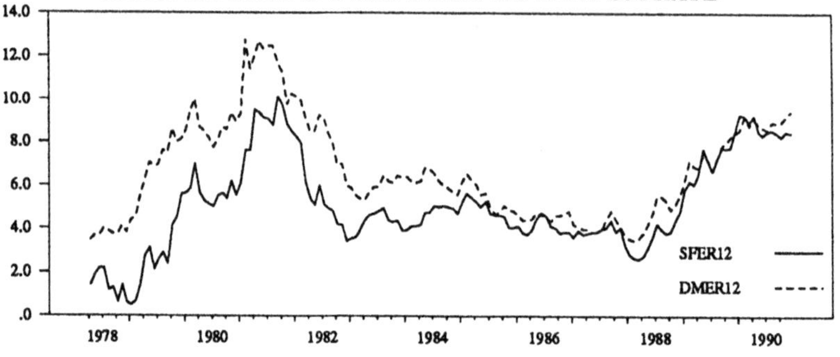

FORWARD PREMIUM AND INTEREST DIFFERENTIAL

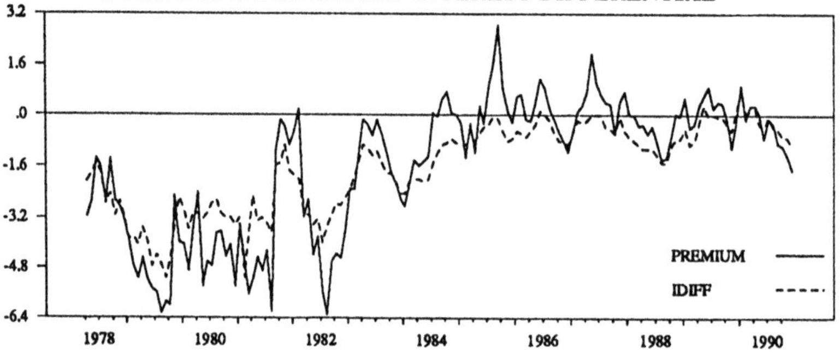

FIGURE 2

12 MONTH EURO SFR RATE AND 12 MONTH ZURICH DEPOSIT RATE

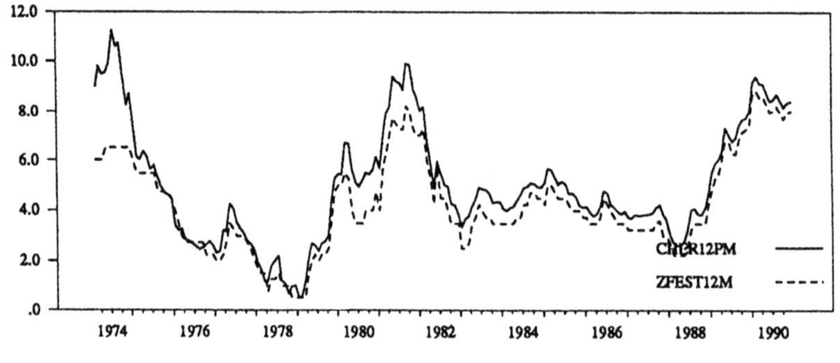

DIFFERENCE

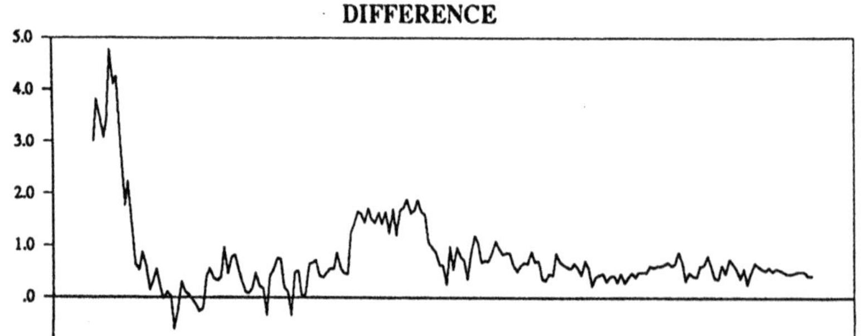

To study the degree of integration of the domestic financial markets with the Euro markets, it is necessary to compare interest rates on domestic deposits with those on the Euro market. **Figure 2** shows the evolution of the 12-month Euro Swiss Franc rate and a 12-month deposit rate in Zurich as well as the differential between them. The Zurich rate is representative primarily of the domestic wholesale market since the minimum balance for deposits with this yield is 100'000 Frs. The figure inspires several observations. The first is that the Zurich rate has been on average about one half percentage point lower that the Euro rate. Three potential explanations for this differential come to mind. One relates to controls on capital flows. If there are restrictions which prohibit or limit capital outflows, a higher interest rate on the Euro Swiss Franc market could not be arbitraged away.[2] On the basis of actual regulations on capital flows, it is hard to believe that this is the real reason for the differential. A second possible reason for the differential in favor of the Euro-deposit rate would be a failure of large domestic depositors to take advantage of higher external interest rates. The implied segmentation of the two markets would then make it possible for local banks to exploit their position as monopolists. Again, this explanation seems unlikely in view of the ease with which large depositors could go off shore. Finally, it may simply be that the interest differential reflects transaction costs for a domestic depositor interested in placing funds in the Euro markets.

The second observation prompted by **Figure 2** concerns the episode from March 1980 to January 1982 when the differential between the Euro rate and the Zurich rate is approximately one percentage point higher than during the rest of the sample. It is hard to explain such an episode other than with reference to the temporary imposition of some form of control on capital movements. According to the comprehensive review of such measures contained in Cosandier (1987) it is however not possible to identify any such controls, so the behavior of the interest differential during this episode remains a puzzle. Concerning the large differential observed in 1974 Cosandier (1987), p. 119, writes:

---

2 Frankel, MacArthur (1988) suggest that controls on capital flows can account for observed off-shore/on-shore interest differentials in their comprehensive study on interest linkages among 24 developed and developing countries. Their data for Switzerland (their table 3) indicate that the domestic deposit rate was slightly higher than the Euro rate on average during the period 1982-86 contrary to what our data indicate. This is presumable a typographical error.

Gaps observed between the rate on Zurich deposits and the rate on London deposits in Swiss francs, particularly in 1974, owe apparently more to the idiosynchrasies of legally tolerated cartel practices in the Swiss banking environment than to specific measures taken by the Swiss monetary authorities. In 1974, smaller banks complaining about the rise in the rate on three-month Zurich deposits have convinced the larger Swiss banks to leave the posted rate at 6.0 percent - a record level then -in spite of the substantially higher rate on London deposits in Swiss Francs. It is known, however, that major domestic deposits have enjoyed considerably more favorable conditions over that period.

The third remark inspired by **Figure 2** is that the volatility of the interest differential seems to have fallen over time. Indeed, if one calculates the yearly standard deviation of that differential over time one finds that there is a significant trend-like reduction during the period covered in the figure.[3] One explanation of this reduction is a greater awareness of local depositors of available opportunities in the Euro market which forces local banks to adjust local interest rates more rapidly in response to external interest-rate movements. In this case the reduction in the volatility of the interest differential points to a gradual increase in the integration of the two markets over time.

On the basis of the data in **Figure 2** we can tentatively assert that the domestic market for large deposits has been quite closely integrated with the Euro-deposit market since the mid-seventies. This is perhaps not surprising given the ease with which large bank clients can make use of off-shore financial services. Smaller clients have less easy access to these services, so whether they are effectively integrated into the Euro markets depends on the degree of competition between local banks for local retail deposits. Figure 3 presents some evidence on this issue. The solid line represents the yield on 3-year term deposits at Swiss Cantonal Banks, and the dashed line is an estimated 3-year Euro-deposit rate.[4] The following characterization comes to mind on inspection of this figure. The domestic rate was significantly lower than the external rate in the beginning of the sample, but the difference has decreased over time to the point where the two

---

3 A regression of the standard error on a constant and a time trend yiels a slope coefficient of -0.00295 with at t-value of -6.90 for the entire sample 1974:2 to 1989:12. Taking out the 1980:3 - 1981:12 episode the slope coefficient is -0.00298 with a t-value of -6.970.

4 More detailed discussions of the reasons for chosing this particular measure to represent the local retail rate and the estimation involved in creating the 3-year Euro rate are contained in Section IV.

FIGURE 3

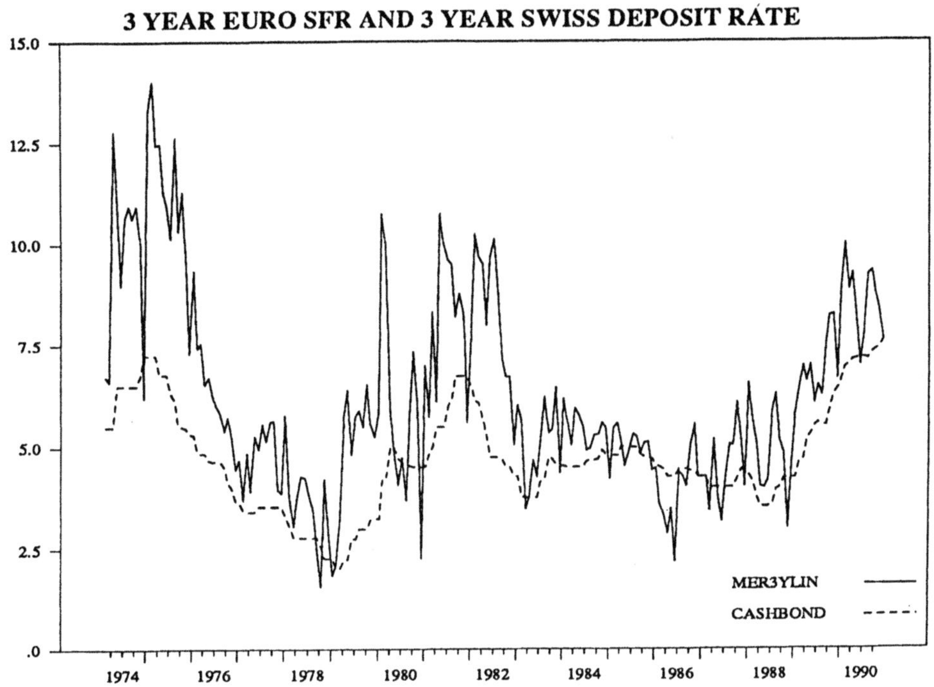

FIGURE 4

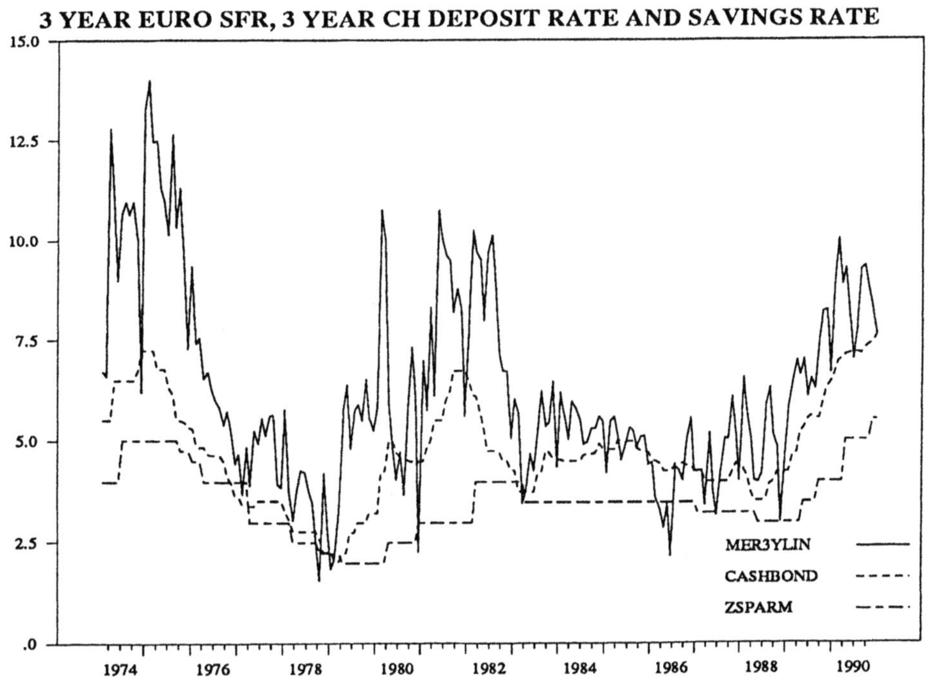

rates are effectively equal since the early 1980ies. A theory of monopoly power of domestic banks based on market segmentation and cartel arrangements that is consistent with the evolution of the interest rate differential in **Figure 3** will be developed and tested in the next section.

Another indication of the difference between retail and wholesale deposit rates is presented in **Figure 4** which depicts the 3-year term deposit rate and the estimated 3-year Euro rate mentioned above together with the interest rate on Savings Accounts in a large Zurich bank. What is interesting here is the much more sluggish behavior of the return on savings accounts than on the other two types of investments, particularly the failure of the savings account rate to follow the upward movements in the 1980-1981 and 1989-1990 periods. The reason for this may lie partly in the somewhat greater liquidity offered by the savings accounts, but more likely it is due to a certain segmentation of the markets. If the latter explanation is correct then one should observe a reaction of deposit volumes to the observed interest differentials. **Figure 5** suggests that this is indeed the case at least as far as the 1989-90 period is concerned.[5] The share of savings accounts as a percentage of the total balance sheet of the reporting banks shows a rather striking decline in these two years in favor of longer-term deposits for which, as we have seen, the interest rates more more in line with the external interest rates.

A possible conclusion that emerges from the previous discussion is that while the domestic market for large deposits is effectively integrated with the off-shore markets, there is some degree of segmentation at the level of small deposits. This segmention has allowed domestic banks to keep interest rates on retail deposits below the competitive level. If this is a correct view, the logical follow-up question is whether local lending rates is also less than fully integrated with external credit markets. Answering this question is complicated by the fact that lending rates incorporate risk premia that are specific to each loan. For this reason we limit our discussion to just two observations. The first relates to the determination of local mortgage rates and their financing. **Figure 6** shows the interest rates on mortgages, savings accounts, and 3-year "bons de caisse". One fact to notice here is that the differential between the first two has been virtually constant over time. This presumably reflects a type of mark-up phenomenon since traditionally the financing of banks' morgage loans has been with savings accounts. However, as we have seen, larger and larger amounts of funds are moving into long-

5 Data on deposit volumes were unfortunately not available for earlier periods when particularly large interest differentials emerged.

FIGURE 5

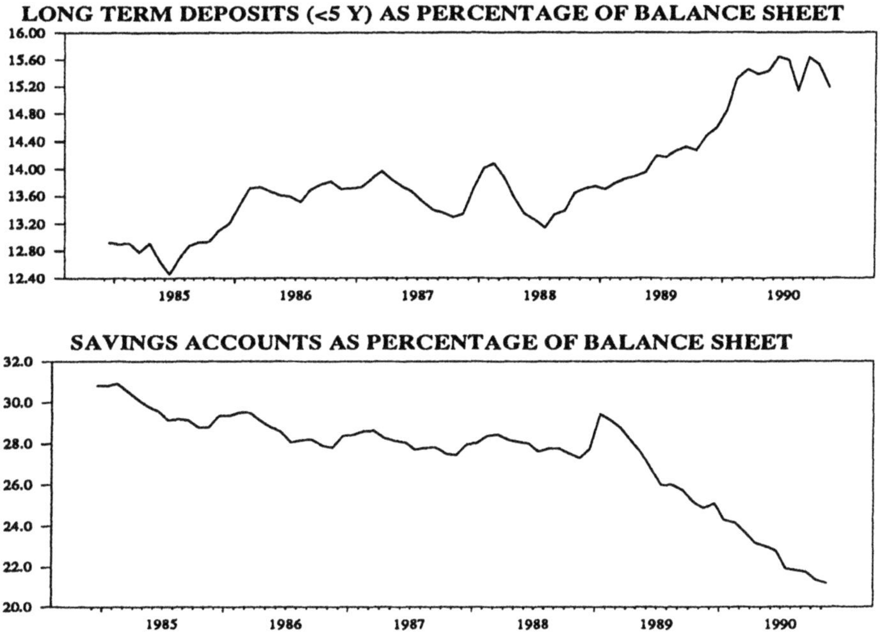

term deposits like bons de caisse and out of savings deposits as a result of the higher yields on the former. This means that the cost of funds for mortage lending is increasingly determined by competitively determined interest rate movements. It would seem to follow that the mortgage rates themselves will have to be determined likewise in which case the lending side of the Swiss financial market will also be integrated with external markets. If Switzerland ever was an island as far as lending rates are concerned, it is not likely to remain so for much longer.

The second observation we would like to make concerning lending rates relates to the question of whether Switzerland is a low-interest-rate country. **Figure 7** shows prime lending rates in Germany and Switzerland. The differential between them must be adjusted by two factors; a one percentage point commission charge should be added to the Swiss rate, and the forward premium on the Swiss Franc (see **Figure 1**) should be subtracted from the German rate. Until about 1984 this premium was on the order of 2-3 percentage points per annum on 12-month deposits. Assuming a similar forward premium for the horizon applicable to the prime rate implies that a substantial proportion of the interst differential vis-à-vis Germany can be accounted for. Since 1984 the forward premiun has declined but so has the differential between the prime rates.

FIGURE 6

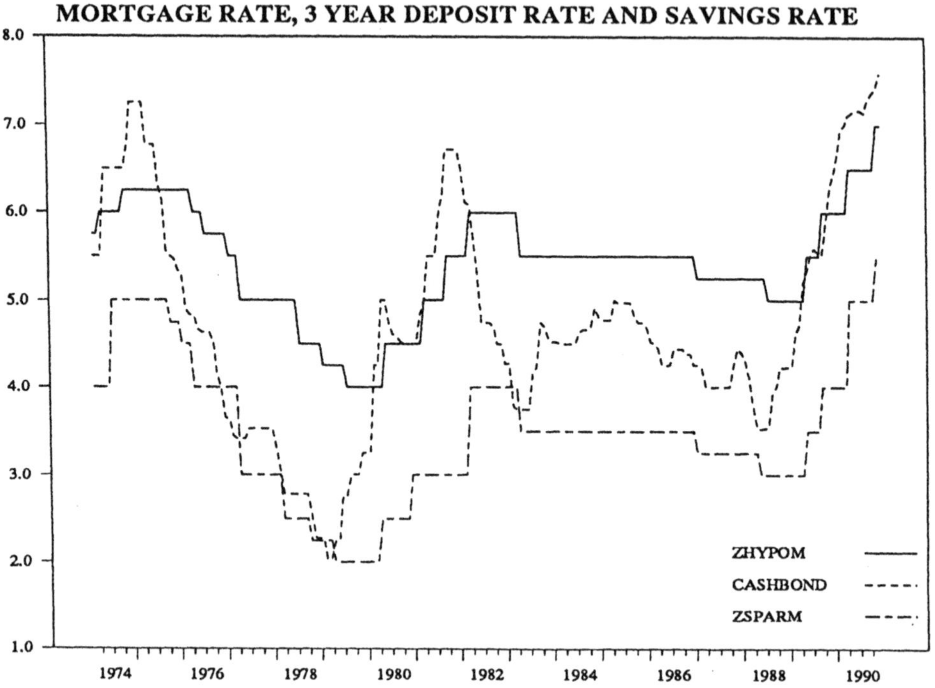

FIGURE 7

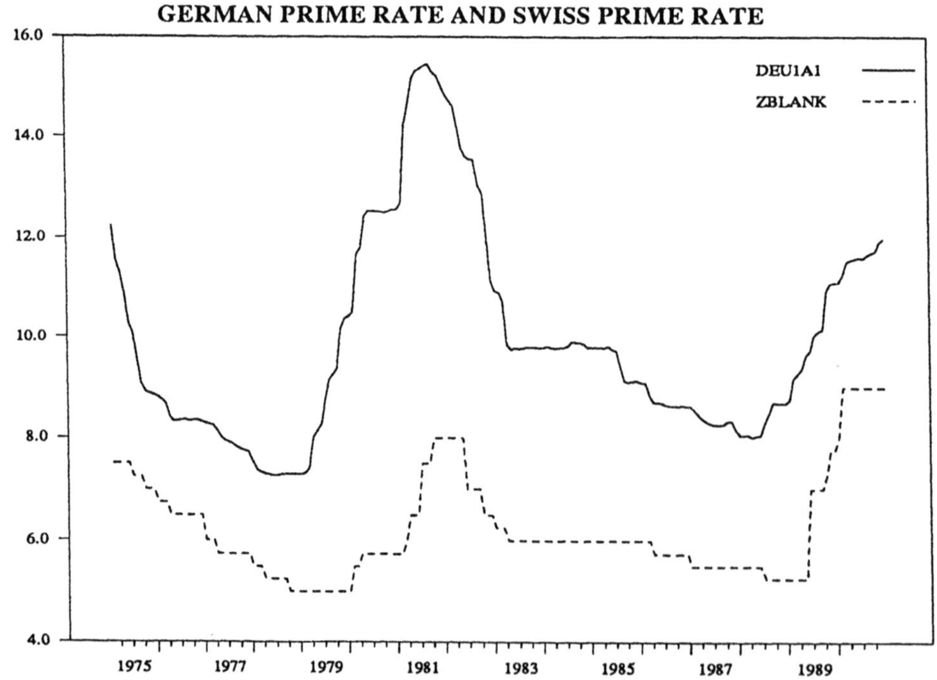

While appropriately corrected German lending rates may still be somewhat higher than Swiss rates, the size of the differential does not appear big enough to justify singling out Switzerland as a country with unusually low lending rates.

III. Monopoly Power in the Retail Market for Deposits?

In this section we study the monopoly power of local banks in the market for retail deposits. Two main hypotheses will be investigated:

1) As a result of cartel agreements and restrictions on competition from abroad, interest rates on deposits in Switzerland have been kept below corresponding deposit rates on the Euro-SwissFranc market.

2) Over time the effective monopoly power of local banks has been eroded.

The procedure that will be followed is first to derive the implications of a model in which a domestic bank with monopoly power accepts deposits at a certain interest rate and invest the proceeds in the Euro Swiss Franc market. The local bank can set its own deposit rate but takes the euro-rate as given. Adapting the model in Barro (1972) allows us to derive the optimal local deposit rate and to draw certain implications concerning the differential between this rate and the Euro Swiss Franc deposit rate. These implications are tested using data on 3-year deposit rates in Swiss Cantonal Banks and on estimated corresponding Euro rates.

1. A Model of a Domestic Monopoly Bank.

We adapt the model of monopolistic price adjustment by Barro (1972). The analytical framework is as follows:

The bank issues deposits with interest rate r. It invests the proceeds on the Euro market at interest rate i. The volume of deposits is X. Processing these deposits is subject to a quadratic cost function

$$C(X) = a + bX + cX^2 \qquad b, c > 0 \tag{1}$$

The demand function for deposits is a negative function of the differential (i - r):

$$X - \alpha - \beta(i - r) \qquad \alpha, \beta > 0 \tag{2}$$

The bank's profits are

$$\pi - (i - r)X - C(X) \tag{3}$$

which it maximizes by choosing r optimally. The Euro-rate i fluctuates randomly.

When there are no adjustment costs associated with changing the local deposit rate, then the optimal value of r can be written

$$r - i - \frac{\alpha + b\beta + 2c\alpha\beta}{2\beta(1 + c\beta)} \tag{4}$$

i.e. the local deposit rate will be below the Euro rate. The differential depends on the degree of integration between the two markets measured by the sensitivity of the demand for local deposits to changes in the differential.

A somewhat troubling implication of this result is the one-for-one effect of changes in i on r for given parameters in the model. Casual observation (see **Figure 3** in the previous section) suggests that the local deposit rates are adjusted less frequently than the Euro rates.

Suppose instead therefore that adjusting local deposit rates is costly. Then it can then be shown that the local monopoly bank will only adjust the domestic rate if the Euro rate moves outside a certain band defined relative to the time of the last adjustment in the domestic rate. Consider **Figure 8**. Suppose that the initial position is one in which the interest differential i_1 - r_1 is equal to the optimal differential in the absence of adjustment costs. An increase in the Euro deposit rate creates an incentive to increase the domestic rate as well. However, if such an adjustment entails a cost, it will not take place until the foreign rate has increased sufficiently to outweigh this cost. This occurs in **Figure 8** at time t=3 when the external rate hits the limit $i_3 = i_1 + h$. The width of the band, 2h, depends positively on the cost per adjustment of the domestic rate and negatively on the degree of persistence of the shocks to the external interest rate.[6]

Figure 8

Hypothetical interest rate movements in the presence of market segmentation and monopoly power

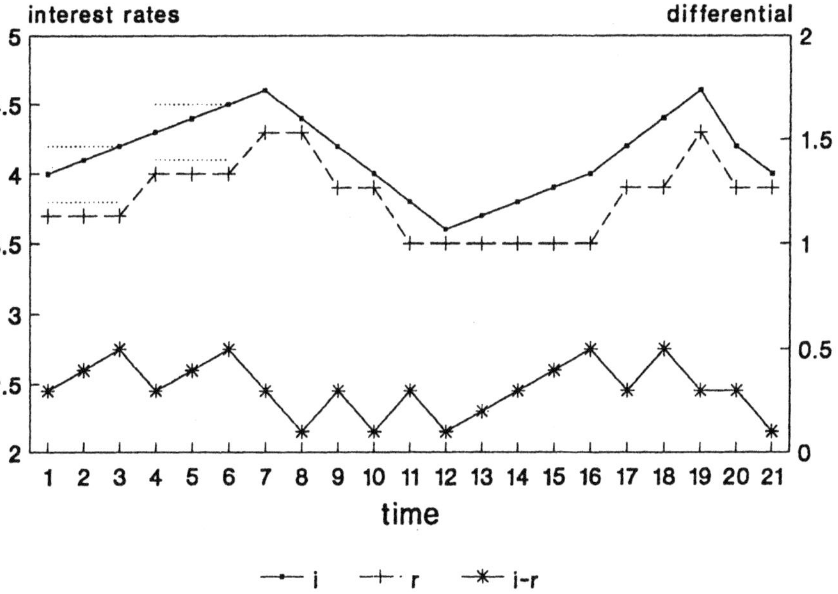

Two implications of the preceding analysis should be retained:

1) The interest differential i - r is not necessarily constant in the presence of adjustment costs. On average over a period of time it should however be strictly positive and be equal to what the optimal monopoly differential would be in the absence of adjustment costs.

2) If monopoly power declines over time in the sense that β in the equation (2) increases, then i - r should on average decline as well.

These two implications will be tested in what follows.

---

6 See Barro (1972) for details.

2. The Data.

The domestic deposit rate used to test the implications derived above was the yearly yield on 3-year "bons de caisse" of Swiss Cantonal Banks. End-of-month values of these series for 24 banks in different cantons were provided by the Association of Swiss Cantonal Banks. Only nine of these series were complete for the entire sample which extended from January 1974 to December 1990. These nine were used in the empirical tests. Comparing the movements of these nine domestic deposit rates made it immediately obvious that they move extremely closely together. As a result, the remaining empirical analysis was carried out using the simple average of the nine complete domestic rates.

The external deposit rate with the same maturity was estimated (see below) by using end-of-month values for 1-month, 2-month, 3-month, 6-month, and 12-month Euro-deposit rates. The corresponding data series were taken from the magnetic data tape of the Swiss National Bank.

The 3-year international reference rate was constructed by using a two-step procedure. First, the coefficients of a linear term structure approximation for the 1, 2, 3, 6, and 12 month Euro-deposit rates were obtained by estimating the equation

$$r_{it} = \alpha_o + \alpha_1 i$$

for every period from January 1974 to December 1990. In this equation r_{it} denotes the nominal rate of return of a Euro-deposit with maturity i at time t. The fitted values turned out to approximate the actual term structure quite well in most cases.[7]

In a second step, the estimated term-structure equation was used to calculate an estimated 3-year Euro-rate. The result has already been shown together with the domestic rate in **Figure 3**.

---

7 The average R^2 was 0.459 and the average standard error of estimate 0.0867. Additional details about these results may be obtained from the authors on request.

3. Methodological considerations.

Taking into account that an estimated international rate is used, the Barro 1972 model implies the following relationship between the international and domestic rates:

$$i_t - r_t = m_t + u_t + v_t$$

where

m denotes the monopoly mark-up determined by the parameters in equations (1) and (2).

u stands for the difference between the short-run changes in i and r which in turn depends in part on the band width 2h discussed in section II.

and

v denotes the prediction error for the international rate of return resulting from the estimate of the term structure on the Euro Swiss Franc market. The variance of this prediction error can be calculated from the estimated term-structure equation.

Our adaptation of the Barro 1972 model implies that m + u should be strictly positive over the whole sample period. In order to test this proposition the sample mean of i - r was calculated and the hypothesis that it was positive was tested using a statistic of the form

$$t = \frac{\overline{(\hat{i} - r)}}{\sigma_v}$$

This test does not allow any conclusion about the relative importance of m and u, but it does allow us to draw conclusions about the evolution of their sum, i.e. of i - r, over time by calculating the t statistic for different sample periods.

A second test deals with the relative importance of m, u, and v over time. From the fit of the estimated term structure equations we know that σ_v becomes smaller over time. As the sum of m and u must be strictly positive, crossings of $\hat{i}$ and r (i.e. changes in sign of $\hat{i}$ - r) have to be attributed entirely to the prediction error v. In the presence of a constant or a declining prediction error as measured by σ_v, we should expect the number of crossings in subperiods of equal length to be constant or decrease over time if m and u were constant. However, if the number of crossings increases over time, then m + u must be declining. In principle, this argument still does not allow any conclusion about the relative importance of m and u. But the combination of the two tests allows us to draw indirect inferences. Changes in the parameters of the demand and cost functions tend to change m and u in the same direction. However, only u is influenced by the variance of i. So if the variance of $\hat{\imath}$ changed over time, this would only affect u. But to attribute the increased number of crossings of $\hat{\imath}$ and r to changes in σ_i may not be appropriate if the sample mean of $\hat{\imath}$ - r changes systematically over time.

4. Results.

a. The first test.

For the first test, the period from 1974,1 to 1988,12 was divided into 5 sub-periods of 40 months each (1974,1 - 1977,4, 1977,5 - 1980,8, 1980,9 - 1983,12, 1984,1 - 1987-4, and 1987,5 - 1990,4). The sample mean of $\hat{\imath}$ - r and the average of the forecast errors (of i) were then calculated for each sub-period. The results were as follows:

	$\hat{\imath}$ - r	σ_v	t
1974,1 - 1977,4	3.003	1.399	2.146
1977,5 - 1980,8	1.590	0.683	2.326
1980,9 - 1983,12	2.002	1.019	1.965
1984,1 - 1987,4	0.121	0.471	0.256
1987,5 - 1990,4	1.285	0.489	2.627

Although the tendency is not monotonic, it seems from these results that the average interest rate differential becomes smaller towards the end of the sample period. To confirm this impression, the interest differential $\hat{\imath}$ - r was regressed on a time trend and a constant. The following results were obtained:

Sample	Constant (t-value)	time trend (t-value)	see	$\overline{R}^2$
1974,1 - 1990-12	2.87 (12.37)	-0.0127 (-6.326)	1.63	.16

b. The second test.

In an **Appendix** we show that the sequence of crossings (i.e. the occurrence of changes in the sign in the interest differential between the euro rate and the local interest rate)

$$\tau_i = inf\{\, t: \tau_{i-1} < t,\ (\hat{i} - r)_{t+\delta}(\hat{i} - r)_{t-\delta} < 0 \,\}$$

for $\delta > 0$ has, in the limit, a Poisson distribution. In order to use the properties of this sequence for a statistical test, the sample period was split into 10 subperiods of equal length. For every subperiod, the number of crossings was calculated as

$$n^j = \{\, \tau_i^j,\ 0 \leq i \leq 18 \,\} \quad for\ j = 1,\ldots,10$$

For our purposes, the interesting question is whether the intensity parameter μ of the Poisson distribution is constant over the sample periods or, alternative, changes systematically over time. So the following competing hypotheses were tested:

H_o: $\mu = \lambda_o$

H_a: $\mu = \lambda_a + \lambda_{1a}t$

where t denotes a linear time trend. The null-hypothesis is a restricted version of the alternative hypothesis, so the likelihood-ratio test can be used to discriminate between them. The parameters λ_o, λ_a, and λ_{1a} were estimated by maximizing the corresponding likelihood function. The results were:

Restricted model		Unrestricted model			$-2\ln(L_o/L_a)$
λ_o	L_o	λ_a	λ_{1a}	L_a	
3.60	$1.281\ 10^{-09}$	1.52	0.38	$5.09\ 10^{-09}$	2.72

The likelihood-ratio test is based on the fact that $-2\ln(L_o/L_a)$ is distributed χ^2 with one degree of freedom. The critical value for this distribution is 2.71 at the 90% level of significance. The value obtained with our data indicates that the restricted model should be rejected in favor of the alternative implying that the number of crossings have increased over time consistent with the proposition that financial integration has increased.

IV. Monetary Policy and the Off Shore/On Shore Interest Differential

If Euro-deposits and local retail deposits are imperfect substitutes due to a certain degree of market segmentation, then one should expect that monetary policy would be able to influence the interest differential between them. If it is assumed that monetary policy in the first instance influences the market for large deposits and the Euro market, then a standard portfolio model would predict that an increase in the money supply would reduce the differential between the euro interest rate and the local retail rate. This hypothesis was tested by regressing the interest differential on a constant, a monetary policy variable and a linear time trend. The monetary policy variable chosen was either the percentage change in M1 or in the monetary base (MB). On the assumption that the interest differential has not been a target variable for the Swiss National Bank, the right-hand side regressors could be treated as exogeneous justifying the use of the least square estimator with correction for first-order autocorrelation. **Table 1** shows the results for equations that included a dummy variable for the period of March 1980 to December 1982, and **Table 2** for equations without this dummy. The coefficents of the monetary policy variable have the expected sign and are significant. The trend coefficient is in most cases not significant. In all cases in which the dummy variable was included, this sign turned out to be positive.

The regressions were also performed over two sub-periods in order to test for parameter stability. In all cases where the dependent variable is the interest differential between the Eurorate and the deposit rate in Zurich, the hypothesis of parameter stability has to be rejected. The coefficient for the monetary policy variable was only significant for the first sub-sample from January 1975 to December 1982. The trend coefficient was always significant and changed signs between the two subperiods. In the second subperiod from January 1983 to December 1990, there was a systematic reduction for the interest differential between the Euro rate and the deposit rate in Zurich. A rather puzzling result, however, is the positive and significant trend coefficient for the interest differential between the Eurorate and the savings rate.

The results in **Tables 1** and **2** suggest that the impact of monetary policy on interest rates has changed over time. This in turn implies that both the speed and nature of the trans-mission of monetary shocks to the rest of the economy have been altered. In principle therefore, both the operating procedures and the entire strategy of the Swiss National Bank may be affected. Further research on these topics will be undertaken in the future.

Table 1a

Dep. Var.	Sample	Δ% M1	t-value	TREND	t-value	SEE	D.W.	$\bar{R}^2$	F(3/186)
DERDP3	T	-0.02332	-3.66	0.00074	0.42	0.105	2.23	0.43	
	S1	-0.03849	-5.49	0.00616	2.90	0.156	2.02	0.52	
	S2	-0.00354	-0.76	-0.00329	-2.66	0.030	1.95	0.29	14.68
DERDP6	T	-0.02243	-3.31	0.00154	0.78	0.077	2.24	0.61	
	S1	-0.03995	-5.39	0.00751	3.26	0.117	2.06	0.66	
	S2	-0.00356	-0.70	-0.00300	-2.05	0.022	1.77	0.44	13.18
DERDP12	T	-0.01868	-2.68	0.00228	1.06	0.062	2.19	0.69	
	S1	-0.03563	-3.97	0.00879	2.87	0.093	2.05	0.74	
	S2	0.00056	0.13	-0.00300	-2.53	0.020	2.00	0.41	11.18
DER12SV	T	-0.10027	-7.14	0.01164	1.52	0.189	1.69	0.95	
	S1	-0.11637	-4.97	0.01959	1.06	0.306	1.74	0.95	
	S2	-0.08325	-5.86	0.02107	2.31	0.078	1.42	0.96	0.41

Notes: **DERDP3** is the difference between the 3 month Euro SFR rate and the 3 month deposit rate in Zurich
DERDP6 is the difference between the 6 month Euro SFR rate and the 6 month deposit rate in Zurich
DERDP12 is the difference between the 12 month Euro SFR rate and the 12 month deposit rate in Zurich
DER12SV is the difference between the 12 month Euro SFR rate and the savings rate
T denotes the estimation period from January 1975 to December 1990
S1 denotes the estimation period from January 1975 to December 1982
S2 denotes the estimation period from January 1983 to December 1990
SEE denotes the standard error of estimation
F(3/186) denotes the F-value of a Chow-test for parameter stability in the two subperiods

Table 1b

Dep. Var.	Sample	Δ% MB	t-value	Trend	t-value	SEE	D.W.	$\bar{R}^2$	F(3/186)
DERDP3	T	-0.01941	-3.20	0.00057	0.31	0.107	2.26	0.42	
	S1	-0.02341	-3.15	0.00673	2.43	0.174	2.11	0.47	
	S2	-0.00695	-0.84	-0.00372	-2.55	0.030	1.96	0.30	6.349
DERDP6	T	-0.01419	-2.51	0.00148	0.71	0.079	2.26	0.60	
	S1	-0.01962	-2.70	0.00801	2.51	0.131	2.18	0.62	
	S2	0.00098	0.12	-0.00250	-1.52	0.022	1.75	0.44	4.956
DERDP12	T	0.00781	-1.50	0.00235	1.04	0.063	2.22	0.68	
	S1	-0.01148	-1.67	0.00931	2.41	0.103	2.12	0.71	
	S2	0.00398	0.53	-0.00261	-1.86	0.020	2.01	0.41	5.347
DER12SV	T	-0.03018	-3.15	0.00872	0.79	0.226	1.43	0.94	
	S1	-0.03356	-2.63	-0.00141	-0.05	0.351	1.54	0.94	
	S2	0.00037	0.02	0.03476	2.32	0.105	1.04	0.94	1.192

Notes: See Table 1a.

Table 2a

Dep. Var.	Sample	Δ% M1	t-value	Trend	t-value	SEE	D.W.	$\bar{R}^2$	F(3/186)
DERDP3	T	-0.02431	-3.90	-0.00031	-0.33	0.105	2.24	0.43	
	S1	-0.03859	-5.58	0.00611	2.95	0.154	2.02	0.53	
	S2	-0.00354	-0.76	-0.00329	-2.66	0.030	1.95	0.29	14.93
DERDP6	T	-0.02386	-3.46	-0.00100	-0.84	0.078	2.26	0.60	
	S1	-0.04091	-5.49	0.00695	3.04	0.117	2.05	0.66	
	S2	-0.00356	-0.70	-0.00300	-2.50	0.022	1.77	0.44	13.06
DERDP12	T	-0.01957	-2.76	-0.00064	-0.43	0.063	2.23	0.69	
	S1	-0.03658	-4.02	0.00789	2.56	0.094	2.03	0.74	
	S2	0.00056	0.13	-0.00300	-2.53	0.020	2.00	0.41	10.73
DER12SV	T	-0.09818	-6.97	0.00657	0.85	0.190	1.69	0.95	
	S1	-0.11228	-4.78	0.01281	0.63	0.307	1.73	0.95	
	S2	-0.08325	-5.86	0.02107	2.31	0.078	1.42	0.96	0.459

Notes: See Table 1a.

Table 2b

Dep. Var.	Sample	Δ% MB	t-value	Trend	t-value	SEE	D.W.	$\bar{R}^2$	F(3/186)
DERDP3	T	-0.02023	-3.36	-0.00089	-0.86	0.107	2.27	0.42	
	S1	-0.02365	-3.21	0.00654	2.42	0.172	2.11	0.47	
	S2	-0.00695	-0.84	-0.00372	-2.55	0.030	1.96	0.30	6.641
DERDP6	T	-0.01476	-2.60	-0.00132	-0.98	0.079	2.29	0.59	
	S1	-0.02009	-2.75	0.00722	2.23	0.131	2.18	0.62	
	S2	0.00098	0.12	-0.00250	-1.52	0.022	1.75	0.44	5.028
DERDP12	T	-0.00837	-1.61	-0.00073	-0.45	0.064	2.26	0.68	
	S1	-0.00120	-1.74	0.00808	2.02	0.104	2.11	0.71	
	S2	0.00398	0.53	-0.00261	-1.86	0.020	2.01	0.41	5.206
DER12SV	T	-0.03039	-3.18	0.00595	0.55	0.225	1.42	0.94	
	S1	-0.03378	-2.67	-0.00547	-0.18	0.348	1.54	0.94	
	S2	0.00037	0.02	0.03476	2.32	0.105	1.04	0.94	1.246

Notes: See Table 1a.

V. Concluding Remarks

The empirical evidence presented in this paper is consistent with the view that Swiss financial markets are becoming increasingly integrated with corresponding international markets. While a high degree of international integration has characterized the environment for large domestic bank clients during the entire period we have studied, the behavior of interest rates relevant for smaller domestic economic units implies that a certain degree market segmentation existed in the 1970ies. This gave domestic banks some monopoly power which was used to drive a wedge between interest rates in Switzerland and interest rates on the Euro Swiss Franc market. The degree of market segmentation has however been reduced during the 1980ies. This diminished the ability of local banks to set interest rates collusively, and led to a closer relationship between external and internal interest rates both on deposits and on loans.

While this brief portrayal of the evolution of competition in local financial markets is compatible with the theoretical model in Section III, a number of refinements of that model could potentially provide more powerful tests of the underlying hypothesis. These refinements include: (i) modifying the assumption that the external interest rate follows a random walk, (ii) modeling the adjustment costs seriously rather than treating them parametrically, (iii) modeling the demand for deposits as a demand for a durable asset, and (iv) modeling also the asset side of the banks' balance sheet in order to get predictions about the optimal setting of lending rates.

The empirical research can also be extended in several directions. Obvious candidates for such research include: (i) studying the evolution of local lending rates in relation both to deposit rates and to foreign lending rates, and (ii) examining the impact of monetary policy actions on other variables than the off-shore/on-shore interest differential.

Finally, it would be highly desirable to investigate whether and in what way the changing competitive environment in Swiss financial markets should lead to changes in the conduct of monetary policy by the Swiss National Bank.

References

Aeberhardt, W., and Zumstein, M. (1990). Zinsinsel Schweiz. Studie No. 13, Bundesamt für Konjunkturfragen, Bern.

Barro, R. (1982). "A Theory of Monopolistic Price Adjustment". Review of Economic Studies, 34, 1, January, pp. 17-26.

Cosandier, P. A. (1987). Switzerland and International Financial Integration, Recent History and New Theoretical Developments. Doctoral Dissertation, Graduate Institute of International Studies, Geneva.

Cumby, R.E. and Obstfeld, M. (1984). "International Interest Rate and Price Level Linkages under Flexible Exchange Rates: A Review of Recent Evidence". In: Exchange Rate Theory and Practice. Ed. by Bilson, J.F.O. and Marston, R. C. Chicago: University of Chicago Press.

Frankel, J. and MacArthur (1988). "Political vs. Currency Premia in International Real Interest Rate Differentials: A Study of Forward Rates for 24 Countries". European Economic Review, Vol. 32, No. 5, June, pp. 1083-1121.

Gaab, W., Granziol, M. J. and Horner, M. (1986). "On some International Parity Conditions: An Empirical Investigation". European Economic Review 30, pp. 683-713.

Genberg, H., Saïdi, N. and Swoboda, A. K. (1982). "American and European Interest Rates and Exchange Rates: U.S. Hegemony or Interdependence?" Mimeo.

Genberg, H. and Salemi, M. (1987). "The Effects of Foreign Shocks on Prices of Swiss Goods and Credit: An Analysis Based on VAR Methods". Annales d'Economie et de Statistique. No. 6/7, pp. 101-24.

Hauser, H. (1991). Integration der Europäischen Kapitalmärkte: Konsequenzen für die Schweizerische Geldpolitik. Schweizerisches Institut für Aussenwirtschafts-, Struktur- und Regionalforschung, Hochschule St. Gallen.

Hermann, W. and Rich, G. (1988). "Zinssätze und Wechselkurse in der Schweiz - McKinnons unischtbare Hand". In: Wechselkursstabilisierung, EWS und Weltwährungssystem. Ed. by Issing, O. Hamburg: Verlag Weltarchiv.

Kirchgässner, G. and Wolters, J. (1985). "U.S.-European Interest Rate Linkage: A Time Series Analysis for West Germany, Switzerland, and the United States". The Review of Economics and Statistics, Vol. 69, pp. 675-84.

Rich, G. (1990). "Comment". In V. Argy and P. De Grauwe (eds.), Choosing an Exchange Rate Regime, The Challenge for Smaller Industrial Countries. Washington, D.C.: International Monetary Fund, 1990, pp. 220-23.

Comment on

Hans Genberg, Thomas Helbling, Salih Neftci: "Monopoly Power in Swiss Financial Markets"

Urs W. Birchler, Werner Hermann

Genberg, Helbling and Neftci analyze retail and wholesale deposit rates on Swiss domestic capital markets. It is an investigation of interest rate differentials. There are two main issues in the paper: one is the degree of integration of Swiss and foreign markets, the other is the consequences of the empirical evidence presented for Swiss monetary policy.

The paper starts off with a brief overview of the empirical literature on the integration of Swiss and foreign financial markets. The authors then describe and compare the development of various interest rates since the mid Seventies. They find that the market for large domestic deposits is effectively integrated with the off-shore market but that there is some degree of segmentation at the level of small deposits. This hypothesis gives rise to a more formal analysis of the relation between Euro Swiss Franc rates and the return on small deposits with banks in Switzerland. A model of monopolistic price adjustment by Barro (1972) is used in order to test the two hypotheses that (a) there is some room for monopolistic price setting - in other words that Swiss retail markets are not fully integrated - and (b) this room is decreasing over time. Empirical tests confirm that both is indeed the case. We share these conclusions. They are also in line with what most observers of the market believe. The paper is an interesting contribution to the ongoing discussion.

The approach the authors choose certainly is an appropriate and convenient way to address the interesting issue of financial market integration. However, by analyzing the differential between interest rates the authors make one implicit assumption: that an observed interest rate differential necessarily means that banks have monopoly power. A direct comparison of the different interest rates is only useful if the corresponding deposits offer the same service, for instance that Euro Swiss Franc deposits deliver the same benefit to an investor as retail deposits. Otherwise a differential could be justified by the different nature of the services. The attribute where the services are most likely to differ is the risk involved. Even if the return is objectively the same, there may be information costs ignored in this paper. A Swiss investor may find it easier to assess the risk of a deposit with a domestic bank than that of a Euro-deposit. In addition, it is easier for a Swiss resident to take legal and political measures to recapture the loss in case of default of a Swiss bank. Therefore it is possible that a Swiss depositor on the Euro market asks a risk premium. We think the implicit assumption of identical service of the deposits in question should at least be made explicit, but we do not think it invalidates the paper.

The costs of adjusting prices prevent banks from immediately responding to the slightest change in demand. The role of adjustment costs could be made more explicit. In the theoretical model chosen the costs of price adjustment do not enter as a separate variable. Therefore the analysis is limited to constant adjustment costs. The stochastic properties of demand changes also plays a role. A profit maximizing bank's reaction today depends on the predictability of future changes. It would be possible to test whether or not changes in the Euro Swiss Franc rates are predictable.

In order to point out the contribution of the paper we would also like to discuss some issues it does not address. The paper does not fully answer all the questions that come to mind when reading the title and the introduction. For example it does not deal with monopoly power in financial markets in general. It focuses on the classic banking business and does not discuss monopoly power in underwriting or securities dealing. Another issue that is not thoroughly explored in the paper is the question whether Switzerland is an "interest rate island". If one compares two arbitrary time series, two kinds of relations between them can be distinguished. One is the short term movement, and the other the longer term development. The notion of an "interest-rate island" usually means that there is no tendency towards levelling out differentials in the long term. Despite that the short term movements can be closely linked. The paper is about long term developments. Therefore a reader might expect an explanation of the low Swiss interest rates which the paper does not provide. Furthermore the paper does not offer an economic explanation why competition actually has intensified (e.g. in the parallel case of underwriting there are well known reasons behind fiercer competition: the deregulation of capital movements by the Swiss National Bank (SNB) and the softer reciprocity stance of the Federal Banking commission). In addition, the issue of capital mobility is mentioned in the introduction but is not explicitly treated in the body of the paper.

An alternative way to tackle the issue raised in the title would be to compare the costs and prices on domestic financial markets. Unfortunately this strategy would be harder to follow because of difficulties to determine the proper costs, but it has the advantage that it is feasible even if there is no comparable foreign market. While this strategy is mentioned in the paper it is only implemented in a short comparison of lending and deposit rates. The authors argue that there were loan specific risk premia. However, since all major banks consider the risk of mortgage lending quite low it should be possible to treat mortgages as a single market. Prime (or interbank) lending rates would be an alternative benchmark if mortgage rates are considered unreliable. The investigation of the Swiss cartel commission and the answer of the Swiss Bankers Association went more in the direction of comparing costs and prices.

Let us add some comments concerning the data used. The paper focuses mainly on three markets: the Euro Swiss Franc market, the domestic market for large deposits and the domestic market for small deposits. The Euro-market is represented by Euro Swiss Franc deposits for 3, 6 and 12 months and by an estimated 3-year Euro Swiss Franc rate. The domestic market for large deposits is represented by the 12-month deposit rate in Zurich. The market for small deposits is represented by 3-year "bons de caisse" of cantonal banks. Almost all cantonal governments legally (and probably all of them factually) guarantee the liabilities of the respective cantonal bank. Therefore "bons de caisse" of cantonal banks essentially are a riskless asset. In part four, 3-, 6- and 12-month deposits in Zurich are used to characterize the retail market. However one has the impression that the same 12-month rate has been used to characterize the wholesale market in part two of the paper. Basing the evidence on a broad dataset certainly adds to the quality of the conclusion. In this case, however, we feel that the amount of interest rates presented is rather puzzling. The readability of the paper would be enhanced if in a first presentation one rate would stand for one market. For the comparison of the Euro-market and the domestic retail market the authors need to have two deposits with equal maturity. They decide to compare observed 3-year "bons de caisse" of cantonal banks with estimated 3-year Euro Swiss Franc deposits. The method of estimation of the 3-year Euro Swiss Franc rate is a valid method if an estimation is required. Yet we do not find the explanatory power of the regression surprisingly high given the fact that the regressions have only three degrees of freedom. Another possible approach would have been to use an observed proxy for a domestic short term rate for small deposits and observed Euro Swiss Franc rates. Some suggestions for such a proxy would be the rate on "Anlagehefte" or on savings deposits. Rates on Anlagehefte with cantonal banks are available from 1980 on. Switching to a shorter than 3-year maturity would have an additional benefit. Because banks are not allowed to raise the rate of "bons de caisse" autonomously a more market based rate could be used. An increase in the rate on "bons de caisse" was and still is subject to approval by Swiss National Bank. Since the beginning of the Eighties the Swiss National Bank has refrained from managing the return on "bons de caisse". Prior to the Eighties the more complicated administrative process took more time. This explains in part why now banks adjust the rates on "bons de caisse" more often than in the seventies. Zimmerli (1983) computed monthly and quarterly adjusted time series (67-81) for "bons de caisse" of the big banks. By making a similar adjustment or using his data one could avoid some of the problems of distorted data.

A last remark concerns taxes. Euro-deposits are tax free whereas domestic deposits are subject to the withholding tax. From the point of view of an investor the pre-tax spread underestimates the interest rate differential. Since the withholding tax can be recovered after one year it is not easy to adjust for taxes but the different tax treatment should be a consideration. Given the different tax treatment the mere existence of the domestic market is evidence of market segmentation.

We said that we subscribe to the paper's conclusions. Let us qualify this in two respects. One result of section four is that the interest rate differential between the Euro and retail rate is decreasing over time. The tests reported in the table (page 298), however, contains more information than this conclusion. It might for instance be interesting to note that the hypothesis of a constant differential in the sub-periods 1977,5 to 1980,8 and 1987,5 to 1990,4, respectively, cannot be rejected at any reasonable level of confidence. Obviously the conclusion of a decreasing trend owes a lot to the large differential at the beginning of the sample period when off-shore markets for the Swiss Franc were first established an when several restriction in the Swiss capital markets were in force. It might therefore be interesting to see, whether a test in the period after 1975 could refute the hypothesis that competition for deposits has been unchanged - maybe even perfect - in the past 15 years.

Another conclusion of the paper is that monetary policy can influence the interest rate differential between Euro Swiss Franc and domestic retail deposits. Regressing this differential on a monetary policy variable and a time trend for different periods leads to the evidence that the impact of monetary policy on interest rates has changed over time. The positive sign of the trend coefficient, however, raises some doubts concerning the correctness of the previous result of increasing integration of on- and off-shore markets. This result might be due to mis-specification of the model (ommission of the policy variable).

In a nutshell we find the paper an interesting one, and it is certainly worth reading. Not only because of the methodology and of the conclusions reached but also because it touches on a lot of interesting issues and stimulates ideas for further research.

Literature

Zimmerli, M. (1983), "Zinspolitik der Nationalbank mit Hilfe von Artikel 10 des Bankgesetzes", Schweizerische Nationalbank, Zürich.

List of Authors

Dr. Julian S. Alworth, Bank for International Settlements, P.O. Box, CH-4002 Basel

Prof. Dr. Ernst Baltensperger, Institute of Economics, University of Bern, Vereinsweg 23, CH-3012 Bern

Dr. Urs W. Birchler, Swiss National Bank, P.O. Box, CH-8022 Zürich

Prof. Dr. Niklaus Blattner, Labour and Industrial Economics Research Unit (FAI), University of Basel, Leonhardsgraben 3, CH-4051 Basel, and Swiss Bankers Association, P.O. Box 4182, CH-4002 Basel

Dr. Andreas Bossard, Swiss Bankers Association, P.O. Box 4182, CH-4002 Basel

Dr. Peter Buomberger, Union Bank of Switzerland, P.O. Box, CH-8021 Zürich

Dr. Ulrich Camen, International Centre for Monetary and Banking Studies (ICMB), Avenue de la Paix 11 A, CH-1211 Geneva 21

Prof. Jean-Pierre Danthine, Department of Econometrics and Economics, Ecole des Hautes Etudes Commerciales (HEC), University of Lausanne, CH-1015 Lausanne

Dr. Thomas Gehrig, Basle Centre for Economics and Business, University of Basel, P.O. Box, CH-4003 Basel

Prof. Hans Genberg, International Centre for Monetary and Banking Studies (ICMB), Avenue de la Paix 11 A, CH-1211 Geneva 21

Prof. Vittorio Grilli, Department of Economics, Birbeck College, University of London, 7-15 Gresse Street, London W1P 1PA, UK

Urs Haegler, Labour and Industrial Economics Research Unit (FAI), University of Basel, Leonhardsgraben 3, CH-4051 Basel

Thomas Helbling, International Centre for Monetary and Banking Studies (ICMB), Avenue de la Paix 11 A, CH-1211 Geneva 21

Prof. Dr. Martin Hellwig, Basle Centre for Economics and Business, University of Basel, P.O. Box, CH-4003 Basel

Dr. Werner Hermann, Swiss National Bank, P.O. Box, CH-8022 Zürich

Matthias Jeger, Labour and Industrial Economics Research Unit (FAI), University of Basel, Leonhardsgraben 3, CH-4051 Basel

Prof. Dr. Oliver Landmann, Programme Director, Swiss National Science Foundation, National Research Programme 28, Möndenweg 77, D-7854 Inzlingen

Prof. Dr. Salih Neftci, The Graduate Institute of International Studies (IUHEI), University of Geneva, P.O. Box 36, CH-1211 Geneva 21

Dr. John Noorlander, Swiss Bank Corporation, P.O. Box, CH-4002 Basel

PD Dr. George Sheldon, Labour and Industrial Economics Research Unit (FAI), University of Basel, Leonhardsgraben 3, CH-4051 Basel

Prof. Alexander Swoboda, The Graduate Institute of International Studies (IUHEI), University of Geneva, P.O. Box 36, CH-1211 Geneva 21

Roland Theiss, Labour and Industrial Economics Research Unit (FAI), University of Basel, Leonhardsgraben 3, CH-4051 Basel

Matthias Wirth, Swiss Bankers Association, P.O. Box 4182, CH-4002 Basel

List of Participants

Dr. Julian S. Alworth, Basel
Prof. Dr. Ernst Baltensperger, Bern
Dr. Urs W. Birchler, Zürich
Prof. Dr. Niklaus Blattner, Basel
Dr. Claudio Borio, Basel
Dr. Andreas Bossard, Basel
Beat Brenner, Zürich
Prof. Pascal Bridel, Lausanne-Dorigny
Dr. Peter Buomberger, Zürich
Dr. Ulrich Camen, Geneva
Prof. Jean-Pierre Danthine, Lausanne
Alberto Eichholzer, Torino
Dr. Emil Ems, Geneva
Dr. Christian Etter, Bern
Doris Frick, St. Gallen
Dr. Alexander Galli, Zürich
Dr. Thomas Gehrig, Basel
Prof. Hans Genberg, Geneva
Prof. Vittorio Grilli, London
Urs Haegler, Basel
Prof. Dr. Heinz Hauser, St. Gallen
Thomas Helbling, Geneva
Prof. Dr. Martin Hellwig, Basel
Dr. Werner Hermann, Zürich
Matthias Jeger, Basel
Prof. Ulrich Kohli, Geneva
Prof. Dr. Oliver Landmann, Inzlingen
Dr. Martin Maurer, Zürich
Prof. Dr. Salih Neftci, Geneva
Dr. John Noorlander, Basel
Prof. Dr. Kurt Schiltknecht, Zürich
Prof. Dr. Bernd Schips, St. Gallen
Wolfgang Schwartzkopff, St. Gallen
Dr. Adelgunde Sengthaler, Zürich
PD Dr. George Sheldon, Basel
Othmar Suter, Basel
Prof. Alexander Swoboda, Geneva
Roland Theiss, Basel
Dr. Rolf Weder, Basel
Matthias Wirth, Basel

Studies in Contemporary Economics

B. Hamminga, Neoclassical Theory Structure and Theory Development. IX, 174 pages. 1983.

J. Dermine, Pricing Policies of Financial Intermediaries. VII, 174 pages. 1984.

Economic Consequences of Population Change in Industrialized Countries. Proceedings. 1983. Edited by G. Steinmann. X, 415 pages. 1984.

Problems of Advanced Economies. Proceedings, 1982. Edited by N. Miyawaki. VI, 319 pages. 1984.

Studies in Labor Market Dynamics. Proceedings, 1982. Edited by G. R. Neumann and N. C. Westergard-Nielsen. X, 285 pages. 1985.

A. Pfingsten, The Measurement of Tax Progression. VI, 131 pages. 1986.

Causes of Contemporary Stagnation. Proceedings, 1984. Edited by H. Frisch and B. Gahlen. IX, 216 pages. 1986.

O. Flaaten, The Economics of Multispecies Harvesting. VII, 162 pages. 1988.

D. Laussel, W. Marois, A. Soubeyran, (Eds.), Monetary Theory and Policy. Proceedings, 1987. XVIII, 383 pages. 1988.

G. Rubel, Factors Determining External Debt. VI, 264 pages. 1988.

B. C. J. van Velthoven, The Endogenization of Government Behaviour in Macroeconomic Models. XI, 367 pages. 1989.

A. Wenig, K. F. Zimmermann (Eds.) 3, Demographic Change and Economic Development. XII, 325 pages. 1989.

J. K. Brunner, Theory of Equitable Taxation. VIII, 217 pages. 1989.

E. van Imhoff, Optimal Economic Growth and Non-Stable Population. IX, 218 pages. 1989.

P. S. A. Renaud, Applied Political Economic Modelling. XII, 242 pages. 1989.

H. König (Ed.), Economics of Wage Determination. XI, 373 pages. 1990.

C. Dagum, M. Zenga (Eds.) Income and Wealth Distribution, Inequality and Poverty. Proceedings, 1989. XIII, 415 pages. 1990.

A. J. H. C. Schram, Voter Behavior in Economic Perspective. X, 274 pages. 1991.

J. B. Woittiez, Modelling and Empirical Evaluation of Labour Supply Behaviour. VI, 232 pages. 1991.

R. Arnason, T. Bjorndal (Eds.), Essays on the Economics of Migratory Fish Stocks. VIII, 197 pages. 1991.

Ch. Czerkawski, Theoretical and Policy-Oriented Aspects of the External Debt Economics. VII, 150 pages. 1991.

D. Stern, J. M. M. Ritzen (Eds.), Market Failure in Training? VII, 233 pages. 1991.

M. Savioz, New Issues in the Theory of Investment. XVI, 216 pages. 1992.

W. Franz 2, (Ed.) Structural Unemployment. X, 132 pages. 1992.

N. Blattner, H. Genberg, A. Swoboda, (Eds.), Competitiveness in Banking. VIII, 315 pages. 1992.

GPSR Compliance

The European Union's (EU) General Product Safety Regulation (GPSR) is a set of rules that requires consumer products to be safe and our obligations to ensure this.

If you have any concerns about our products, you can contact us on ProductSafety@springernature.com

In case Publisher is established outside the EU, the EU authorized representative is:

Springer Nature Customer Service Center GmbH
Europaplatz 3
69115 Heidelberg, Germany

Batch number: 10726298

Printed by Printforce, the Netherlands